The Old Home Place
at the foot of the hill
Mondray, Ky.

CHILDREN'S PICTURE BOOKS
BY PHILIP DALE SMITH

OVER is not UP!
Illustrated by Donna Brooks
(1995)

Nighttime at the Zoo
Illustrated by Gwen Clifford
(1997)

The Rabbit and the Promise Sign – with Pat Day-Bivins
Illustrated by Donna Brooks
(1998)

Little Tom Meets Mr. Jonah—with Pat Day-Bivins
Illustrated by Donna Brooks
(2000)

For information about Philip Dale Smith's
speeches and training programs, contact
him at the address below, e-mail at
smithdale2@aol.com or by phone at
253 847-9441

Published by Golden Anchor Press
PO Box 45208
Tacoma, WA 98445

Turn Back Time

Turn Back Time

ISBN: 1-886864-02-0

Printed in the United States of America

Turn Back Time

A NOVEL BY

Lisa Kay Hauser &
Philip Dale Smith

Golden
Anchor
Press

Tacoma, Washington

ACKNOWLEDGMENTS

A book is always the work not just of the author, but also of those who have meaningfully influenced her. Out of the multitudes who have so touched my life, I hereby express deep gratitude to the following who in special ways have had a part in this book—with apologies to those unintentionally omitted:

To John Orville & Ethel Louise Smith, whose story it is—though highly fictionalized.

To my Mom and Dad, Philip Dale and Mary Jo Smith, for endless rereads, editing, encouragement, and just being there for me. And of course, Dad should get at least a bit of credit for being my connection to the above two who inspired this story—and for being my coauthor!

My heartfelt gratitude goes to three special friends who read each word almost as soon as it was written and cheered me on along the way: Mary Francis, Debi Towns, and Michelle Welsh, my favorite journalist.

To those who contributed to research and story development: Bobby Anderson, Gayle Carver, Paul Camplin, Pat Day-Bivins, Joanna Fox, Dennie Harper, Karen Harper Lain, Jeanie and Harold Morris, Reginald Rhoads, Jerry Roberson, Sandy and Charles Short, Dawson Smith, Judge Philip Stone, June Trimble, Carl Lendle Mullins, Ann Vincent, the folks from Greenville, Kentucky's Harbin Memorial Library—especially Linda Brown, and the unnamed source who helped Dad unravel the mystery as to who actually committed the murder in the ambush at Ebenezer. Also to Muhlenberg County's two newspapers, the *Leader-News* and the *Times-Argus,* and the Owensboro *Inquirer,* for carrying news releases in which the authors requested information to help in developing the book.

To Susan Vaughn we express special gratitude for the use of the sketch of "The Old Home Place at the Foot of the Hill"

To the wise women who understand the written English language far better than I: Helen Harris, Loretta Sorensen, and especially Susan Titus Osborn. Thanks for gentle editing. To readers of the manuscript who gave us valuable feedback and helped us get rid of some of those gremlins that creep into a text: John Bos, Ann Brazile, Brenda Brewer, Martha Brown, Cindy Pavey, Linda Sandlin, Linda Howell, Lourie Kelley and Karen Smith. Also kudos to Rowena Hanson for invaluable service in getting the manuscript into final form.

And finally, my thanks to my big brother, Kent, and all the aunts, uncles, and cousins who help keep the story alive by striving to live the example that Ma and Pa set for all of us.

PREFACE

We found special and delightful challenges in creating this story. While the book is fiction, we've incorporated much that is real about the people, mines, and mining towns of Muhlenberg County, Kentucky as they existed during the Great Depression. We wanted the story to be true to its setting and circumstances, but at times, to make it easier for readers without knowledge of mines to follow the story, we modified mining terminology slightly. We've included a glossary. It should help, not only with terms related with mining, but also with the slang of the day and words not used today that were "hand-me-downs" from previous generations. We created an imaginary mining community, Coaltown, Ky., to be the scene of several key happenings in the book. But the book is mostly about people: people facing difficult times with fortitude, joy, and love.

To fit the plot, some actual happenings were moved forward or backward from the dates when they occurred. For example, many early efforts to unionize the mines took place in the 1920s rather than in the 1930s. A strike-related ambush near Ebenezer happened in 1936, not in 1934 as portrayed in the story. The man killed was a miner, not a management man. The struggle for unionization was as bitter and bloody as we've described it. It devastated families and communities, sometimes causing rifts and hard feelings that continue to this day. We've tried to present, without taking sides, various views held by the people of that time.

This book was inspired by the lives of John Orville Smith and Ethel Skipworth Rhoads of Drakesboro and nearby Mondray, Kentucky. As it is a novel, a large part of it comes from our imaginations. But woven into the fabric of the story are many bits of history and much family lore. It is true, for example, that in his younger years Smith really was the short-fused, fast-fisted, hard-drinking gambler we've portrayed him as being. Then he met Ethel Rhoads. Her gentle love tamed him. But that's getting ahead of the story. We hope you'll find it fascinating.

DEDICATION

To Ma & Pa.: Together their roots twined and went deep into the soil and grew a family tree that is a living legacy of their love. To Daddy and Mama for carrying on the tradition. To Richard who understood my need to tell the story. And to Tracie, Ricky and Garrett, my own torchbearers to the next generation.

—Lisa Kay Hauser

To Rhea Nell Rhoads Bowman Spurlin: As fine a big sister as a little boy (or grown man) could possibly have. For the special love we share. For the popcorn balls, divinity candy, and chocolate fudge I enjoyed as a child and the southern cookin' I still enjoy. For being, as a little girl, the inspiration for Dulcie in this novel.

—Philip Dale Smith

PROLOGUE

Deep underground in Coaltown Mine, in one of the myriad passages that honeycombed Muhlenberg County, Kentucky, Smith Delaney made his way through the darkness. He could feel the mine's dampness and smell its stench. His mouth and throat filled with the air's cold bitterness. A quarter of a mile to go, and he would be at the face of coal where he would earn his next meager paycheck.

Above ground, the surrounding countryside was poor—dirt poor, but coal rich. Even the air held the acrid scent of coal. There was money to be had in the mines, but also treachery and death. Not much wealth trickled down to the men who dug the black bituminous coal out of the ground. Vast areas had been dug and scraped, leaving deep scars on the land. Huge heaps of inferior grade leavings were piled in ugly gray-black mounds, lying about the county like mock mountains. Coal dust was everywhere.

It was land that had been predominantly settled by immigrants from England, Ireland, and Europe. Many had come west when Kentucky was still Indian Territory. Their language was full of colorful Old World terminology. These multigenerational families, through heritage and faith, had deep loyalties and strong ties to God, church, family, and neighborhood. Farms and mines were their livelihood.

Just as his father, uncles, and brothers had done before him, Smith Delaney slogged doggedly through the darkness to where, with pick and shovel, he and others on the "hoot-owl" shift would mole their way into the face of coal for a ten-hour stretch.

This ain't no way to live, he thought. *No way to live, just a way to die. Maybe die quickly. Or maybe to die slow and miserable. Surely a man was created for better'n this.* As Delaney moved, his awkward, stooped posture and uneven gait under the low ceiling caused the carbide light on his head to bob up and down.

The vein of Number-Nine coal at Coaltown Mine was four feet, eleven inches thick. Delaney, five-feet-nine inches tall, was narrow-waisted and broad-shouldered. Years of swinging a pick and shovel had hardened his body and developed his massive biceps and forearms. He found no consolation in still being strong and powerful, or in the fact that, due to his small stature, it was easier for him to work there than it was for taller men.

The mines will get me: a fire damp explosion, other gases, a cave-in. Or coal dust will clog my lungs and smother the life outta me like it did my dad, and is doin' to Eldon Stoneworth and most of the rest of them older men workin' down here. I gotta get out. Somehow, I just gotta get outta here.

A distant shriek of pain and terror jolted Delaney from his dismal reverie. *That's not a human. That's a bank mule in trouble!* he thought. His brow furrowed into a frown. *Sure's the world, Jeb Sawyer's on one of his rampages again.* Smith crouched lower and broke into an awkward but rapid trot. Soon he could hear the slap of a whip accompanied by the pain-filled whinnies of the mule. Running through a breakthrough and rounding a corner, he could see the scene at a distance. It sickened him. The tiny old mule, harnessed to the coal car, couldn't get away—yank at the traces as it might. With his left hand, Jeb Sawyer, the huge mine boss, gripped the mule's head by the bridle. With the whip in his right hand he flailed the animal. The mules' eyes rolled wildly in its head as it collapsed, writhing and twisting, to the ground. The five miners working the face of coal stood slack-jawed in dismay, their picks and shovels at their sides. The changing expressions on their faces told Delaney that they were looking past Sawyer and watching his bobbing light rapidly approaching. But Sawyer didn't see or hear him.

14

"Get up, you miserable excuse of a mule. Get yourself up and pull that there coal car. You hear me? You ain't a layin' down on me, or my name ain't Jebidiah Sawyer. I'll cut you to shreds! I'll turn you to hamburger for these lazy, no account, good-fer-nothin' miners. I'll ... "

The steel grip of Smith Delaney's left hand clamped Sawyer's wrist as again he drew back the whip. Delaney spun the big man toward him, and in the same motion, he began an uppercut that swept in an arc beginning near his feet. His fist crashed flush into Sawyer's face. The bully's head lunged upward into the low ceiling. He crumpled in the muck.

Smith stepped over him and knelt by the mule. "Easy, Boy, easy. I'm gonna get you outta here. Easy!" He began unhitching the mule. A couple of the miners joined him.

"All right, Delaney! All right!" said one miner. "He deserved what you give 'im and then some. Wish I'd a done it! I prob'ly would've, if you hadn't."

"Better hush up, McKinney," said another miner. "Sawyer might come around and hear you."

Smith Delaney continued to talk to the mule. The animal calmed and gained footing on shaky legs. Smith held the bridle and gently stroked the animal. The mule quivered under his hand. He called to an older miner who was arranging the loose harness, "Eldon, I'm takin' Smokey out and turnin' 'im loose. I'll send somebody down with a new mule. You throw some water in Sawyer's face. When he comes to, tell 'im not to start yammerin' about how he's gonna fire me. I know I'm fired. And I ain't comin' back this time."

"You done the right thing, Smith," said Stoneworth. "I'll take care of Sawyer. We're obliged to you."

Smith didn't respond. He walked away, leading the old mule. He had plenty of time to think about his plight at they trudged the dank, dark, three-quarters of a mile to the elevator cage that would lift them to the surface. *Fired. Fired again! Out of work again.* His grip tightened around the harness. *Where to now?*

15

Not another mine! Hit the road again? Back to gamblin'? I'm good at cards. Back to runnin' bootleg whiskey? Good money, but a man can get hisself killed or, worse'n that, put away.

Smith shook his head in frustration. *At this point in my life I shoulda found me a wife—and have me a bunch a little kids to love. Before I know it, I'll be forty years old. Ain't I ever gonna get my life turned around? Surely this ain't all that's meant to be for me—But what else is there?*

Hattie eased down into the chair. She rubbed the small of her back with one hand and her swollen belly with the other. Her labor had begun in the dark of the early morning. Already, her back was aching in time with the rhythm of her breathing. She could feel the pressure pushing down, down, down. Soon, she'd have to walk up to Radburn's Store and have them call her sister to come for Dulcie and bring the midwife. Someday she might have a phone of her own. But this was 1933. The Depression was deepening and a phone was a luxury she couldn't afford.

Even before sunup the heat was stifling. Beads of perspiration trickled down between her breasts. She pushed her dark hair off her forehead with the back of her wrist. Loose tendrils wrapped around her damp arm as she pushed it back into place. Her hair was so dark it was almost black. Her deep-set eyes were the same color as her hair. With a sigh, Hattie pushed herself up from the chair and walked to the counter. She stirred up biscuit dough and with a rolling pin pressed it out into a round on the floured enamel work surface. With swift efficiency she cut biscuits with the circle of tin that her husband, Jack, had made from a clean Pet Milk can. He'd been so careful to turn the top edge back so it wouldn't cut her hands. Earlier she had prepared the pie tins with bacon grease. Now it only took a moment for her to turn the biscuits in the grease, flip them over and place them in the pans and into the oven. She quickly fried the eggs. She worked flour into bacon grease in the still-hot, black cast-iron skillet and added milk, stirring in salt and pepper as the gravy thickened. When it was bubbling, and just the right consistency to pour over the biscuits, she moved the skillet to the back of the stove where it would stay warm. Now, all was ready.

Soon her little girl would be stirring, but right now there was time for a quick cup of coffee. She spooned a careful amount of sugar into the blue enameled cup she had carried up the one step from the kitchen onto the screened-in back porch where the table and chairs were. Hattie loved this morning ritual of sitting and looking out at the trees, listening to the birds greet the morning. Here she could escape the sweltering heat and feel the breeze as it passed through the porch. She watched the purple martins swoop down to their two-storied, many-holed birdhouse. Single bluebird boxes scattered across the back of the acreage encouraged those birds to settle there and raise their babies in the spring.

"Mama," Dulcie's curly dark head peered around the doorframe. "Dulthy hungwy", she said as she climbed onto the porch.

"Are you, Darlin'?" Hattie asked. "Well, it's a good thing Mama made you somethin' to eat then, isn't it?" She struggled to her feet, giving the three-year-old a quick hug. Then stepping back into the hot kitchen, she removed the golden biscuits from the oven and made a plate for her little girl. She helped Dulcie up on the four-legged wooden stool and sat down again. They held hands and Hattie said, "Lord, we thank you for this food, this day, and all our blessin's. Be with us as we go on through the rest of it. In Jesus Name, Amen."

"Amen," Dulcie echoed.

Hattie smiled at the little echo. *How mighty is the faith of a little child,* she thought. *Lord, let my faith be like that, too. Especially today.*

After they had eaten, Hattie washed and dressed Dulcie and tied on the child's sunbonnet for the hot walk up the road to the little store on the edge of town. She'd washed the few dishes quickly in the old dishpan with water from a bucket she'd drawn from the box well on the outside porch. *Daddy knew what he was doin' when he put that well on the porch,* she thought. *But, oh, what it must be like to turn a knob and have water in the house!* Her sister Carrie had water in her house. It was a pure pleasure to turn that handle and see it rush right down into the sink. And it ran right back out down the drain. You didn't have to haul it in or haul it back out. Gene, Carrie's husband, said someday most everyone would have running water in their homes, but Hattie wasn't so sure. Seemed like a big luxury for poor folk.

She took her sunbonnet off of a hook on the porch and loosely tied it under her chin. She opened the screen door, then took the child's hand. As she walked, Hattie gazed across the yard at the rutted road running up the hill, then glanced back over her shoulder at the old house where she'd grown up, and where she and Jack had come to live after their wedding. Hattie loved the azalea bushes and lilacs her mother had carefully tended from the time she was a young bride until her death. Hattie had kept them pruned and added a few more in the last few years. It was peaceful there, sheltered by soft hills on three sides and by the steep ascent into town. Looking back up the path where she was going, she thought, *When Daddy built the house down here, was he thinkin' to keep the world out, or us in? Some of both, I reckon.* She smiled at the thought of the many trips she'd made up and down the path beside the road that led to Drakesboro, with her daddy's big, rough hand gently holding hers just as she now held Dulcie's.

"See that bug up there on the wild rose, Dulcie?" Hattie asked, pointing out a small insect. "That's a mayfly. Don't it have funny wings, all stickin' up like that? And that white flower over yonder? That's Queen Ann's lace. It looks just like a piece of fancywork for a Sunday dress collar. I reckon that's why they call it that, don't you?"

Dulcie had the two middle fingers of her left hand in her mouth. Her huge brown eyes took in all they saw. "Whath's that?" she lisped around her fingers, looking at green growth on a half buried, rotted log along the path.

"That's moss. It's like a carpet of green, isn't it? I read in a book about a man that made an outdoor room in a beautiful forest. It had a carpet of moss on the floor. He made himself a place he could go and just feel God all around him. Wouldn't that be somethin' to see? I hear there's big churches in places all over the world that have colored glass windows and big stone walls and statues with real gold on 'em. But I think I'd like that man's moss-carpet room in the woods better for worshippin' the Creator than any of those old man-made buildin's."

As they walked, she continued to point things out to the child. It was her way. She talked and explained what she could and was always careful to show her respect for the world of nature around her.

After they crested the hill they passed the homes of several friends and neighbors in the quiet little community. Hattie told Dulcie who lived in each house as they went by. She nodded at a house to their right. "That's where the Sumners live. They're the ones who helped us when the snow blocked the road last winter. They're good folks." Later Hattie asked, "See that little place set back over there? That's Miz Shropshire's place. She's always so sweet." Without thinking about it, Hattie was planting seeds of security in Dulcie's mind: they were surrounded by people who cared about them.

The walk was only a mile or so, but it took its toll on Hattie. She had to stop once as a contraction caught her off guard. She was relieved to see the store come into view. The little bell over the door tinkled as she pushed her way into the dim interior.

"Be there in a minute," came the voice of Annie Radburn from the door to the backroom that led to their living quarters.

20

"Here I am—Hattie, what are you doin' walkin' all this way, and your time almost on you? Come set yourself down."

The storekeeper bustled over to help Hattie into a chair set at a table in the corner of the store and fussed over Hattie and Dulcie. She lifted the little girl up onto one of the stools at the counter and gave her a penny candy. "There now, Dulcie, you jest set and let your Mama talk to me a minute."

"Miz Radburn, I don't have a penny to pay for that candy. I didn't come to shop today." Hattie held her head up, but she was deeply embarrassed.

"Why, Honey, did I ask you to pay for that candy? That's a gift to Dulcie for brightenin' my day with that smile and those dimples of hers," said Mrs. Radburn with a smile.

"Well, thank you, then. I can't stay but a minute. I wonder if you'd call Carrie and see if she'd come after Dulcie." She added quietly, "I'm thinkin' it's my time."

"Mercy sakes alive, and you walked all the way up here? Didn't I tell you not to sell Mr. Jack's truck 'til after the baby come?"

"Miz Radburn, I had to pay for Jack's buryin'. 'Sides, I don't know how to drive, so it wouldn't of done me any good to'ave kept that old heap of tin. Jack just barely kept it going, and half the time I think it was my prayers that got him home—not that old truck." Hattie smiled at the older woman. "Seems to me sellin' it made more sense than keepin' it. Now, do you think it'd be all right to call Carrie?"

"Oh, of course it's all right, but then I'm gonna have Mr. Radburn run you back down home in his Dodge. Mr. Radburn! Mr. Radburn! Hattie Crowe's here and you're gonna drive her home. You hear me?"

Harwell Radburn poked his head around the corner from the backroom and said with a twinkle in his eye, "Oh, yeah? What's in it fer me if'n I do? Is Dulcie gonna give me some sugar?" Dulcie hopped off the stool and ran to Mr. Radburn, throwing her arms around his thighs.

"Hi," she said.

"Hi, yourself, youngun. Whatcha got there? Did Annie give you a candy? Good thing. I'd take her to the woodshed if she forgot to give my girl a candy!" He threw a mock glare at his wife and scooped Dulcie up for a quick hug. Dulcie giggled when he scraped his beard on her soft cheek.

"You scwatchy!" She squealed.

Mr. Radburn laughed and shifted her to his hip. "You wanna listen to the ocean?" he said, picking up a large pink shell from the shelf behind the counter. "Hold it to your ear, Darlin'. You hear that? That's the ocean!"

Dulcie's eyes grew large as she listened to the rush of sound from the shell. A shy smile spread across her face.

Hattie also smiled, remembering listening with wonder to the same shell when she was a child not much older than Dulcie. Annie's parents had run the store back then, and Annie was just a teenager.

Annie clapped her hands and laughed outloud, "Good gracious, Mr. Radburn. I don't believe there's hardly a youngun in the county ain't heard the ocean in that shell. When my cousin sent me that shell all those years ago I never dreamed so many would get to see it and imagine the ocean while alistenin' to it."

Harwell replaced the shell and turned back to Hattie. "What are you fine ladies doing out on a hot day like today, and so early, too? Did you bring me some eggs, Hattie?"

"No, sir. Not this time. I just come to see if y'all would call Carrie for me."

Annie Radburn turned a fine shade of pink and said quietly, "Well, it ain't nuthin' for men to be thinkin'on, but we need to get Miz Carrie to come pick up Dulcie, 'cause ... well, 'cause Hattie's got some bizness to take care of that ain't fittin' for a youngun to be in on." She tilted her head toward Hattie and cut her eyes swiftly to her belly then back at Harwell.

Harwell's face blazed as pink as Annie's. "Oh, I see. Well, then, uh, I reckon you best git on the phone to Carrie while I go

22

start the car." He turned to Dulcie. "Wanna come with me, Punkin'?"

Solemnly she nodded her head. "All righty then ... " Out they went through the door in the back toward the old shed where he kept his car under a tarpaulin.

Annie reached for the phone. She rang the exchange and asked for Carrie Beckwith. In just a moment she was connected.

"Carrie, Honey, Annie Radburn callin' you. How're you? Fine, just fine. How's your Mr. Gene? Fine. That's fine. I'm just callin' you to let you know you need to come. It's Hattie's time. Now, on the way could you stop for Ma Richards? We don't want Hattie havin' this baby by herself. 'Course you will. All you Stoneworths are good younguns. I always said your mama raised the sweetest bunch of children in the county. Wish she was alive today. I'd tell her to her face. She was the kindest woman, never turned nobody away fer nuthin'. Always up to the church doin' and takin' care of things. I'm right proud to be shirttail kin to her even if it is just by marriage."

Hattie gasped as a sudden contraction took her breath away. "Miz Radburn, 'scuse me, but I think I need to get back home soon," she hissed through her teeth. "Could you just ask Carrie to be careful and to hurry?"

"Mercy, you're laborin' and I'm conversatin'! Sakes alive, what's the matter with me? Carrie, you come right away, and stop for Ma Richards. I'll keep Dulcie with me, and Mr. Radburn'll drive Hattie home in the Dodge. Now, don't stop to get your sisters. I don't think there's time."

With that, Mrs. Radburn hung the receiver on the hook. "Now, don't argue with me, Hattie Crowe, Dulcie will stay here, and Carrie will come to you with the midwife. After you're all ready, Carrie can come for your little girl and bring her back home. You need wimen-folk at a time like this, and I know how close you and Carrie are. 'Course, all you Stoneworths are close."

As Annie rattled on, she was helping Hattie out the door to the waiting car. She plucked Dulcie off the front seat and eased Hattie in. As the car crunched down the gravel road she was prattling on to a big-eyed Dulcie as though the child were a little old lady from the Thursday morning ladies' Bible Study, "Just the finest bunch of folks this county ever laid eyes on. I'm proud, I tell you, just right proud to be shirttail kin, even if it is by marriage ... "

Hattie gritted her teeth as the Dodge dropped into a deep rut. Pain flamed around her middle and caused her to suck her breath in. She reached one hand up to grip the door handle.

Harwell Radburn reached over and patted her other hand. "Did you ever hear a woman could talk like my Annie? She can go on and on and not say nuthin' at all. She's a good 'un, though. She'd break her own heart afore she'd hurt another soul. She sure loves you and your Dulcie. I reckon if she's said it once she's said it a hundred times 'If I coulda had a daughter, I'da wanted one just like Hattie Stoneworth Crowe!' I'm mighty fond of you too, Hattie. We feel powerful bad about your Jack. He was a good man. We couldn'ta been prouder when he was made deacon of the church, if'n he'd been our own boy. "

Hattie closed her eyes and laid her head back on the seat. She would not cry. Not now. There was too much to do when she got home to give in to a fit of the sorrowfuls. But, oh, how she missed Jack today. *Of course, If he was here to help,* she thought, *he'd be all fumblefingers, tripping over his feet and getting in the way the whole time.* She thought of him on the day Dulcie was born. *He pert near burst his buttons he was so proud of that baby girl.* She'd heard of men that got angry when their wives had a girl first, but not Jack. He'd whooped and hollered and fired off the shotgun to let the world know how proud he was. Waste of good ammunition, but it made Hattie smile to think of it now.

Mr. Radburn pulled up the slope next to the house, as close as he could get to the door so Hattie wouldn't have far to walk.

24

"Can't help you with much more here, Hattie, but I could chop some wood and bring in a load, if you're needin' some."

"No, thank you, Mr. Radburn. My brother, Forrest, cut and stacked plenty last week. I brought some in this morning when I first started ... well, you know, when I realized. I sure appreciate the ride, though."

"Oh, that's fine then," Harwell quickly said. "I'll just let you get on with your, uh, work then. Carrie'll be here anytime now with Miz Richards, and she'll let us know after ... well, anyway, you come to us if you need anything, now.

He backed carefully down the slope and eased up the hill. Hattie turned and walked slowly into the house. *Okay, Lord, it's just You and me. I'll do my part, and you do Yours.* She knew she had a little ways to go, so she set about straightening things. Old Ma Richards was the best midwife in the area, but she was a little on the abrupt side and wouldn't think anything of criticizing the way Hattie kept house if she thought it weren't up to snuff. It wouldn't do to give her anything to talk about.

Hattie took out of her bureau drawer a clean baby gown, an outing flannel baby blanket, and little flannel booties all edged with careful feather stitching. She'd worked hard on the little clothes and knew they were beautiful. Mama had taught her to sew almost as soon as she could hold a needle.

She'd done most of the work while Jack slept. He'd slept a lot the last few weeks before he died. The cave-in at the mine that had cruelly crushed him hadn't killed him quickly. He'd lingered for almost two months before the end came. She'd sat by his bed for hours on end as he labored to breathe. That's when she'd made the baby clothes. Jack had been so happy they were having another baby and proudly inspected each little piece of clothing as she finished it. He'd been her anchor, and she and Dulcie had been his whole life. Some days Hattie still half expected him to come roaring through the door. "Where's my girls?"

Hattie slid down in the rocker as a tear slipped down her cheek. *Jack, how'm I gonna do all this by myself? Raise these babies and take care of all that's needin' takin' care of? How'm I gonna do it when I'm missin' you so? Oh, Jack, why'd you have to go and die?* She cried quietly for a minute, then took a deep shuddering breath. *Well, that's that then. I'll just do it, 'cause I have to. There's nobody gonna do it for me.*

She got up and poured water from the pitcher on the washstand onto a clean towel and bathed her face. Then turned back to the bureau. She pulled out two white cotton nightgowns. One for the labor and one for afterward. Ma Richards was particular about cleanliness though some thought her foolish. Hattie gathered up clean sheets and toweling and tied two dishtowels to the wooden uprights on the headboard of the bed. Then she went into the kitchen to start water to boil. She boiled her scissors and laid them out on her nightstand on another clean dishcloth. She went to the closet under the stairs and retrieved the stack of soft white cotton strips she'd need after the baby came. Then, when everything was ready, she made a pot of coffee and poured a cup. Walking out on the porch, she sat down to wait.

Well, Lord, it's gonna be a big job, but I think we can handle it. Or at least, You can. I'll just let You do the work. It'd be real nice if You could make it quick work, though, if it wouldn't be askin' too much. She grimaced as another contraction shook her body. *Whew! They're comin' swift and sure.* Hattie bit her lip as the pain slowly passed, then took a deep breath. *I... I thank You for being with me. Be with Dulcie, too, up at Radburn's, and Father, if you could just give Jack a message, could You let him know I'm having the baby today? I reckon he'd like to know.*

The car that came over the hill a little while later was crowded with women. All but one had dark hair, dark eyes, and sweet faces. Five Stoneworth women and one gray-haired mid-

26

wife. Ma Richards looked pained, squashed as she was between Carrie in the driver's seat and Lalie on the other side. Marva, Willa and Chloe sat in the back seat. The noise those six women put out was incredible.

"Hattie, what are you doin' sittin' there?" asked Carrie.

"Hattie, why aren't you in bed?" chimed Marva.

"Hattie, did you put a knife under the pillow to cut the pain?" asked Willa.

"Hattie, did you eat?" added Chloe.

Hattie started laughing as they piled out of the car and headed for the screen door.

"Let's see, I'm drinking coffee. I don't feel like going to bed yet. No, I saved the knife for Ma Richards. How're you, Ma Richards? Thanks for coming. And ... what was the last question? I remember. No, I didn't eat today. Just had a little coffee. Carrie, I know I heard Annie Radburn tell you not to take the time to pick up your sisters. Don't you ever listen?"

Carrie gave Hattie a gentle squeeze. "Mama always made us look out for you 'cause you was the least'un. Just seemed nat'ral to round up the girls to look after you today. I only had to make two stops 'cause Marva, Chloe and Lalie were planning a trip to Greenville to go shoppin' and were all at Lalie's house gettin' ready to go when I got Annie Radburn's call. And Willa, she'd just stopped at my house for coffee. You know, Hattie, I don't believe I said a thing to Miz Radburn except, 'Hello, fine, yes ma'am, and, well bye then'. She was talkin' so fast I could hardly understand her, but I got 'Hattie, Ma Richards, and you've got to come.'"

They all laughed because each had spent considerable time with the storeowner's wife over the course of their lives and knew what a verbal tidal wave she was.

Ma Richards gave all the girls a hard look and said, "You girls orta be a little more respectful of your elders and them that serves you. Where would we all be right now if Annie Radburn hadn't been kind enough to call? Carrie Stoneworth Beckwith, you need to learn to curb your tongue. And you, the oldest of this family, carryin' on like that!"

"Ma Richards, you're right. I'm plum 'shamed of myself. We all love Annie. Please forgive me. You know how my tongue runs when I'm excited."

"Humph! Ain't for me to forgive, but you're settin' a fine example is all I'm sayin'."

Carrie turned and winked at Hattie, who bit her cheeks and looked down to keep from laughing. Oh, it was good to have the girls here! And even Ma Richards. It had been so long since there'd been any laughter in the house.

Hattie's breathing shallowed, and she gripped the edge of the table hard. Her eyes suddenly seemed to lose focus as she tried to breathe through the pain that racked her body. A rush of water forced its way between her legs. She looked at the wet porch floor. "Oh my!" She sighed. "I reckon y'all made it just in time."

"Fiddlesticks!" said Ma briskly. "We got here with plenty of time to spare. You ain't dropped that baby on its head yet. Lalie, don't stand there with your mouth open! Help me git your sister into a nightgown and into that bed. Carrie, you carry my bag. Marva, you start a pot of tea with the packet in my bag. No, the other packet. That one's for bowels. Willa, pour me a cup of that coffee with a smidgen of sugar. Make that two smidgens. And you, Chloe, get my Bible and read to me from the book of John. I don't care where. I just love John."

Instantly, everyone was in motion. Each person had a job to do and did it swiftly and carefully. Hattie was undressed, put into a nightgown and put to bed before she realized she had her shoes off. Marva was pressing a cup of Ma's special tea into Hattie's hands while Willa was placing a cup of heavily sugared coffee into Ma's. Carrie was standing on one side of the bed gently stroking Hattie's hair back. Chloe sat down in a straight backed chair and read quietly, "In the beginning was the Word ... " Lalie straightened and restraightened the little baby clothes that were waiting. Everything was under control.

Hattie's labor was intense. The Stoneworth girls carried the kitchen chairs into the bedroom and sat in a circle around something that Hattie couldn't see. They worked quietly, but with lots of good humor. Each would take her turn coming to the bedside to see to Hattie for a few minutes. They offered words of encouragement during contractions and quietly rubbed her wrists in between. Hattie knew she was blessed. As she rested between contractions she looked around at her sisters and knew that Annie Radburn was right. They were the "sweetest bunch of younguns in the county."

Ma also looked around the room. She'd delivered every one of the Stoneworth girls. The Stoneworth boys, too. There were three of them: Eldon, Forrest and Berkley. She shook her head and said, "I reckon your brothers'd be here too, if'n y'all didn't know I don't brook no men at a birthin'. Them boys sure are partial to Hattie. 'Course, everyone's partial to you, Hattie. You bein' the least'un an' all. Ain't you the tiniest little thing? Don't b'lieve you stand five foot tall, do you, girl?"

"Just barely." Hattie answered.

"Can't weigh more'n a hunnerd pounds, neither, not countin' the baby. And here you are ready to give birth any minute! You was the only one of your mama's babies I was ever afraid of losin', you know. You was so little when you was born, I was mortal afeared you'd die. But you didn't just surprise me by livin', you've done real good. You love your family, the Good Lord, all the wonders of nature, and life in general. Yep, you've done all right and I suspect you'll do fine by this little one you're about to bring out into our world."

Ma rose creakily from the chair next to the bed and went to the kitchen to pour herself another cup of coffee.

"Ma," Carrie whispered as she followed the old midwife. "Hattie really is awful little. I'm scared if she has a big baby it'll tear her apart."

Ma glared at Carrie. "You let me do the worryin'. I'll take care of her if she tears."

Carrie grimaced at the thought and Ma laid a hand on her arm.

"Listen here, don't you even think about goin' back in that bedroom with *that* look on your face. Dulcie was a purty good size baby, and Hattie birthed her without much trouble a'tall. Reckon she'll be just fine. We'll just have to wait and see. Won't hurt none to pray, though."

Before Ma sat back down in the old rocking chair by the bed with her handwork to busy herself during the wait, she carefully placed a paring knife under Hattie's pillow. "Now, I don't know if'n I b'lieve in this bizness or not," she said. "They say the knife'll 'cut the pain'. Maybe it does, maybe it don't."

Lalie watched the old midwife pat the corner of the pillow where she'd tucked the knife. "If'n you don't believe in it, why'd you do it?"

"Reckon 'cause my Mama done it, and her Mama afore her. I'd just as soon not be the one to break the tradition. It's a comfortin' thing to birthin' women. No one never asked me not to do it, so I reckon I'll jes' keep right on adoing it. If it makes the laboring wimen feel better, it's worth its weight in gold."

Between contractions, Hattie watched her sisters as they finished what they were doing and put their project away. She was mildly curious but figured they'd tell her when they were ready. Maybe they were making shirts for the boys for Christmas presents, or working on a quilt. You'd think they'd let her see it if it was a quilt, but maybe they just didn't want to bother her right now.

Time passed slowly 'til Ma sent Chloe and Lalie to the kitchen to make lunch for the rest of them. Just as they were leaving the room, Hattie let out a gasp. Carrie helped her reach the knotted dishtowels that Hattie had tied to the headboard earlier. Ma moved to the bottom of the bed and reached up under the sheet.

"Mmm hmmm, yup, it's time. You push now, girl. Like you've never pushed before."

Hattie pushed and panted and pushed and panted for what seemed like forever. The sisters gathered in a half circle to pray for Hattie and her coming baby. Ma frowned and waited. Finally, she said, "There's a head ... It's comin'. Push, Hattie!" Hattie pushed, and there he was. All chins and wrinkles. A sweet baby boy. He was purple and mashed-looking and, oh, so beautiful. Ma gripped his ankles, held him up, and smacked his little bottom. He started to cry, and so did the rest of the house. Ma shook her head. Then she blinked her eyes hard to remove a suspicious wetness that had suddenly formed there. With the surety of experience, she tied off the cord and cut it, rubbed the baby in a towel, and wrapped him in a blanket. Then she laid him in his mother's arms.

"There he is, girl. You done good, real good. Lookee there! Don't he look just like Jack Crowe?" Ma chuckled. "Well, Jack told me back in the spring if I didn't bring him a boy this time, my reputation would be pure ruined 'cause he'd already told everyone I was agoin' to."

Everyone laughed through their tears and crowded around to see the baby. Hattie said, "Jack's boy ... I think he should be Jackie Stoneworth Crowe. That's a fine name. Do you think Jack would like it?"

Carrie hugged her little widowed sister. "Honey, he'd love it."

Ma moved back down to the end of the bed to deliver the afterbirth and then shooed the rest of them out of the bedroom. Willa washed the baby on a towel that had been heated in the warming oven of the stove. She dressed him in the little gown and booties, wrapped him in a blanket and brought him back to Hattie. Ma called to Chloe to bring Hattie another cup of her special tea and to Lalie to bring the cradle down from upstairs.

31

Hattie had cleaned it and made it ready the day before, so they just needed to move it into the bedroom.

Carrie was talking quietly to Hattie whose eyes were drooping. Ma took the baby and settled him into the cradle. She took Carrie by the arm.

"Out of here, girl. Your sister didn't cry out once the whole time she was laborin'. She's exhausted fightin' those pains. You get out to the kitchen and see to that lunch I sent those others to start a while ago. I'll be out in a minute."

Ma sat down on the edge of the bed. She didn't allow much softness between herself and the women she helped. It was too hard when you lost one of them or one of their babies, but she felt a special bond with Hattie.

"Well, girl, you done it." She roughly patted Hattie's hand. "Answer me this. Why didn't you holler like any one of them girls in there woulda done if it had been them, 'stead of you?'"

"Ma, they worry over me so. I just didn't want to scare 'em no more than they already were."

Ma hooted with laughter. "Ain't you the limit! You may be the least'un, but I b'lieve your heart's the biggest of all them Stoneworths!"

"Oh, Ma," cried Hattie, "that's just *exactly* what Jack used to say!"

The old granny, unexpectedly choked with emotion, cleared her throat, "Go to sleep. You're tired." She stalked from the room.

Hattie gazed at the tiny baby in the cradle beside her bed. *Lord, It's me, Hattie Crowe. You done good work today. Thanks for givin' Jack the message and for letting him send one back to me through Ma Richards. Ain't You somethin'.*

2

Eunice Ruby Crowe descended on them like bad news on a dark day. It was obvious she had worked herself into a state of near hysteria by the time she got out of the truck driven by her brother, Ferd. As she made her way to the door, he had to support her.

"Now, now, sister, don't take on so. You're gonna make yourself sick," Ferd said as he helped her into the best chair on the porch.

Carrie and Willa greeted her politely. They were all careful what they said to Jack's mother. The woman took offense easier than anyone they'd ever known.

"How do, Miz Crowe? Awfully kind of you to come. Hattie's sleepin'. She had a fine, healthy boy a little bit ago. We were just fixin' to send Chloe up to Radburn's to call the family with the good news. Would you like some coffee? How 'bout you, Ferd?"

"No ma'am, thanky. I b'lieve I'll jes' step out in the yard while y'all visit," Ferd replied.

"Carrie Beckwith, I find it hard to b'lieve you were going to send anyone to call me," whined Eunice. "I had to hear it was Hattie's time from Annie Radburn when I went into the store for a pound of bacon and a sack of flour. It just about mortified me beyond redemption to hear it from an outsider. You know that woman's always thought she was a little better'n the rest of us. She just lorded it over me that Hattie had come to her instead of me when she needed help. Like I wouldn't have taken poor little fatherless Dulcie into my home when she needed someone to watch her. I'm so ashamed I could die."

Carrie rolled her eyes at Willa and went to get the coffeepot.

"Miz Crowe, I've never known Annie to put on airs," said Willa. "Besides, your house is almost another mile and a half beyond Radburns. Surely you didn't expect Hattie to walk all that way with a three-year-old, and in labor besides. I know it must have been hard for you to find out at the store, but we really were fixin' to send Chloe up to call. The baby's only been here an hour, and we're just now gettin' settled down to cookin' so Hattie won't have to when we go home."

"She wouldn't have to do none of the cleanin' and cookin' if she'd just let me move in here and take care of her and those poor fatherless children. I've just been waiting for the baby to come so she'd see how much she needs me. Jack would have wanted me here to help, but Hattie's just been hateful about the whole thing. 'No, Mother Crowe, I think it's best if I stick to the routine that Dulcie's used to. They's been too many changes already.' I know Jack's just rolling in his grave that she's bein' so stubborn. It ain't seemly for a woman as young as Hattie to be alone, even if she is a widow. It'd be better for all concerned if she'd bend her back a little and let me come down here with her. Surely y'all can see that it would be the perfect solution to the problem."

Carrie returned with the coffee, listening to Eunice harp at Willa about Hattie. She plunked the coffeepot down on the table, a little more roughly than was necessary, and glared at Hattie's mother-in-law.

Eunice was a pinched looking woman. Her hair was scraped back into a tight bun on the back of her head. Her long nose appeared to slice her thin face in half. She was severe from top to bottom. All the Stoneworths were amazed that laughing Jack Crowe had been this humorless woman's son. It just didn't seem possible. She wielded Scripture like a weapon and brought destruction wherever she went.

At the dinner after Jack's funeral, Eunice had announced that she was moving in with Hattie. That was just the way she was. She didn't ask if Hattie'd like her to come. She stood up and announced it to all within earshot. All her fine talk of Christian duty was nothing but hot air. Hattie knew she'd end up waiting on Eunice, hand and foot, for the rest of her life. So far, she'd been able to hold her ground, but it wasn't easy standing against Eunice. She could suck the joy out of Hattie in five minutes flat.

"Miz Crowe, there's only one bedroom in this house. Where would you sleep? It would be awfully crowded for you with Hattie and Dulcie and Jackie all in one bedroom," Lalie said as she joined them on the porch.

"Well, now, I'll just tell you where I'd sleep. I could take the bedroom, and we could move my little divan into the front room, and Dulcie could sleep on that. Hattie could have that big old couch that Jack insisted on buyin'. The baby will be in his little cradle for quite a while yet ..."

"You expect a woman who's just given birth to give up her bed to you?" said Ma Richards as she stepped up on the porch. "My, my, aren't you a fine piece of work!"

The rest of the Stoneworth girls watched from the kitchen door.

"If you think I'm gonna stand by and let you railroad that young lady out of her bed when I just delivered her a fine baby, you've got another think coming. She's gonna stay right where she is. If you want to sleep on that couch, that's up to you, if you can get Hattie to agree. But Hattie's not gonna move one step out of that bed without my say so, and I ain't agonna say so anytime soon to you or the Queen of England or anyone else in the state of Kentucky, so you can just get shet of that thought right now!"

Two Stoneworths had coughing fits, and three others had suddenly become fascinated by their aprons. No one spoke for a minute, and then Carrie asked brightly, "More coffee anyone?"

Eunice Crowe went beet red from up under her old hat to the Victorian collar of her dress.

"No, thank you. I reckon I'll just see my new grandson and be on my way. I know when y'all get together there's no reasoning to be had. I warned my Jackie about you Stoneworth girls when he first took up with Hattie. I told him, 'Jackie, you'll be in for the worst henpeckin' of your life if you marry up with her 'cause it won't just be her! It'll be the whole lot and litter!' I'll come back when Hattie's alone. Then we'll see how things are gonna be. Now, if y'all don't mind I'd like to see my grandson."

As soon as Chloe brought the sleeping baby out to her, Eunice started in again. "Oh, you poor fatherless boy. How you'll *ever* survive in this world is beyond me. Don't you worry, precious. Grandma will take care of you." She carried on over the baby with wet, noisy sobs. The family sighed with collective relief when she gave the baby to Carrie and swept from the porch saying, "Tell Hattie I want to talk to her when things are quieter around here. Come on, Ferd." And Eunice was gone as quickly as she had come.

Ma Richards blew out a breath and muttered something about "that woman would try the patience of a saint." Then she said, "Carrie, Hattie's gonna have a time when it gets out she had that baby. Every mother in Muhlenberg County who's got a baby with 'thresh' is gonna be linin' up at the door for him to blow in their babies' mouths. By the time he's old enough to blow, they'll be coming down here in droves."

It was a superstition that a child born after his father's death had only to blow into the mouth of a baby with thrush for healing to begin. Unfortunately for Jackie, it was a strongly held belief for many of the hill folks. They were steeped in the traditions of a simple people in a simpler time when professional medical help was very limited.

Ma Richards continued, "Anyway, in a couple of years you might remind her to be on the lookout for anxious mamas with

36

white-mouthed younguns. I reckon I'm 'bout ready to go. Carrie, if one of you will stay with Hattie, Chloe can drive me home in your car and come back for you later."

"Of course, Chloe can run you home," said Carrie. "And I'll talk to Hattie about the thresh babies. Here, Chloe, take my keys and run by my house and get the little bag I packed, and bring it to me. I'm staying here tonight. Gene thinks he'll die without me, but I'm sure he'll survive. My girls can get supper without me and do the washin' up after, so they'll all be fine 'til tomorrow."

Chloe nodded and took the keys and turned toward the door.

"Wait, I'm still thinking," Carrie continued. "Oh, stop at Radburns and pick up Dulcie on your way back. Hattie'd just kill me if we forgot to bring Dulcie home. After we eat, you can take the girls home and keep my car 'til tomorrow if you'll come for me around noon."

As usual Carrie had organized all their lives in a few brief sentences.

Chloe threw her head back and laughed. "You think you got us all raised up to mind you, don't you? Well, one of these days, we ain't none of us gonna do as we're told. Then where'll you be?"

Chloe was the tallest of the Stoneworth girls. Slender of form and fair of face, she was the only one except Carrie who could drive. They had all been surprised when Chloe told them she wanted to learn, because she was also the quietest. It was just so unexpected coming from shy Chloe. She and her husband Ray had four children. Like three of the other girls' husbands, Ray was a miner. He was also a good man who loved Chloe and the children beyond belief. Chloe only had to look at something once for Ray to try to buy it. She'd had to learn to tell him "no" when he'd reach for his wallet. All of them had heard her say, "Ray, Honey, that's real nice, but I don't need it. It's just not my style." It sounded kinda funny when she'd said it about a new Sears and Roebuck washing machine.

Ma went back in to check on Hattie one more time before she left, and then she and Chloe loaded her bag into the car and headed back to town.

Willa and Marva went to the garden to pick vegetables for the supper table. Lalie dug through Hattie's sewing basket 'til she found an apron with a torn pocket to mend. She gathered up needle and thread and walked out to sit on the porch-swing.

When Carrie saw everyone else was occupied, she looked in on Hattie. She was surprised that Hattie was awake gazing at her baby. "Well, did you sleep, Least'un?"

"Not much, not with Mother Crowe coming in like she did." Hattie looked up and smiled wearily. "I s'pose I shoulda come out to see her, but honestly, she just pushes and pushes… Carrie, how'm I gonna keep that woman out of this house? She would be the death of all that's peaceful in my life, and Dulcie's, too, for that matter. She fusses over her 'til she makes her cry, then fusses *at* her. And can you imagine not liking Annie Radburn? I don't understand Eunice. She wouldn't smile at a laughin' contest. I know she misses Jack as much as I do, but honestly, sometimes I just want to poke her."

"You're not the only one that'd like to poke her," replied Carrie. "I thought I'd just die if she said one more 'poor fatherless children' to me. She's just awful. How did Jack stand it growin' up in her house?"

"He said as long as he said, 'Yes, Mama. I know, Mama,' they got along pretty well. I just don't think I could do that for more than a few minutes before I'd be findin' me a sharp stick." Hattie laughed at herself. "I know that sounds awful. You know I'd never ... She means well. I've been praying for her and about her. Sometimes that's all that gets me through."

Carrie cautioned, "Try not to think about her anymore. You got that precious new baby to think about instead, and he's gonna wake up anytime now and want to be fed. You try to rest a little bit longer while we get supper ready. Chloe's taking Ma home and bringin' Dulcie back, so it'll get lively again in a little bit. Rest while you can."

Carrie smoothed Hattie's hair back. As she walked back into the kitchen, she chuckled to herself at the thought of sweet little Hattie chasing Eunice with a stick.

She let her gaze wander around the room. Jeb Stoneworth had built the house before he'd married Lettie. It was the house where they grew up together and raised their children. In those early days the two rooms upstairs had four bedsteads for the children, three for the girls on one end and one for the boys on the other. There was so much joy in that house! Then after Mama died when Hattie was ten, Daddy just seemed to give up. He said he was tired, so he went to bed. Six months later they gathered at the cemetery to bury him beside his wife. Carrie had a little girl of her own by then, but she came and packed up Hattie, Lalie and Berk and took them home with her. She and Gene Beckwith raised them with the same kind of love that Jeb and Lettie had given so freely when they were alive.

Carrie loved the kitchen in the old house. It was rectangular and had a door on each wall. One door led up one step to the screened-in back porch that ran the width of the house; one led from the end of the kitchen to the outside porch where the box well and porch-swing were. Another door went to the dining room, and the last one led into the bedroom. There was a small white enamel table-and-chairs set. A matching Hoosier hutch had a work surface. It had flour and sugar bins built right in, and the glass doors above rattled when you opened or shut them. Closing her eyes, she focused on the fragrance of the good kitchen aromas.

Carrie was tall, but not as tall as Chloe. At forty-five, the laugh lines around her eyes were becoming more pronounced. Last year, she'd cut her waist length hair and gotten a permanent wave! Gene said she was "purtier'n a speckled pup." She'd blushed and told him to "go on!" but she'd been tickled. She was a little on the plump side but not too much. She had the same dark hair and deep-set eyes as all the rest, but her features were softer. It was hard to pick a favorite out of the Stoneworth girls, but most said they'd sure like to be respected the way Carrie Beckwith was. She was a fine woman in a family of fine folk.

Lalie came in from the porch and sat down across the table from Carrie. "Did you see Eunice Crowe's face when Ma Richard's was tearin' into her?" she asked.

Carrie nodded, "I seen her and it worries me more than I like to admit. She's a menace."

"Oh, I don't know 'bout that," Lalie responded. "I think she's just lonely. If she weren't so all fired mean to Hattie, I think I'd feel kinda sorry for her."

"All I know," said Carrie, "is that I was mighty glad Ma Richard said what she did. Otherwise, I woulda had to figure out a way to keep her from movin' in here tonight."

Lalie laughed. "There's enough of us, if we'd had to, each of us could have blocked a door. Can't you just picture Eunice runnin' around the outside of the house tryin' to get in with one of us in each doorway?"

"Eulalie Ruth Stoneworth, you be nice," Carrie cautioned, but the corners of her mouth twitched until a giggle escaped. "She'd be fit to be tied!"

"Hey, you know what she needs, Carrie? A husband! She's been a widow a long time now. There's no reason she shouldn't get married again. She's a real good cook. She keeps a clean house. Maybe we orta start prayin' for her to find herself a nice man. Then she'd be too busy to meddle with Hattie."

Carrie grinned and nodded vigorously, "And while you're prayin' for this miracle man, pray he's hard of hearin' so he'll stay more'n five minutes."

The other girls were coming in now. Marva and Willa had picked enough peas to feed an army. They begged a cup of coffee and went to sit on the screened-in porch.

"Whew! It sure is hot out there!" Marva said, wiping her face with a napkin. "I believe we'd have roasted if we'd stayed out there any longer. Hey, Lalie, hand me that bowl and I'll shell them peas while we're settin' here."

Marva was the cutest of the Stoneworth girls. She had the deepest dimples anyone had ever seen. She had married young to the preacher's oldest boy, Conroy Fenton. They had never been able to have children, but my, how they loved all their nieces and nephews. Carrie said if there were ever natural-born parents it was Marva and Conroy. Conroy preached nearby in Beech Creek. Their church was small but active, and Marva was its heart. She did everything from teaching Sunday school to cooking and taking food to the shut-ins, and always with those dimples flashing.

"How long you reckon it'll be 'fore Chloe comes back with Dulcie?" Willa asked.

"I s'pose it'll take about an hour or so. Why? You got plans for the evenin'?"

Willa blushed prettily, "No, I don't have plans for the evenin'. I made a ragdoll for Dulcie, and I'm anxious to give it to her. I was thinkin' with her mama havin' a new baby, she might be needin' one, too."

"Willa! If you ain't the sweetest thing. Wish I'd thought of that!" Marva cried. "Why, if I was three years old and my mama had a new baby, that's just what I'd want. Will you show it to us?"

Willa walked back into the kitchen and returned with a paper sack. As she reached inside she said, "Now, I was thinkin' on it, and it come to me that she might want the same kind of baby her mama had, so I didn't put but just a little hair right on top of its head. I made two sets of clothes, one for a boy baby and one for a girl baby. That way we can dress it like a little boy just like Jackie." She pulled out the little doll and the doll clothes she'd made. Carrie, Marva, and Lalie all exclaimed over the doll, and oohed and ah'd about the clothes while Willa dressed him. It was a thoughtful gift from a thoughtful aunt for a little girl who might be feeling a little put out with the real new baby brother she was about to have thrust at her.

Willa said, "I thought I'd save the other set of clothes for the next baby doll I make, and then I'll be almost done with it before it's even started."

Lalie looked Willa up and down. "You know what you need to do, Willa? You need to find you a man and have you a bunch of younguns of your own. There's gotta be at least one man in Kentucky that meets your standards."

"I'm sure there is. He just don't happen to be throwin' hisself down in my path, beggin' for my hand in marriage. I'm almost thirty years old. You'd think some old codger'd be willin' to take me on."

"Hmmmm. There's always that Dawson Hastings at Depoy," Lalie said coyly.

Carrie hooted with laughter, "Oh, yes, him and his seven younguns. They'd prob'ly take you on. You bein' such a good cook an' all."

Willa lowered her eyes. "Dawson's a good man. It's a shame he lost Caroline like that. She was gone before a body hardly knew she was sick."

"Wiiiiilllaa! You are *not* makin' eyes at Dawson Hastings, are you?"

"No, of course I'm not. I'm not makin' eyes at anyone, but he is a good man. I feel right bad for him and his ... " Willa pinched up her face, changed her voice into a fair imitation of Eunice Crowe, and said, "poor motherless children."

All the Stoneworth girls howled with laughter.

Carrie replied in her best Ma Richards voice, "Why, Willa Stoneworth, you oughta be ashamed of yerself. Talkin' that away about your elders. What would your mama say?"

The afternoon wore on with much of the same patter as the women worked around Hattie's house. There wasn't much to be done, as Hattie kept a clean house, but there were always

42

little things to do. Marva took down the heavy portieres that hung from the door that led from the dining room to the front room and took them outside to shake any dust out. She knew Hattie would have to stand on a chair to take the curtains down and put them back up again. Lalie brought in another load of wood. Carrie drew fresh water from the well and peeled a mountain of potatoes. She sent Lalie to the smokehouse for a ham and cut thick slices to fry with the potatoes.

"Y'all are just too good to me," said a voice from the bedroom door. Hattie stood there looking around at all the activity in her little kitchen. "I coulda got supper on."

"Hattie Stoneworth Crowe, you get right back in that bed," came the reply from five older sisters at once. They shooed her through the door.

"Y'all wait, now," said Hattie. "I'm not sick. I just had a baby. I made supper for Jack the night Dulcie was born. I'm fine."

By then she was all tucked up in the big bed again.

"You ain't doin' nothin' 'til tomorrow," said Willa. "Why do you think we're here? So you can wait on us? Not likely."

Carrie said, "Marva, go get that project we was workin' on. Now's as good a time as any to pass it on to Hattie. Now, Hattie, I know you said to give all Jack's shirts away to someone who might need 'em, but I just couldn't, so I had this idea that we'd make a quilt for the baby so he'd have something of his daddy. I hope you don't mind, but I asked the other girls and they all agreed. Here, Marva, let me show her."

Carrie carefully spread the half-size quilt out on the bed for Hattie to look at, and pointed to a square. "See, that one there is his gray work shirt, and that's the white Sunday shirt. That one's his second best, and there's the blue work shirt. We cut 'em up into squares, and all of us pieced a few nine patches. We used a sheet for the stripping and the binding. You're not mad, are you?"

Hattie sobbed as she gathered up the quilt and pressed it to her cheek. "Oh, Carrie! I wanted Jackie to have somethin' of Jack's, so I saved his pocketknife, but he won't be able to have that for a long time yet. This is perfect. Thank you so much. Just look how much work y'all did! It's beautiful. I love it, I do—I just can't seem to quit cryin' is all."

All of a sudden, Hattie's sobs were joined by a new little voice crying right along with her. Baby Jackie was awake and hungry. His little face was all scrunched up, bright red. Little fists flailed against the air. His mouth was wide open as he announced his displeasure.

"Would you listen to that boy holler? I reckon he's gonna be a powerful singer when he grows up, just like his daddy." Hattie wiped her eyes and reached for the baby. She unbuttoned her nightgown and settled him at her breast. As she eased back against the pillows she softly sang,

"In the pines, in the pines, where the sun never shines,
and we shiver when the cold wind blows.
Little girl, little girl, what have I done
To make you treat me so."

As the old song went on, altos and sopranos, contralto and tenor all blended in womansong as the sisters joined in and watched Hattie feeding her baby for the first time. Each sang well alone, but together they were wonderful.

"I remember mama singin' that to you when you was a baby," Lalie said slowly. "I think one of my favorite memories of this house is all of us singin' in the front room. And Daddy and Mama singin' in the kitchen when I was dressin' for school. Hearin' that song again ... can't you just feel 'em right here with us?"

"I think they are." Hattie said quietly, "I hear Mama when I get up of a mornin'. I'll be settin' on the porch with my coffee and I hear her, plain as day, singin' *Whispering Hope* or *Jesus, Rose of Sharon*. I hear Daddy out by the smokehouse bellowing out *Bringing in the Sheaves*. I know they aren't really here, but I remember it so clearly that some days, well, I think it's a gift from the Lord just to remind us of how He knows what we need. I guess He thinks I need to remember where I come from, so He lets me hear a little bit of heaven on earth. I've even heard Jack a couple of times since he's been gone."

"Course you hear 'em, Honey," Carrie said. "We all do. You're right about it being a gift. Sometimes we need to be wrapped up tight in His love. I reckon it might be upsettin' if He was to sing to us in His voice, so He sends a voice we know. One that'll be comfortin' instead of frightenin'. At least that's what I figure. Don't you reckon He knows how much those old songs mean to us? 'Course He does."

Jackie was full, and Hattie patted his little back until he burped. It was a big ol' burp that seemed too big for such a little body. It broke the solemnity that had drifted over them all.

"Well, if that's not a boy! He sounds like a miner already," Marva said.

"No, I don't think he'll be a miner," said Hattie. "Someday, the veins of coal are gonna play out. I'm thinkin' I don't want my youngun underground. I think he'll go to school and be a lawyer or a doctor. Maybe even a preacher, like your Conroy, Marva."

With the baby's future settled, the women tucked Hattie back in with her Bible, and they returned to the kitchen.

"See about stirring up some biscuit dough, Lalie," Carrie said. "I'm gonna set down for a minute with this coffee. It won't be long 'til Dulcie's here, and then there won't be another peaceful moment 'til bedtime."

In the bedroom, Hattie closed her Bible and let her eyes drift shut. *Lord, when You made this family You knitted together a treasure. I'm powerful proud to be part of it, Father. Help me to bring joy to those around me and to always remember where I come from.*

3

Hattie was slipping her feet into her old felt slippers when she heard a car pull up the drive. A minute later the booming voice of Forrest Stoneworth sounded through the house.

"Where's my baby sister? Where's that baby boy? I heard he looks just like his best lookin' uncle. That being me, of course."

Marva called out from the kitchen, "Y'all are just in time for supper. Come on in."

"Well, sure we're in time for supper. Vida's got a powerful appetite, and she said she knowed you'd be cookin' so we better hurry."

"Oh, go on with you, Forrest," said Vida, his wife. "You was the one what had to come down here and see that baby. I told you we shoulda waited 'til tomorrah or the next day and give the folks a chance to settle in. Marva, don't think you need to feed us. I got a pot of beans on at the house just waiting for us to get back."

Hattie smiled as she picked up the baby and walked to the doorway with Jackie on her shoulder.

"Well, here he is, Forrest. This what you come to see? Ain't he purty?" She turned the baby in her arms so the newcomers could see his little face. She smiled up at her big brother. "What do you think? Don't he look like Jack?"

"He sure does, Hattie. Look at those little fingers."

Vida was expecting her first baby in a few weeks and looked at the baby wistfully. "Oh, ain't he sweet? He's not bigger'n a minute. Lookee there, Forrest."

"You want to hold him, Vida? I'm thinkin' maybe I need to sit down for a bit."

"Course I do. Forrest, get Hattie that chair."

Forrest moved fast for a big man. He grabbed the chair and spun it around, then scooped up Hattie and the baby and gently sat her down.

"Don't move, Least'un'. You ain't got no color in your face. What're you doin' up anyway?"

"I'm fine, just a little tired. I've had me a few things to do today."

Forrest's big hands took the sleeping baby from Hattie and passed him to his wife. He put his hands on his Vida's shoulders and looked over. "Hattie, I b'lieve he's the finest boy you ever had."

"Course he is, you goon. He's the onliest boy I ever had."

"Well then, there I go bein' right again." Forrest grinned the famous Stoneworth grin and walked over to the stove where he snitched a fried potato.

"Get outa there, Forrest, or I'll whomp you with this spoon." Carrie chased her brother out onto the side porch where he plopped himself in the swing.

"It's too hot in that kitchen, anyway," he hollered at the backdoor. "Too many wimenfolk to suit me."

Vida grinned, "Y'all know he worships the ground you walk on, don't you? I never knew a man who loved his family the way he does. Guess that's why I fell for him. Couldn't have been his good looks." The last words were spoken in a much louder voice.

"Watch it, woman!" Forrest was so easy going that it was fun to tease him and take his teasing in return. He was the family character, always looking for fun.

Just as things settled down from the arrival of Forrest and Vida, Chloe came bumping up the driveway.

"Mama, Mama!" Dulcie's little body flew from the car into the house. "We havin' a birfday party?" she asked when she saw all the aunts. "I here. I have cake?"

Forrest crouched low as he came back into the kitchen. Growling, he grabbed up the little girl and held her close a moment. "It sure is a birthday party. You got you a new baby brother, and it's his birthday. Wanna see him?"

"Nope," said Dulcie, barely glancing at the baby. "I want cake."

Vida handed Jackie to Lalie and said, "Give her to me, Forrest, and go get the cake outa the car. Aunt Vida knows what you like, Darlin'. I brought you a cake. It's not a jam cake like mama makes, but I think you'll like it. It's got coconut on it. I think your mama's gonna want you to eat supper first, though."

Chloe came through the back door with a sack of sugar and one of flour. "She ate so much stuff up at Radburn's, I don't think she'll be able to eat anything else. Annie and Harwell spoil her somethin' awful. She was settin' on the counter eatin' licorice right out of the candy jar when I got there," Chloe said with a laugh. "Hey, Vida. I'm glad y'all are here. 'Sides the fact you brought cake, it wouldn't have been the same without you. Hattie, Annie sent you these." Chloe put the flour and sugar on the table. "She said they was a gift for the baby, and she wouldn't take 'no' for an answer."

"Supper's ready," said Carrie. "Lalie, you, Marva and Willa help me carry in this food. Forrest, go get a pillow for Hattie to sit on. The rest of you find a place to sit."

Forrest winked at Hattie and did as he was told. "She gets bossier the older she gets," he whispered as he helped Hattie to her chair in the dining room.

They blessed the food and filled their plates. The rumble of conversation seemed to float over Hattie as she looked around the room at her family. Then she heard Forrest say, "I think he's a good man. I know he's got a reputation, but underneath all that, he's real solid. Those folks from that part of the county are God-fearing and loyal. I don't think there's a really bad one in the bunch. Some of 'em are a little wild, I grant you, but there's none better."

"Who's that your talkin' about?" asked Carrie.

"If you wasn't chewin' so loud you'da heard me," Forrest responded with a grin. "Smith Delaney—you remember him? I think he was in school a couple years ahead of me. Maybe in Eldon's class?"

"I remember him," said Chloe. "He was in my class for awhile 'til he quit comin' –about the sixth grade—I think. Always thought he was nice, but he was wild when we were in school and for a while after, too. Didn't he join the army?"

"Sure did. I b'lieve he lied about his age and got in when he was sixteen. As far as I know, that's the only dishonest thing he ever did."

"See there, Willa? There's a nice man, just about the right age for you." Lalie couldn't resist a little teasing. "I bet you could turn his head if you tried."

"I'm not lookin' for a man. I told you that earlier. Sides, I got my cap set for those 'seven motherless children' in Depoy, remember?"

Forrest looked confused. "What are you talkin' about? Are you seein' somebody with seven children?" he asked.

Hattie laid her hand on Forrest's arm and waited for the women to stop laughing.

"You mean you hadn't heard, Forrest? Willa's sweet on Dawson Hastings. They's just about ready to set a date."

"You are not! Are you really? Well, Dawson's a good man, but with all them kids ... "

The house rang with laughter. Carrie held up her hand. "Y'all stop! I can't eat and laugh at the same time. Shame on you, Hattie! Forrest, Willa's not walkin' out with nobody. We was givin' her a hard time this afternoon, and somehow Mr. Hasting's name got brought up and, well ... anyway ... what's all this about Smith Delaney?"

50

"Nothin' much, just that he's lookin' for work, and I was askin' Marva if she knew anyone in Beech Creek that might need a hired man."

"Shoot, the only person I know who *really* needs a hired man is Hattie."

"What?" Hattie's head jerked up. "I don't know, Marva. I'm doin' all right on my own. I don't have a lot of money to pay for a hired man."

"You're doing fine, Honey, but what about the roof on the smokehouse? I know Jack was fixin' to get it done this spring. Your garden needs attention, and the fencerow down at the end of the field's leanin'. You gonna do all that by yourself and watch two babies?"

"I not a baby, I big girl!" Dulcie said from her stool. "I help Mama."

"Yes, you do, Darlin'." Hattie turned back to Marva. "I don't know," she repeated. "But I'm not sure I'm wantin' anyone else on the place."

"Hattie, you got to have help, and that's all there is to it. You got that backroom in the smokehouse. The boys could help you fix it up with one of the bedsteads upstairs. I know there's an old dresser of Mama's and Daddy's up there, too. He'd probably be glad for homecooked meals and a nice place to stay. You wouldn't have to pay him much."

"That's good, 'cause not much is 'bout all I've got. Forrest, are you sure he's a good man? I wouldn't want no one drinkin' and cussin' around my younguns."

"He'd know better than that around any of us, Hattie. I'll talk to him and see if he's interested. If he is I'll bring him by on Saturday. Will that suit you?"

"I… I guess it'll have to," Hattie said. "Seems like y'all got it all settled anyway."

Carrie frowned, "If you don't like the looks of him when he comes, you don't have to hire him, Hattie. Nobody's gonna make you. It's just that you do need help, especially now with the new baby and all." She rose from the big oak table and started clearing away the dishes.

Carrie continued to talk as she worked, "Hand me those biscuits. I'll set 'em in the warming oven. Now listen. Smith Delaney comes from good folks. I'd heard he was out of work but didn't really think nothin' of it. What happened to his last job, Forrest?"

"You know how it is at the mines. Men are laid off all the time for not more than looking at the strawboss crossways. He got into it with ol' man Sawyer for beatin' a bank mule. I guess he told Sawyer to quit hittin' the poor ol' thing, and when he didn't, Smith like to took him apart. I heard Sawyer had him throwed off the place. Then somebody else said that wasn't true, that Delaney quit and walked out before he could be fired."

Hattie shuddered. "When I think about the conditions in the mine, it just makes me sick. If it hadn't been Jack crushed in that cave-in, it would've been someone else, and I don't guess it'll be long 'fore it happens again." She blinked hard and twisted the napkin in her lap. "It was hard enough losing Jack, but to know it coulda been avoided with just a little bit of money spent to shore up the ceiling. If he hadn't lingered so long and suffered so much ... I just hate to think who'll be next. Seems like the men get younger and younger goin' down the mines, as the old ones don't last."

Forrest reached over and placed a large hand over her small one. "A man's gotta make a livin', Hattie. We all live with knowing the whistle's gonna blow, and there's gonna be another cave-in, explosion, or other disaster. It's just the way it is with minin'. Coaltown ain't much worse than any of the others. Sawyer's a bad egg, and he gets away with it. I reckon that's the way it is when you marry the owner's sister. And you get 'Assistant Manager' tacked on after your name, to boot. Not much we can do to change it 'cept pray and be as careful as we can when we're underground."

Forrest knew the dangers of the mines as well as anyone, and talk like Hattie's made him decidedly uncomfortable. He rubbed the fingers of his right hand over the stubble of beard on his jaw. In his hurry to get to his little sister's house, he hadn't shaved. "We make a reasonable good wage. And we got roofs over our heads and food on the table. If word gets out that you're talkin' against the mines, all us Stoneworths could find ourselves out on the dole. You be careful who you're talkin' to."

"You know I wouldn't say it outside the family," said Hattie, "but you can't tell me you ain't thought the same thing. I even heard you and Eldon talkin' about it. Y'all were talkin' when you was sittin' with Jack's body. You thought I was sleepin' but I wasn't. Y'all were even talkin' about joinin' the union or startin' one of your own like others have done."

"Hattie, I'm tellin' you that's dangerous talk! Just last week there was a man over at Central City got hisself horsewhipped for talkin' union. There's been murder, too. Not around here, but it's happenin' in the eastern part of the state, especially around Harlan."

"Wait a minute, Forrest," said Willa. "I heard about that killin' at Bevier—they say it was for not much more than just talk."

"That's right! Hattie, you and the other women best be keepin' your mouths shut. You could get yourself and them babies burned out, or worse." Forrest was getting agitated. "Looks like the time's here when you're in trouble with some folks if you're for unions, and in trouble with others if you're agin' unions."

"Hush, Forrest Stoneworth. You're scarin' her, and me, too," Carrie scolded. "Hattie knows better than to stir up trouble."

Union talk was whispered wherever miners gathered but in most circles never discussed out loud.

"What me and Eldon was sayin' was just grief talkin'," said Forrest. "We wasn't serious about startin' nothin'."

"Smith Delaney ain't a union sympathizer, is he?" Marva asked as she wiped down the surface of the big oak table. "He wouldn't be bringin' no trouble on Hattie and the babies if he come here, would he?"

"Don't think so. Everybody knows ol' man Sawyer's a hothead, and not too many people put much stock in what he says. Sawyer got what was comin' to him. That Smith Delaney don't abide no mistreatment of animals. He don't abide anything he sees as unjust. I reckon he figured if Sawyer's low enough to beat an old wore-out mule he'd be low enough to do just about anything. Sometimes I think the coal mines won't never change unless somebody steps up and takes 'em on. The coal companies always make the rules and we... we just gotta live with 'em, like it or not."

The coal company controlled their lives in so many ways. It paid their salaries—or not. It gave them credit at the company store when money was tight, as it always was. Somehow, when payday came there was never quite enough to pay back the company. So you needed more credit to make it until the next paycheck. So the cycle continued. You always seemed to be in debt to the company, one way or the other.

"You don't owe nothin' to the store, do you Hattie?" asked Willa.

"No, Jack was smart that way. We do most of our buyin' up at Radburns. Jack'd never let us buy nothin' from the company store without cash money. He said chargin' was a surefire way to be a slave, and he wasn't gonna give up his freedom to nobody. He had that bit of money from when his granddaddy died, and when things were tight, we used a little of it. I've still got some laid by, and with selling that old truck, I didn't have to go into debt for the funeral neither. I been selling eggs to Annie Radburn and doin' some sewing for folks. So far, I'm all right."

The table had been cleared. The girls did the washing up quickly and quietly. Any talk of unrest at the mines sobered most folks, as it did them.

Forrest put his arms around Vida from behind and rested his chin on top of her head. "Well, I reckon we better be gittin'

54

back up the hill and headin' for home. I'll be out Saturday mornin' with Smith. You think about whether you want him or not."

"Dulcie, come here to me," Willa called. She took the little girl into the front room, sat down on the couch, and pulled her up in her lap. "I got somethin for you." She reached into the bag where she'd put the ragdoll. "Lookee here. Your mama's got a new baby and so do you."

Dulcie's eyes were big as saucers. "Baby for me?" She held the doll, slid to the floor, and jumped up and down. Then she scrambled up in the big rocking chair. "I rock da baby," she said.

"That's right. You gotta take good care of your baby. He needs lots of lovin'. What you gonna name him?"

Dulcie concentrated a long time, then she said, "I name him Hat."

"Hat? Why Hat, Honey?" Willa looked puzzled.

"Mama's baby haves daddy's name. My baby haves Mama's name!" Dulcie said proudly.

"I guess that's right. Yup, that'll do just fine," said Willa with a smile. "Youngun, you are sharp as a tack! Nothin' gets by you."

Lalie walked in on the tail end of the conversation.

"Whatcha got there, Dulcie?"

"This my baby. His name is Hat. He vewy good boy like Mama's baby."

"Yes, I can see he's a good baby. Honey, your mama wants you. Can you run in there and see her?"

Dulcie slid to the edge of the rocker and hopped down. She scooted around the corner and out of sight holding her doll by one foot.

"What do you think of Hattie takin' on a hired man?" Lalie asked Willa.

"I don't know. I reckon she's gonna have to do somethin'. Eldon and Forrest have families of their own to look after, and I know they been down here a lot tryin' to help. I'm just thankful she's got the house. At least she don't have to worry about bein' turned out."

"Ain't it the truth. I've always thought it was a shame, turnin' the womenfolk out of the company houses when their men get sick or killed. Hattie'd been in a bad way if she'd been in a company house."

"Well, she wasn't, and thank the Lord for it. Jack and Hattie put this old place back together with sweat and hard work."

"I know. Carrie and I thought they were crazy to want to move down here, but when they asked if they could try, it seemed like we had to let 'em. They did a real good job. Don't you know Daddy would be proud to see it standin' so clean and tall?"

"I always thought it was nice when Berk was livin' here, but let's face it, it had fallen on hard times by then. And a man just don't keep a house clean like a woman. As much as I miss Berk, I think I'll always be glad Nan didn't want to live so far from her mama 'cause look how good it turned out for Hattie."

"Uh huh. Remember how heartsick we were when Berk said he was going to Louisville to live. Now, I think I understand why that happened. God knew Hattie was goin' to need a safe place to live. Guess that goes to show you Who's really in control." Lalie looked up as Chloe came to the door.

"Y'all, I'm fixin' to go. Marva's just about ready, too. If you're wantin' a ride, better come on. I need to get home 'fore Ray thinks I run off with the Tinker."

"Ha! He'd come after you if you did!" laughed Lalie. "All right, let's go say our good-byes. I know you got to run all over the county droppin' us off."

Soon they were loaded up and heading for home. Hattie, Dulcie and Jackie were all kissed goodbye.

Willa said, "Be sweet, I'll see you soon."

"Let us know if you need anything," said Lalie as they went out the door.

Carrie bathed Dulcie, told her the story of Daniel in the Lion's Den, and tucked her into the bed she'd shared with her mother since Jack's death. When Dulcie'd finally closed her eyes, thumb in her mouth and arm hooked around her new ragdoll, Carrie left her and went to find Hattie.

Hattie was nursing Jackie on the porchswing. The swing jiggled a little as Carrie sat down beside her.

"Well, I'm glad they were all here," said Carrie, "but I'm glad they're gone now, too. I'm about wore out. How 'bout you, Honey?"

"I'll live, I reckon. I'm tired, but it's a good tired. It's been an awful long day. You and the girls was so good to come."

"It won't be long now 'til we're in the middle of it again at Forrest's. Vida's lookin' fit to pop anytime. Ain't she sweet? I'm so glad he got him a good woman. I think I worried over all you kids marryin' up with the wrong kind more than anything else after Mama and Daddy died. Every one of us did good with our choices, though, don't you think?"

"Yes, ma'am, I do." Hattie shifted the baby to her other breast. "We wouldn't none of us brought shame on the family, Carrie. Why would you worry 'bout that?"

"Hattie, there's all sorts out there that talk big and even act like they're good folk, but behind closed doors they beat their wives or drink or both. Look at poor ol' Mamie Dunford. If she comes in to church with a black eye one more time ... It just makes me so mad! And to look at Deke Dunford, you'd think he was the sweetest man in the world. He's gonna kill Mamie one of these days—you mark my words—and there's nothin' nobody can do to stop it. It's that kind of thing that scared me, I reckon."

"I see what you mean. You know what's really scary? One time at Bible study, I heard Miz McPherson say a man wouldn't hit his woman if she didn't need hittin'. I b'lieve there was another woman there that agreed with her. Can you imagine thinkin' like that?"

"'Course not. But we didn't never see that kinda carryin' on when we was growin' up. Daddy'd have cut off his arm 'fore he'd have hit Mama, but if he had beat her, maybe Eldon and the boys would have thought that was the way to act." Carrie shifted in the swing, setting it to rocking sideways. "Hattie, I know this is changin' the subject, but would you really object to havin' a hired man?"

Hattie bit her lip. "I don't guess so. I just ... well, it seems awful soon to have another man on the place. Jack's only been gone for three months."

"Nobody's askin' you to marry him, Hattie."

"I know. I guess I'm a little concerned how it'll look to the folk, and you *know* Eunice Crowe is gonna have a fit. I won't let her move in, but I'll take in a strange man. Course, I guess if I let her move in too, it wouldn't look unseemly to have him here."

"Don't you do it! Don't you even *think* about doin' it. She don't need to move in here. She's just wantin' to get her hands on Mama's things. She'd turn herself inside out if she thought she could tell folks she's livin' at the Stoneworth homeplace. After all her fine talk of Annie Radburn puttin' on airs, she's the one that tries to make out she's better'n folks!"

"I know that, Carrie. I'm just trying to keep the peace. You don't know how hard it's been trying to hold her off and not make an enemy of her. Jack wouldn't have wanted that, and neither do I."

Hattie got up and walked back through the side door into the kitchen and through to the bedroom. She reached down and pulled the covers up over Dulcie, then carefully laid the sleep-

58

ing baby down into the cradle. Carrie watched her from the door until she came back to the kitchen.

"You're lookin' a little peaked. Why don't you get ready for bed, and I'll get the kitchen ready for the mornin'.."

Hattie nodded, then wrapped her arms around Carrie. "What would I do without you? You've been my sister, my mother, and my friend. I know I'd just be lost if you weren't here to give me what for."

"What? With all your other sisters you think you'd miss me?" Carrie laughed softly into the hair of her baby sister, holding her tight. "I think you'd do just fine. Mama and I raised you up to get by no matter what the circumstances, and you've had to do that. I'm powerful proud of you, Darlin'. Now, let go of me 'fore I start to bawlin' and wake up them younguns."

She gave Hattie a gentle push toward the bed and turned away. "Sleep well, Hattie."

"I think I will. You gonna be all right in the front room?"

"Uh huh. I've slept on worse than a couch before. Remember the time ... " They talked quietly back and forth between the rooms as Carrie hooked the latches on the screen doors, then turned down the kerosene lamps and blew them out. Slowly everything quieted, and Hattie heard the springs on the big couch give as Carrie lay down. She could hear the crickets and the cicadas humming outside. The old house creaked as it settled down for the night.

Lord, I know You're there watchin' over. Would You help me decide what to do about Mr. Delaney? I ... I ain't sure, Lord. It just seems like an awful big thing to have him come here, and I know it'll tear Mother Crowe from one end to the other. Help me make the right choice.

4

Hattie rose early Saturday morning. She sat down in the quiet of the porch and tried to think of reasons why she should hire Smith Delaney.

Eldon and Forrest had put in a crop of corn for her before Jack died. Jack had always planted corn as a cash crop. It was late summer now, and she'd need help with the harvest.

It wasn't just the harvest she'd need help with though. Marva was right about the smokehouse roof. It definitely needed fixing. She and Jack had put off tackling the outbuildings until they had gotten the old homeplace back in order. He had bought all the materials to fix it last fall with the corn money, thinking he'd do it this year. But this year Jack was gone. The roof wouldn't last another winter and everything inside would be damaged. The temporary patches he'd put on last fall were just barely keeping the rain out.

The fence *was* in bad shape. Firewood and coal would have to be bought and hauled in. She could use help with the garden. There was plenty for a hired man to do.

Even knowing all that, Hattie was reluctant to hire Mr. Delaney—or anyone else.

Why couldn't things just go on the way they were? Forrest and Eldon would keep on helping her ... but Hattie recalled the conversation she'd had with Rose Ellen, Eldon's wife, the afternoon before when they'd come down to see the baby and help clean the smokehouse.

"Hattie, you know Eldon and I'd do anything in the world for you. I wasn't gonna say nothin' about it, but I'm worried

61

about Eldon. He's been up coughin' every night for the last couple weeks. I think the coal dust is gettin' to him."

When Hattie's eyes grew large with fear, Rose Ellen had continued, "Now, I don't think it's real bad, but Honey, he's got all he can do to keep up at the mine and around our place. When Carrie told me you were thinkin' on hirin' a man to come help out around here, it sure made me feel better. I just want you to know it'll ease Eldon's mind not havin' to worry over you."

"Eldon never said a word ... "

"'Course he didn't, and he never would. You got enough on your plate right now, but Eldon's my husband and ... well, when Carrie said you was thinkin' about takin' on Mr. Delaney, it just seemed like an answer to prayer."

Not my prayer, Hattie thought as she swirled her coffee absently.

"Think on this, too," Rose Ellen continued, "When Vida's baby comes, she's gonna need Forrest more than ever. She don't have a mama to come be with her. He's not gonna want to leave her."

"No, I don't reckon he will."

"It ain't that we ain't willin' to help. It's just that if you got the chance to hire somebody, well, it'd just make it easier on everyone. You wouldn't be alone out here anymore, either. I 'magine there's been a time or two since Jack's been gone you've wished there was a good man around."

Hattie thought of the night in June when a truckload of drunk men had come tearing down the hill whooping and hollering, their truck spinning around and off the edge of the road. They got it on again and headed back over the hill. They hadn't done anything except make a lot of racket, but it had scared Hattie. It had scared her badly enough that she'd slipped out of bed in the dark, loaded Jack's shotgun and watched until they'd turned around and headed back toward town. You could never tell when a bunch of liquored-up men might turn ugly. It had taken a long time for her hammering heart to slow down.

Rose Ellen had changed the subject after that, and it wasn't long 'til Eldon had come in from moving the furniture she'd chosen from the attic. Hattie had a hard time putting the conversation out of her thoughts. Rose Ellen wasn't one to worry needlessly. If she was concerned about Eldon, there was reason to be.

Hattie laid her head down on the table and prayed: *Lord, I don't want to do this. I ... I just want to turn back time and have Jack here with me and the babies ... I know that's not gonna happen, but I don't want another man here. Yet, I don't want to be a burden on my family either. You seem to be openin' this door, but I'm not wantin' to walk through. Help me to know this is Your will. I'm not so certain. What if he ain't clean? What if he don't like my younguns? What if he don't know You, Lord? And what's Eunice Crowe gonna say? It's gonna be bad, Lord. I just know it will!*

Hattie lifted her head. Crossing her arms on the table, she put her chin down on them. She looked out at the wakening dawn. The birds were beginning to sing. Closing her eyes, she continued to pray: *Help me, Father. I can't do this by myself, and I ain't wantin' this man to come. Help me make the right decision even if it's not what I want.*

Smith Delaney looked out the window of Forrest's beat up old truck and wondered what he was doing there. Why was he even considering being a hired man for a widow woman? He was a miner, not a hired hand. There were other mines in the area; he could go to one of those. He knew the answer to the question. He was sick of it. Sick of the dust. Sick of the dark. Sick of the death. He didn't want to die coughing up coal dust like most of the old men he knew, including his own father. He guessed it wouldn't hurt to go see the woman. It probably wouldn't come to anything anyway, and nobody was going to make him take the job. He'd see what it was about and then decide.

The truck jounced down the hill and up beside the house. Forrest jumped out of the truck, and yelled, "Hello, the house! Hattie, you there?"

"I'm here." Hattie opened the screen door. Dulcie hid behind her mother's skirts and peered at the stranger getting out of the truck.

"Smith, this here's my sister I told you about, Hattie Crowe. Hattie, this is Smith Delaney."

"How do, Miz Crowe."

"Mr. Delaney."

Smith was stunned. This beautiful young girl was Forrest Stoneworth's widowed sister? He'd been expecting someone older, and definitely not so pretty. She couldn't be more than twenty-two or twenty-three years old. She was the widow? Sympathy shot through Smith like an arrow. *Someone needs to be taking care of her. Just look at her, with her hair so shiny and those big dark eyes.*

"I'm right sorry to hear of your loss, ma'am," he said. "Sounds like you've kinda got your hands full around here."

"Thank you. I guess I do. Please come in. We'll set out here on the porch where there's a breeze if you don't mind."

"That'll be just fine," replied Smith.

"Hey, Hattie, where's the baby?"

"He's sleeping."

"Guess I'll have to make-do with my number one girl then. Come here, sugar."

Dulcie ran to her Uncle Forrest and let him pick her up.

Hattie led the way back to the table, sat down, and motioned for the men to sit.

When they were seated she said, "I've never hired anyone before. I'm not real sure how to go about it. Maybe you could tell me a little about yourself."

64

"I'm not a real big talker, ma'am, but I'm from the Old Hebron-Mud River area. I'm a hard worker and I do an honest day's work for an honest day's pay. I'd do right by you if you take me on." *What am I doing? I'm practically begging this woman for the job.*

"I don't reckon I could ask for more than that. Is there anybody that would recommend you? I mean... somebody we know?"

"Well, ma'am, I don't know. I know Forrest, and I'm on noddin' acquaintance with Gene. I worked with your brother, Eldon, too, at Coaltown."

"I guess I meant someone outside the family who'd vouch for you."

"Let's see... You know Annie Radburn? Up at the store in Drakesboro?"

"Yes, sir."

"She's my cousin on my mama's side." Smith's eyes twinkled. "Poor Annie. She's always been so quiet and shy. Reckon she's about the only one I can think of on the spur of the moment like this."

Hattie smiled at his ridiculous description of Annie Radburn. "That's all right. I reckon that'll do. Did Forrest tell you what I can pay you? I know it ain't much, but I'm a good cook, and I'd make sure you don't go hungry."

Forrest jumped in at this point with eyes twinkling. "I don't know 'bout that; she pert near killed me one time with her biscuits. And one time her gravy's real watery and the next it's lumpy."

Smith grinned, "I'm sure it'll be fine. I understand you got a room for me to stay in?"

"Not in the house." Hattie blushed and said quickly, "It's in the back of the smokehouse. I guess you'll want to see it."

When Smith nodded, they rose and made their way to the old smokehouse. It was used mostly for storage these days. The building was divided in half down the middle by a strong wooden partition. The back half had two windows and a door that led onto a small roofed porch.

Hattie opened the door and held it for the men. Smith gestured for her to go in ahead of him.

"It's clean, and there's a bed, a dresser, and a washstand. I guess it don't look like much, but I tried to make it comfortable. We'll put in a stove for the winter if you're still here. See, there's already a chimney. I think there's a couple of chairs on the other side. You can have one for in here and one for the porch if you like."

"It's just fine, ma'am. In fact, it's a lot nicer than some places I've stayed. I'll take those chairs. And thank you."

"When ... um ... when do you think you'd like to start?"

"I reckon I could move in tonight if that'd be all right with you."

Hattie took a deep breath. "Oh. You'll want to go get your things. Forrest going to drive you back down here?"

"No, ma'am. I have a truck. He'll run me on home, and I'll come back down in that. Is there some place you want me to park it?"

"Anywhere is all right, I guess."

Forrest looked from Smith to Hattie. "Well, now that we got that settled, you need anything? I can stop at Radburn's for you and have Smith bring whatever you need back when he comes."

"I guess I do need coffee as long as it's on your way."

"I'd be glad to stop on my way back, Miz Crowe. Do you want me to put it on your account?"

"No, sir! If I can't pay for it, I don't buy it. I'll get you the money." Hattie tilted her chin in the air, turned, and went into the house.

"She's a little prickly, ain't she?" asked Smith.

"Who? Hattie? I've never knowed her to be," Forrest answered. "She's been through an awful lot, with losin' her husband and havin' a new baby, though. She might be a little touchy right now. You watch out for her, will you?"

Smith didn't have time to reply before Hattie was back with her purse. She carefully counted out the coins for the coffee and handed them to Smith. He tucked them into his pocket.

"Miz Crowe, can I ask you somethin'? What's your little girl's name? She's a purty little thing."

"This here's Dulcie." Hattie said, thawing a little toward the man.

"How do, Dulcie? I'm Smith."

Dulcie slid completely behind her mother, then peeped around her skirt.

"I reckon I'll be back around five. Will that be all right?"

When Hattie nodded, Smith and Forrest got into the truck and pulled out.

Hattie slowly let the breath leave her body. She didn't think she'd drawn a full breath the whole time the men had been there. She didn't remember saying, "You're hired", but she'd got herself a hired man anyway. How did that happen? She shook her head. The deed was done. She'd just have to make the best of it.

The bell over the door at Radburn's rang as Smith went in. There were several people in the store, and it took a few minutes for Annie to notice him.

"Hey, Smith. How're you?"

"I'm fine, Annie. You doin' all right?"

"Fit as a fiddle! What're you doin' in Drakesboro? I don't generally see you 'til Granny's birthday in September."

"You'll be seein' more of me now. I'm working for Miz Crowe."

Annie looked at him as if he'd suddenly grown a third arm.

"You ain't! Well, well, well! I'll tell you one thing, cousin, you cut yourself a mighty big chaw if you're takin' on Miz Crowe. Why, that woman's meaner'n a striped snake. You ain't gonna last very long workin' for her. Not with your temper."

Smith was shocked, "She seemed nice enough to me ... "

Annie leaned across the counter and locked her gaze onto his. "Well, maybe she was durin' the hirin', but I'm tellin' you, you're gonna have to watch your tongue 'cause she ain't gonna take no lip off'n you ... "

"That little thing?"

"She may be short in stature, but she's big on hateful! Why, you shoulda heard what she said to me just last Tuesday. She carried on like a scalded cat!"

Smith couldn't believe what he was hearing. Hattie Crowe had seemed so gentle and reserved, but Annie seemed awful certain about what she was saying. He guessed it must be true.

All of a sudden, Annie burst out laughing. "Wheweee! I'd like to be there when you get enough of her. I've never known you to bite your tongue. I 'magine you'll give as good as you get. It'd be a sight to see! And if anyone deserves a good comedown, it's Miz Crowe."

They talked of mutual family for a few minutes, then Smith paid for the coffee he'd come for and headed for Hattie's. *It just figures I'd get m'self hired on with a harpy.* He shook his head. *We'll just see how long this lasts. It's a low-down shame, though. She's awful purty.*

Thirty minutes later Eunice Crowe marched into Radburn's just as Annie was about to lock up for the day.

"I'll have a pound of coffee."

"Coffee? Oh, but ... "

"What's the matter? My money don't spend here? Somebody else's greener'n mine? If you Republicans don't want Roosevelt paper, I got Coaltown Mine flickers." She extended her hand with several brass disks etched with the Coaltown mark.

"No, no ... 'Course your money's fine, Miz Crowe, but ... I mean, wasn't Smith just in here buyin' your coffee?" Annie was confused.

"Smith? What are you talkin' about? Nobody bought nothin' for me." She smiled with feigned concern. "Is the heat gettin' to you?"

"No, but ... he said he was workin' for Miz Crowe, and I thought ... "

"Ain't nobody workin' for me! Have you taken leave of your senses? You're talkin' nonsense!" Eunice stopped in the middle of her tirade as a glimmer of the truth dawned on her. "Annie Radburn, you start from the beginnin' and tell me what you heard. Don't you leave nothin' out!"

For once in her life, Annie was speechless. She couldn't very well repeat what she'd said about Eunice to Smith. She stammered, "My, my cousin, Smith Delaney come in here. He said he was workin' for Miz Crowe. Natr'ly, I thought he was talkin' 'bout you, but he must've been talkin' 'bout Hattie."

Eunice snatched up her purse, whirled around and slammed out the door. Faithful Ferd was waiting in the truck.

"Take me to Hattie's!"

Hattie heaped a plate with porkchops, mashed potatoes, gravy and biscuits and carried it out to the smokehouse. Smith answered the soft knock.

"I fixed you a plate. You can bring the dishes down to the house later. The screen door'll be unlocked. You can leave 'em on the table on the porch."

"Yes, ma'am. Thank you, I will." Smith breathed in deeply to catch the rising aromas of food. "Smells mighty good."

Hattie turned toward the house then back again. "I'd like to go to worship in the mornin'. I was wonderin' if you'd take me and the children in your truck?"

"If that's what you want," he replied. He hadn't been to church in years, but if Hattie wanted to go, he'd take her.

"Good. That's settled then. Well, goodnight."

Hattie was cutting paperdolls for Dulcie a little while later when she heard the roar of an engine cut through the quiet.

"Set there, Darlin', while I go see who that is." She dropped a kiss on Dulcie's forehead and went to the door. Her heart sank when she saw who was marching toward the house. She hoped Eunice hadn't heard about Smith yet.

"Mother Crowe ... "

"Don't you 'Mother Crowe' me!" Eunice's shrill voice cut through Hattie like a knife. "I just heard you're movin' a man in down here, and my Jack not even cold in the ground! You ain't gonna do it, Hattie. I'm tellin' you, you ain't! You ain't gonna bring shame on his memory!"

"Mother Crowe, I'd *never* do that! You know I wouldn't. Please calm down. Let me explain ... "

"Ain't no explainin' needed. I got it on good authority you moved a man in here, and I'm gonna put a stop to it."

"I didn't 'move a man in here'. Not the way you're sayin' it anyway. I need help with the place and ... " Hattie realized her mistake the instant the words left her mouth.

"Oh, I see! Now you need help, but you didn't need no help from me. You need 'man' help," Eunice hissed. "I ain't gonna stand for it! If you don't put him off the place *tonight,* I'm gonna call the law. They'll take them younguns you're so partial to and give 'em to decent folk!" The veins on Eunice's neck stood out like ropes.

"You ... you don't mean that! They wouldn't take my children just on your say so," Hattie cried, panic filling her voice.

"Yes, they would!" Eunice was vicious now. "I'll tell 'em how you brung a man out here, and they'll name you unfit. See if they don't!"

Smith had heard enough. He strode out of the shadows where he'd been standing and watching since the truck pulled in. He'd witnessed the whole scene.

"Scuse me, ma'am. I think you've said 'bout enough. Let me help you to your truck." He took a firm grip on Eunice's arm and propelled the sputtering, stammering woman to the waiting Ford. He put her inside and closed the door firmly, then leaned in the window.

"This your woman?" he asked Ferd.

"Sister."

"Uh huh. She's ready to go home now."

"Yeah, thought she might be."

Ferd started the truck just as Eunice found her tongue again. "You remember what I said Hattie Stoneworth ... "

Smith cut her off. "Well, bye now. Thanks for comin'. Y'all be careful now. See you in church ... " He kept up a steady one-sided dialogue, that cut Eunice off every time she tried to open her mouth, until Ferd had the truck pointed back in the direction of town.

"I take it that's the *other* Widow Crowe?"

Hattie sagged against the side of the porch. She looked like she'd been slapped.

"Miz Hattie, you all right? Now, don't you go worrying 'bout what that old woman said. She's just blowin' smoke." Smith couldn't believe how protective he felt about this woman he'd known for less than a full day. He wanted to take her in his arms and hold her until the fear was gone. He knew that was out of the question. If she didn't kill him herself, her brothers would. He made up his mind to stick close by the house for a while though.

"Could they take my younguns?" Hattie asked in a voice tight with emotion.

"I reckon they could if you was breakin' the law. You ain't, are you?"

"Course I'm not."

"You ain't got a moonshine still on the place, do you?"

"No!"

"Well then, you take good care of your kids? Feed 'em and love 'em and the like?"

"Yes, of course."

71

"Hmmmm ... then, I'd say your younguns are purty safe."

"But ... "

"I heard her. Miz Hattie, I got a feelin' that woman's fairly well known around these parts. I don't imagine too many people put much stock in what she says. She'd have to prove you been immoral to get them younguns, and since you ain't been ... " Smith grinned. "Did you see her face when I said 'see you in church'?" He chuckled. "Thought she was gonna have a fit right then and there!" He laughed out loud.

Hattie was suddenly furious. How could he possibly laugh at a time like this? She whirled around and let the screen door slam behind her.

Smith laughed all the way back to the smokehouse. This job was turning out fine. Just fine.

5

Hattie had spent a restless night. She knew she wasn't her best that Sunday morning. It had taken everything she had to dress herself and the children, find her Bible, and walk out the door.

"Miz Hattie, might be best if I was to drop you and the younguns off at the door when we get to the church. Y'all can go on in, and I'll just slip in the back and sit with Clarence Hunt. He still sit on the back pew?" Smith negotiated the gravel road with careful precision.

"Yes, he does. Always has as long as I can remember."

"Me and Clarence go way back. We started back-pew sittin' when we was boys up at Old Hebron church. When everybody'd stand for the openin' song we'd sneak out and play in the woods behind the church 'til the invitation song. Then we'd slip back in. We got away with it for a long time. At least we did 'til my Mama figured out what we was doin' and took a switch to me. I ain't been real partial to church-going since," Smith grinned.

Hattie wasn't in much mood to laugh. "I reckon that could put a man off going," she said absently. All she could think of was Eunice being at church. She hadn't ever missed a church service that Hattie could recall. *Please, Lord, don't let her make a scene in front of everyone!* Hattie reached up to adjust her collar with shaky fingers.

"Anyway, I was thinkin' that there ain't no point in stirrin' up a hornet's nest by walkin' in together. I got a feelin' Miz Crowe's gonna be lookin' for any cause to make trouble. We'll try not to give her one. Now, if I was you, I'd go in and sit right in the middle of your brothers and sisters. That way she ain't likely to come at you. She won't be wantin' to get into it with you with all them there to take up for you."

Hattie always sat with the family, but she resented that Smith was telling her what to do. "I'll sit where I always sit. I don't need to be told."

"No, ma'am, I didn't reckon you did. I'm just thinkin' how to get you through this with the least bit of fuss. No offense intended." *Good,* he thought, *she's gettin' her dander up. That's better than walkin' in lookin' ashamed.* "You just do like you always do, Miz Hattie. You'll be fine."

"I will!" she snapped.

Dulcie looked from Mama to Smith. Mama didn't get mad very often, and Dulcie didn't like it when she did. "Mama? You mad at Mr. Baloney?"

"What? Oh. No, Honey. I'm not mad at Mr. *Delaney.* I've just got a lot on my mind. Look over there at that big house. That's where Mr. & Mrs. Billy Bridges live. Did you ever see such a house? They got electric lights! Doesn't it look fine? See the curtains? They're made of real lace. I think they're awful purty. How 'bout you? Mr. Bridges is one reason Drakesboro has such good streets. He's always usin' Black Diamond's workers and equipment and slack from the mine to make 'em better." She was talking a mile a minute but couldn't seem to stop.

Hattie took a few deep breaths to calm herself down. She'd not let anyone see her looking so distraught. She hadn't done anything wrong, and she wasn't going to hang her head! The more she thought about it, the more she was determined to act like everything was fine.

The truck bumped to a stop at the door of the Jackson Chapel Church, and Hattie got out. She reached one hand back to help Dulcie down, then straightened Jackie's blanket.

"I'll be in directly," said Smith. "I don't b'lieve I'll go to Sunday school, but I'll be in for the worship service."

"That's ... that's fine."

Hattie walked toward the familiar faces of friends and family. They looked the same as always. There were the Graysons, the McPhersons, Mamie Dunford, with fresh bruises on her arms, and Carrie, Willa, and Chloe.

Carrie hurried to her.

"What's wrong?"

Hattie should have known she couldn't fool Carrie. "I'll ... I'll tell you later. I don't wanna talk right now. You seen Mother Crowe?"

"No, not yet. Why?"

"I was just wonderin', that's all. We better go in." The family moved toward the door.

Jackson Chapel was a one-room building. Its wooden pews were hard and scarred from years of use. Bare wood showed in spots where the shellac had been worn off. The room was strung with wires across its length and breadth. Long brown curtains were hung from the wires. During Sunday school, the curtains partitioned off separate "rooms". Hattie took Dulcie to Miz Fenton's corner and left her there. They moved down to the front of the building where the adults met. Hattie could hear Miz Fenton leading the youngest children in song. Hattie and her sisters slipped into a pew.

Brother Fenton led the adult group in prayer. He opened his Bible and began a discussion of the Book of Acts. Hattie was just beginning to relax and enjoy the message when Eunice appeared. As usual, she was dressed all in black. *She even looks like a crow,* Hattie thought and felt instantly ashamed.

Eunice glared at Hattie, then turned to the preacher.

"Brother Fenton, I got a question to put to you," Eunice interrupted. "Ain't it a sin for a man and a woman to live together without being married?"

Eli Fenton looked shocked. "Why, of course it is, Miz Crowe."

"And if you was to get word that one of your flock was livin' in sin with a man, it'd be your Christian duty to do somethin' about it, wouldn't it?"

Hattie was horrified. *Don't do this, Eunice. Please don't do this. Lord, I'll die right here, if she does!*

"Well, I reckon it'd be my duty to go visit with 'em and find out what was goin' on before I did anything. Now, If they were willin' to repent and make things right ... "

"But, say they didn't repent. You'd have to put 'em out of the church, ain't that right?"

"If they didn't repent? I reckon I might have to ... "

"And if the woman had younguns. Wouldn't you have to go to the law and say how they's bein' ruined by the morals of their mama? It would be your duty, wouldn't it?"

"I'd purely hate that, but ... "

"Uh huh, and you'd make sure their reputations was ruined in this here county, wouldn't you?"

The preacher frowned and paused a moment before he answered, "Well now, I don't know about that. The way I see it, they'd have ruined their own reputations. That wouldn't be my doin.'"

Carrie had heard enough. It hadn't taken her long to figure out what was going on.

"Brother Fenton, what if a woman was alone in the world, and she hired a man to come take care of her land and her buildin's? That wouldn't be wrong, would it?"

"No."

"And as long as he didn't live in the house with the woman, couldn't nobody say nothin' about it, right?"

"Well ... it wouldn't be the best situation even if he wasn't livin' in the house, but if they were both good, God-fearing folk, livin' moral lives, I guess there wouldn't be nothin' to say about it."

"All right ... and if *someone* tried to stir up trouble for those folks by say, startin' talk, that'd be a sin, ain't that right?"

76

Brother Fenton purely hated gossip. It was one of his favorite themes. "I'd be mighty put out with anyone who'd start talk about it! 'Let him who is without sin cast the first stone'," he quoted.

"Thank you, Brother. That's all I wanted to know."

Eunice was purple. She was so angry. Hattie saw her stare daggers at Carrie, but Eunice clamped her mouth shut and didn't say another word.

Brother Fenton said, "Now, if we can return to the Second Chapter of Acts we'll go on."

Hattie wanted to slide under the pew. She knew her ears were burning. She glanced around the room. Every Stoneworth was lookin' fit to kill. There was a storm coming, and Hattie knew she was going to be in the center of it.

When Sunday school was over and the worship service had begun, she tried to take comfort in the familiar rituals that had been such a part of her life. The service started with an old favorite hymn, and Hattie let herself be comforted by the familiar words:

Rock of Ages cleft for me,
Let me hide myself in Thee.

Hide is right, Lord. I just want to hide! The service went on. Hattie found herself wondering if Smith was sitting on the back row. Over and over her mind ran through the scene that had played out during Sunday school. She wasn't able to concentrate on the sermon.

Annie Radburn looked fit to be tied. She fidgeted on the pew until Harwell reached over and patted her hand. As soon as the last hymn was sung and the closing prayer said, she marched down the aisle and grabbed Smith by the arm. She dragged him outside and around the corner of the church.

"Smith, why in the world did you let me think you was workin' for Eunice Crowe? Why didn't you tell me it was

77

Hattie? That woman 'bout made mincemeat of her this mornin' during Sunday school. Don't you know nothin' bout the Stoneworths? They're good folk, Smith. Real fine."

"Annie ... "

"Hattie's just the best little thing. You ain't got no business working for her. You gonna ruin her reputation and make her life miserable. Now, I ain't never cared whether you and Colt took a drink once in a while or caroused a little, but Hattie'll care. It'll pure tear her up if you behave like that. You hear me? And the rest of them Stoneworths ain't gonna be real happy neither."

"But, Annie, I ain't makin' no claim on her. I just ... "

"Now, I love you, Smith, you bein' kin and all, but you ain't good enough for the likes of Hattie. I'd never've introduced you to her. She's just as fine as they come and you ... well, you got your temper, and you don't think nothin' 'bout gettin' liquored up." She paused, took a breath, looked hard at Smith and continued, "You just ain't good enough for her."

"Annie, if she'd have me, I'd quit all that. I wouldn't touch another drop of liquor. I'd quit gamblin', too. I'd flat out tear myself up doin' right by her. You just wait and see."

"I don't believe you could! A man can't change his stripes like that. Don't you hurt her, Smith. I'll ... I'll never forgive you if you do!" Annie turned on her heels and stormed off, almost in tears.

Smith slowly walked back around the side of the building where the congregation was coming out.

"Smith, you old dog!" said Clarence Hunt. "I couldn't believe it when you sat down next to me in there. How long's it been?" Clarence seemed genuinely tickled to see Smith.

"I don't know. A while I reckon. You been up to anything good?"

"Not much. You?"

"Not much. I'm workin' for Hattie Crowe. Just started yesterday. I'll be livin' down there on her place from now on."

"Yeah, I heard you was let go at Coaltown again. I'm real sorry to hear that. It's a cryin' shame the way they run that mine. If they was all like Mr. Duncan's Graham-Skibo mine, you wouldn't have to worry none about conditions."

"He's a good man, Mr. Duncan is," said Smith, "but he can only hire so many men. Reckon we'd all work for him otherwise. I don't know why the other mines don't follow his lead."

"The way I see it, things are gonna get worse 'fore they get better. You hear they're tryin' to unionize at ... "

They talked of mines and miners and reminisced about some of the pranks they'd pulled as boys until Smith saw Hattie walking toward him with Dulcie in tow.

"You 'bout ready?" he asked.

"How do, Miz Hattie." Clarence pulled his cap off his head and held it between his hands. "You got you a real good worker in Smith here. Ain't nobody works harder than he does."

She nodded. Smith shook Clarence's hand and slapped him on the back. Turning, he walked with Hattie to the truck. He scooped Dulcie up onto the seat and then helped Hattie in with the baby.

As they pulled out onto the highway, Hattie caught a glimpse of Eunice's pinched face. She quickly looked away.

Smith saw the silent exchange and wondered what had happened during Sunday school. *I reckon she'll tell me if she wants me to know.*

"Mighty fine singin' this mornin'."

"Yes, it was," Hattie replied.

"I always liked that song. You know, 'When The Roll Is Called Up Yonder I'll be There'? It can get the roof to raisin' when it's sung right. 'When the roll…"

He started in on the chorus of the song. Hattie looked at him sideways. He didn't have a bad voice. In fact, it was a pretty good one. He sure was getting into it. Dulcie sang along while Smith tapped his fingertips on the steering wheel in time to the music. "When da woll is called up yonder I be deeeeeeere."

On second thought, I'll just ask her right out. She can al-ways tell me to mind my own business. "Miz Hattie, I got somethin' to ask you. My cousin Annie had a few things to say to me after service this mornin'. She said Miz Crowe made a scene durin' Sunday school. That true?"

Hattie explained what had happened and was surprised when Smith laughed.

"That Carrie is a character! I reckon she put ol' Eunice on notice."

"I don't think so. Eunice isn't that easy to stop. She gets somethin' in her craw, and she'll get it out or choke to death tryin'."

"Well let her choke, then."

"Mr. Delaney, Eunice Crowe is my Jack's mother. I'll thank you to remember that. She's these babies' granny, and I got to live with that." The strain of the last hours was starting to tell on Hattie. "I got to keep the peace with her if it kills me tryin'. Don't you understand?" Tears suddenly sprang to her eyes. "Oh, shoot! Why am I even talkin' to you?"

Smith's heart nearly broke at the sight of her tears. He pulled the truck off to the side of the road where there was a little grassy clearing.

"Dulcie Darlin', will you go pick your Mama some flowers for her Sunday dinner table? See them yellow ones over there? They'd be real purty." He lifted the little girl across him and set her on her feet. She scampered happily into the field.

"Miz Hattie, I promised Annie I wouldn't do nothin' to hurt you. I meant it. If my bein' on your land's gonna make you cry, I'll clear off today, as soon as we get back. But, I just want to say that it don't matter whether it's me or another man working for you. You're gonna have trouble with Miz Crowe no matter what you do. So, I guess it's up to you. You gonna let her push you around or you gonna stand up to her?"

"I ... I don't know. I don't feel like I can fight her anymore. I know you're right but she's ... she's just so ... " She let the

80

sentence trail off.

"Well, you let me know what you want me to do. Now, dry your tears. That little girl'll be back in a minute, and she don't need to see her mama cryin'." He handed her his handkerchief. "Listen. I ain't always lived the way I should. I ain't always done things the way my mama raised me to do. I reckon I ain't in the same league as you Stoneworths, and some folks might think they got reason to point their fingers at me. And maybe they do. But if you want me to stay, I won't do nothin' to bring shame on you and yours."

Hattie looked deep into Smith's blue eyes. She believed him. He was a kind, compassionate man. Look how he'd taken up for her last night and how he'd gotten Dulcie out of the way so they could have this talk. "I ... I want you to stay."

"Then I'll stay."

"Ferd, I want you to do somethin' for me," commanded Eunice. "I'm thinkin' you need to go out to Coaltown Mine and talk to Mr. Sawyer. Find out why that Mr. Delaney was let go. Then I want you to go down to the poolroom and shoot you a game or two and, just casual-like, ask around about him there, too."

Eunice wiped her hands on her apron. "I been thinkin' there's gotta be a way to get him off that property. I'm gonna move in down there one way or the other, but him bein' there is complicatin' things."

"I don't know, Sister. I've heard tell of them Delaney boys. By all accounts, they're real clannish. I don't think they'd take kindly to my meddlin'." Ferd preferred to take the path of least resistance. No point in working up a sweat unnecessarily. If he could change Eunice's mind, it'd be worth the effort.

"All the more reason to find out what you can. I don't care whether they like meddlin' or not. They're nothin' but white trash, anyway. I want any dirt you can dig up on him, and I want it soon as you can get it. Come tomorrow, you're gonna drive me over to the sheriff's office, and I'm gonna have me a little talk with him, too."

"Now, Sister, you ain't really gonna make trouble for Hattie, are ya? She was a good wife to Jack, and she's a good mother to them kids. And for all you know, she ain't doin' nothin' wrong."

"She moved him in there without a second thought, but she wouldn't let me move in with her—and me them babies own grandma! Don't you even think about taking up for her, Ferd Barnett! This here's my house, and you'll find yourself out on your ear if you don't do as you're told. You want to go back to diggin' coal?"

Ferd looked offended. He reached down and grasped his suspenders from where he'd dropped them as soon as they'd gotten home from church. He lifted them back to his rounded shoulders. He had come to live with Eunice after her husband died. Over time he'd just stopped going out to work at the mine. Finally he just stayed home. Mostly he hung out on the porch and whittled, though he drove Eunice wherever she wanted to go and did a few things for her now and again. It was an effort though.

"I reckon it's a nice day for a drive out to Coaltown," he replied, shuffling toward the door.

Hattie stood behind the house and looked out over the field. Another day without Jack had ended. After putting the children to bed she'd come out for a few minutes in the quiet of the dusk.

"You got a mighty purty piece of land here, Miz Hattie," Smith's quiet voice came out of the shadows.

"I've always loved it. My Daddy built the house for my Mama when they were courtin'. We were all born in this house." She turned back toward the house. "See that big oak down there in

82

the corner of the front yard? Jack was always gonna hang a swing for Dulcie in that tree. I wouldn't let him last year 'cause she was too little. Now I wish I had."

"I could do it for you, Miz Hattie."

"No, that's all right. I don't guess it's important. We got the porch-swing. I was just thinkin' out loud."

"Ma'am, when I was gettin' those chairs outa storage yesterday evening, I saw a good length of chain. It wouldn't take nothin' to hang it. I could notch a board so it wouldn't slip off the chain, and Dulcie'd have a fine swing. It seems a shame for a little girl not to have a swing."

Hattie hesitated. She didn't want this man doing the things that Jack had been going to do. It almost seemed like he was trying to take Jack's place. Still, it wouldn't be right to make Dulcie lose out on having a swing just because Smith wasn't her daddy.

"I reckon that'd be all right if you got time. Don't rush to put it up. There's no hurry."

"I'll do it first thing in the morning. The summer's passing fast. We want her to have time to enjoy it."

He's right. Time's passing so fast it seems to be whizzin' by me. This time last year we was getting ready to harvest the corn and buying materials for the roof. We were planning the rest of our lives together. Who'd have ever dreamed what would happen between then and now. I sure didn't. I just thought we'd go on and on 'til we were old together. Hattie shivered.

"You cold, Miz Hattie?"

"No, I'm fine. Just thinkin'. I reckon I'll go in now. Good night, Mr. Delaney."

"Miz Hattie, before you go, I just want you to know I'm glad you're lettin' me stay. It'll work out. You'll see."

"I hope you're right. Good night."

Hattie went through the house putting things right for the morning. She blew out the lamp and climbed into bed with

Dulcie. Tonight she felt hopeless. She didn't even feel like praying.

Smith watched the light go out in the house and then walked into his room. He pulled off his boots and stretched out on the bed.

Lord, You ain't heard from me for a while. It's Smith. There's a little gal in that house down there with a broken heart. Worse yet, her spirit's 'bout broke in two. Her man's gone. She's got trouble with his kin. I know she ain't got much money. Now, I don't expect You to do nothin' for me, 'cause You know I ain't done nothin' to deserve it, but could You help her? She's so good, and she loves You. You can just see it shinin' in her eyes. She needs You, Lord. Real bad. Well, I reckon that's all I got to say. Thanks for listenin'.

6

Hattie stood at the kitchen window and watched Smith on the roof of the smokehouse. He had peeled away the old layers of shingles and laid bare the undersheathing. Carefully, he'd rolled out tarpaper and tacked it down. Now he was shingling. His bare chest gleamed with sweat as he worked under the hot August sun. His flat cap was pushed back on his head as he tipped his chin back to drink deeply from the Mason jar of water that Hattie had taken him earlier.

Dulcie was bouncing on the bottom rung of the ladder. She chattered away and questioned every move he made. He always answered patiently. Once in a while he'd peek over the side, just to make her giggle. Through the open window, Hattie could hear their conversation.

"Whatcha doin' now?"

"Nailin' down shingles."

"Why?"

"So the rain won't get inside."

"Why?"

"'Cause if the roof leaks, everything inside'll get wet."

"Oh. Can I come up now?"

"No, ma'am. It's too dangerous up here. You might fall off. Then your Mama'd be mad at me."

"Can I come up one more step?"

"Don't think so, Sugar. You're too short a horse to be climbin' ladders."

"I not a horse!"

"You're not? Let me look at you ... " Smith leaned over the edge of the roof and gazed at the eager face looking up at him. "Hmmm ... you got a mane of hair and a velvety nose and dark eyes. Your ears ain't exactly right for a horse, but ... " Smith rubbed his chin as though carefully considering the creature below him, "Lemme see your teeth."

Dulcie curled her lips back and showed him all her baby teeth.

"They don't look quite right neither. You got hoofs?"

"Noooooo! I gots feets. See?" Dulcie held up one little bare foot and wiggled chubby toes at Smith. "Dem's feets."

"I reckon they are at that. Guess you're right. You ain't a horse after all. Don't know what I was thinkin'."

"You're funny!" Dulcie dissolved into a fit of giggles.

Hattie smiled at the nonsense and walked away from the window. She hated to admit it, but Smith was nice to have around. Dulcie was crazy about him. Hattie hadn't thought much about how the little girl must miss having her daddy around. She'd figured Dulcie was so young she probably wouldn't remember him much. It was obvious to her now, though, after seeing Smith interact with her, that Dulcie very much craved a man in her life. As she had so often in the last few months, Hattie wished she could turn back time to before the accident. If only—so many "if onlys."

Jackie fussed from his cradle, and Hattie went to pick him up. He was a good baby and didn't cry much. Quickly she changed him and sat down to nurse him. All the while she crooned a lullaby her mother had sung to her.

> When the shades of night are softly creeping,
> Down across the garden at the zoo.
> Children would you like to take a peek in
> At the sleepy lions and kangaroos?
> Rosalie, the polar bear is slumb'ring.
> Hear the parrots talking in their sleep.
> And the monkeys off their perches tumbling,

One by one lie huddled in a heap.
Good night, Mr. Elephant.
Tigers, cease your play!
Lie down and you're sure to dream,
That you're roaming in the jungle far away.
Sleep well, Missus 'Rangutang.
Good night, zebras, too.
When another day is breaking,
You will all of you be waking,
In the zoo, in the zoo.

Jackie dozed and nursed, and nursed and dozed. Hattie loved the quiet with him. He was such a precious gift, just as Dulcie had been. She lifted him to her shoulder and patted his little back. He burped, then snuggled close. The feel of his fuzzy little head beneath her chin was a cherished treasure. The sleepy baby pushed away from her shoulder and raised his wobbly little head to look at her. She smiled as he concentrated on her face. His mouth was a perfect little "o".

"Know what, Jackie? There's a whole world of wonder waitin' just outside that door over yonder. There's trees, flowers, bugs, and all sorts of things. Wait'll you see the stars peekin' at you from the dark on a cold winter night. Sometimes it looks like they're winkin' at you."

Jackie looked like a sleepy owl. He blinked and solemnly regarded Hattie's face. He seemed to follow every word.

"We'll go for walks, and I'll tell you the names of all the trees. Just like my Mama told me. You and me'll have a great time. Your big sister knows most of 'em already, but you, you got a lot of learnin' to do. It won't be long, and you'll know 'em all, too. We're gonna have us the best time. You just wait and see.

"Next summer we'll go to Horton's Chapel for the 'Singing'. They have one there every summer. Folks from all over come in their Sunday clothes, and they sit in the church and sing one song after another, new ones and old ones. Brother

Roy up there can lead anything. Sometimes it's so purty it makes me cry. It's just like all the angels in heaven come down."

The baby's eyelids had started the gradual downward slide that spelled naptime. She snuggled him against her and rocked quietly until he was completely asleep. Wishing she could stay with him all afternoon, Hattie sighed, and then she carefully rose and tucked him into the cradle.

Once again her eyes strayed to the open window and to Smith as he nailed shingles to the roof. He wasn't a large man. In fact, by comparison to any Stoneworth man, he'd be considered small. He was maybe five feet, nine inches tall and slender of build.

Without his shirt on though, you could see the muscles he'd developed across his chest, back, and arms by swinging a pick in the mines. The muscles rippled with each blow of the hammer. Skin stretched tightly over well-defined flesh and hard sinew. The muscles of his upper arms bulged like softballs as he clenched his fist around the hammer and brought it down to strike a nail.

Hattie blushed and turned her back to the window when she realized she'd been staring.

What's wrong with me today? I just seem so flighty. Can't seem to get nothin' done for lookin' out that window. Smith seems like a nice enough man. He's been here three weeks now, and I haven't seen any signs of the wild streak everybody seems so worried about. Can't say I've got any reason to complain 'bout him. He's real responsible. Look how he chased Eunice off that first night. He sure didn't have to do that. Coulda just stayed up there in the smokehouse and left me to face her alone. It really weren't his place, after all. I ... I reckon, I'm glad he did, though. I don't know what I would'a done if he hadn't. 'Course, it never would'a happened in the first place if I hadn't hired him, so he prob'ly felt obliged to do somethin'. That's the kind of man he is. Takes responsibility real serious like.

Hattie carefully carried a pot of beans to the countertop and spooned them into a serving bowl. She took cornbread from the warming oven and placed it on the table. Then she went to the well and pulled up the bucket that held a jar of cold milk, chilled by the icy well water. She wiped the outside of the jar with her apron and poured the milk into a pitcher. When she'd set the table on the porch, she called Dulcie and Smith to eat.

"Y'all come on in. I've got lunch 'bout ready."

"I comin' Mama."

"I'll be right there, Miz Hattie."

Smith stopped to wash the sweat and grime off his body and arms, then slipped his shirt on. Hattie had been fixing him a plate and bringing it outside to him, but today, she held the door open to the screen porch.

"You might as well eat with us. It's awful hot out there."

"Much obliged, ma'am. It feels real good here in the shade with the breeze blowin' through."

"Thought it might. You set here, and I'll dish up."

Hattie fixed a plate heaped with beans and cornbread, slices of ripe tomatoes from the garden, and her own bread and butter pickles. She handed it to Smith and then prepared a smaller version for herself and another for Dulcie. When all was ready, she reached for Dulcie's hand. Dulcie reached for Smith's. He hesitated for a moment, then took the little hand in his and reached for Hattie's. She blushed, then slowly extended her hand to his. He closed his fingers around hers, completing the circle, and bowed his head expectantly.

"Lord, we thank You for this food. We thank You for Your many blessin's. We ask You to forgive our sins and help us to serve You better. In Jesus name, Amen," Hattie prayed.

"That was real nice, Miz Hattie. I heard you and Dulcie prayin' the other mornin' and I thought that's the way it ought to be done. Just real straight, like talkin' to a friend."

"Why it *is* like talkin' to a friend, Mr. Delaney. It's exactly like that. Don't you ever pray?"

"Yes'm, I do, but more in my head than out loud. I reckon I figure the good Lord don't need me to say the words to hear what's in my heart."

"I s'pose that's right, but don't you reckon He'd like to hear 'em once in a while?"

"Never give it much thought. S'pose so, now that you mention it." Smith took a bite of beans and cornbread, savoring it slowly. "This sure is good. I b'lieve I've eat more since I been down here than I have since I lived at home with the folks."

"You work hard. You got to eat good to keep up with the work. That's what Jack always said."

"He was a lucky man."

"Thank you." Hattie didn't know what to say. She was still a little uncomfortable being alone with Smith. She took a sip of the cold milk and turned to help Dulcie.

"Miz Hattie? You reckon you could drop that 'Mr. Delaney' business and just call me Smith? After all, I told Dulcie she could call me Smith. Somehow, I like that better'n havin' her call me 'Mr. Baloney'." Smith chuckled. "If'n she's gonna call me 'Smiff', it seems kinda funny for you to keep callin' me 'Mr. Delaney'."

Hattie didn't respond. She just looked at him with her big brown eyes.

"I mean, we ain't strangers no more, what with me livin' here and all," Smith said as he flashed her a lopsided smile.

"I'm not sure that would seem proper to folks, said Hattie."

"You still worried about Miz Crowe? She ain't been around since that first night."

"That's what worries me. I'd almost rather she was settin' here on the porch. At least I'd know what she was up to."

"Shoot! Don't you go losin' no sleep over her. She's like a hundred other old women with nothin' else to do but meddle in other folk's business."

Jackie woke up and started to cry. Hattie looked at her half-eaten food regretfully and then started to rise to go get him.

90

"Let me fetch him. You eat. I was so hungry I 'bout swallowed everything whole. You finish."

Smith didn't wait for an answer. He slipped past Hattie into the house and moved toward the sound of Jackie's cries. In just a minute he was back and settled into his chair with the baby in his arms. He hooked an ankle over his knee and laid Jackie in the pocket made by his crossed legs.

"Whatcha fussin' about, Feller? What is it? You got the weight of the world on your shoulders? Don'cha know that's Mr. Roosevelt's job? You ain't worryin' about this here Depression, are you? Well now, you just leave that to the Democrats, boy. They think they got it all figured out. Don't believe it myself, but it ain't for you to be worryin' over."

Hattie watched with amazement. The same strong hand that had tightened around the hammer a short time ago, now gently stroked the fuzzy hair on the baby's head. A tiny fist tightly gripped one rough finger. The coal miner with the wild streak was baby talking to her boy. It was a little hard to see him there doing the things that Jack would have been doing, had he lived, but somehow it seemed right, too.

Dulcie watched Smith talking to the baby and looking at him eye to eye. "Smiff?" she said.

"Yes, Honey?"

"Jackie don't know what you talkin' about."

"That's right, but he knows I'm sayin' somethin' to 'im. He's workin' on it. He don't know the words, but he knows somethin's goin' on. Just watch—in a minute he'll have so much to sort out that he'll turn his head and quit lookin' at me and figure on it a while. Then he'll look back at me. You just wait and see."

Smith started talking to the baby again, and sure enough, in a little while Jackie diverted his eyes and was quiet and seemed to be deep in thought and ignoring them. After a bit, he again focused on Smith, who had continued his patter.

"Oh, you're a smart little feller, that's what you are, a mighty smart little feller."

"I'm smart, too!" said Dulcie, hopping down from her chair and coming over to lean against Smith.

"You can say that again!" he responded, as he freed a hand from under Jackie and gave her a hug. "And you're a good helper, too."

"How much longer 'til you get the roof finished?" Hattie forked a bite of red-ripe tomato into her mouth.

"Lemme see ... I figure I should have it done by Friday. Shouldn't take me any longer than that."

"You're doin' a real good job. Dulcie's not botherin' you, is she?"

"I not a bother, Mama. Smiff said so. I askted him."

"You're no bother at all, Darlin'." Smith turned to Hattie. "No. She's a pleasure to have around. I'm used to workin' with men folk who don't think much about what they say or how they say it. Sometimes that gets a little old. Dulcie's a nice change. I just can't always answer her questions is all."

Hattie laughed. "I know what you mean. She keeps me on my toes."

"Me an' Smiff is fixin' da roof so da rain don't come inside."

"That's right. We sure are."

"I gonna help him all day."

"Well, not all day," said Hattie, "'cause after you eat, you're gonna take a nap. When you wake up you can help some more."

"Mamaaaaaa. I not tired."

"Wheweeeee! I sure am," Smith jumped in. "A nap would be mighty fine right about now. That sun's hot, and I got me a full tummy. I sure wish I could take me a nap, too."

"You do?"

"Yes, ma'am. I'd just set myself down under that tree out there and sleep for an hour or two, then I'd wake up feelin' good and strong."

"You would?"

"Uh huh."

"Mama, I done now. I gonna take a nap!"

Hattie looked from Dulcie to Smith and back again. Nap time had become a challenge lately, but today Dulcie was ready to go to bed without an argument just because Smith said he'd like to take a nap. He'd worked a full-fledged miracle, right before her eyes.

"All right. Let's wash your face and hands. Smith, will you be all right with the baby 'til I get her down?"

"Why sure. We're talkin' politics, ain't we, Feller?"

Jackie looked perfectly content in Smith's lap, so Hattie led Dulcie into the house. Quickly she wet a cloth, wiped the little girl's face, and helped her wash her hands. She stripped the little dress off over her head and laid her down in the bed.

"Mama, the music box?"

"Sure, Honey. I'll get it."

Hattie took the round blue metal music box from her dresser, carefully wound it, and lifted the lid. The melody floated through the room. She'd started playing it for Dulcie when she was a baby, and now it was a tradition that Hattie treasured as much as her little girl did.

"Night, Mama."

"Night, Honey." Hattie responded as she kissed the sweet little face and went back to the porch.

"So anyway, once you get to be growed up a little more, we'll do us some huntin'. How'd that be? Hmmmm? You like the sound of that?"

"You takin' him huntin' already?"

"Well now, we solved all the politic problems, so figured we'd just work on havin' us a good time for awhile. Didn't we, boy?"

Jackie looked at Smith solemnly and hiccuped.

"He's so wide awake. His eyes are open and everything."

93

Hattie laughed. "He's not a puppy or a kitten. 'Course his eyes are open. They're born with 'em open."

Smith grinned, "You don't say? Well, ain't that somethin'!"

"I b'lieve you're teasin' me, Mr. Dela... Smith."

"I b'lieve you're right. Reckon I'd better give this youngun back 'fore I get too comfortable and take that nap I told Dulcie I was needin'."

Hattie looked at Smith. He did look a little tired. Maybe she was working him too hard.

"If you need to rest, you don't need to..."

"No, ma'am. I'm fine. Just lazy is all. Good food, good company. Makes me sleepy every time. Well, Jackie, reckon it's time for you to get back to your Ma. She's crackin' the whip again. Better watch yourself, boy. She'll have you haulin' coal 'fore you're out of short pants."

"Thanks for holdin' him so I could eat. Seems like every time I get ready to eat a bite, someone hollers for me. If it's not Jackie, it's Dulcie. It was real nice of you."

"Anytime, Miz Hattie." Smith pulled his cap out of his waistband and tugged it down over his forehead. "I'll be up yonder on the roof, if you need me."

Smith whistled a tuneless little ditty as he worked on the roof. She'd let him in the house! Well, not exactly in the house. She'd really only let him onto the porch, but it was a start.

The last three weeks had been the best in Smith's life. He'd worked hard, but it had been rewarding to work for Hattie Crowe. She smiled her gentle smile and spoke so sweetly.

Only once had he felt uncomfortable at the old house under the hill. Once, during the second week he'd been there, Hattie had come out to the porch in the middle of the night when the heat and humidity had been stifling. He'd been dozing in the shadows on the smokehouse porch, and she'd never known he was there. Her lovely face had suddenly crumpled, and she'd laid her head on the table and sobbed. Smith's stomach had twisted at the sight of her broken heart. He'd wanted so badly to hold her, to comfort her.

Now, as he nailed a shingle down he thought, *Someday— someday, I'm gonna make you mine, Hattie Crowe! I'm gonna dry your tears, and somehow, I'm gonna wipe the sad right outa your heart. You just hang on a little while longer, Darlin'. Someday...*

7

The late summer slipped into fall, and with the fall came rain—great driving sheets of rain that turned the roads into impassable quagmires of mud. Rain filled every crevice and fissure. Many mines were flooded. Men couldn't work. Unrest at Coaltown and other mines grew. Coaltown Mining Company demanded rent from the workers who lived in company houses even when there was no work and no way to earn the money to pay the rent. People were evicted from their homes. Those who had raised a cash crop, like Eldon and Rose Ellen, were the lucky ones. They were able to pay, but just barely. And for those that did, the crop cash was their gettin'-through-the-winter money. When it looked like the tension couldn't get any worse, influenza hit the county. It seemed to fly through the countryside, picking and choosing who would live and who would die. The miners were restless, and their wives were exhausted. Men turned to drink and meanness to get through the dark days.

Smith and Hattie had fallen into a comfortable routine by now. She cooked and took care of the children and the house; he took care of the land, the buildings, and the animals. He'd brought in as good a harvest with the corn as could be had, but corn didn't bring much that year. It would be a long winter.

One night in October Hattie woke up. She was thirsty, so thirsty. She crawled out of bed and staggered to the kitchen. *Water. Have to have some water. It's there in the bucket, but the bucket is so far away!* Hattie dropped to her hands and knees and crawled across the floor. Each square in the linoleum looked bigger than the last. *Just a little further, Hattie. Keep going. Got to get the water.*

Hattie paused. She could no longer recall why she was crawling across the floor. She knew she needed help but couldn't quite remember why or who was there to help her. Then she remembered. Hattie changed directions and crawled back across the floor to the door of the screened porch. It seemed to take forever to pull herself up the step and onto the porch. *Got to get help. Smith ... Smith will help me. He'll come and get the babies and help me with 'em. He's a good man. Smith ...*

She crawled across the porch floor until she reached the outer door. Slowly, carefully she reached up and pulled herself up from the floor to unhook the door latch, She stumbled through the doorway. *Just a few steps now. Just a few steps now.* With each rasping breath she repeated the words to herself until she tripped on a branch and fell face down in the mud. Then she crawled again, through the mud and the muck . The porch outside Smith's room loomed ahead. *I'll just rest a minute, just one little minute. Then I'll go on.* She laid her head down. It felt so good to rest. The ground was soft and cool against her hot skin.

The babies are waitin'. The babies are waitin' in the house, she thought. Once more she raised her head and moved forward on her hands and knees. She didn't feel the rocks bruise her flesh or the sticks jab into her. She pulled herself up onto the porch and collapsed. One hand reached out and struck the porch-floor over and over again. Smith opened the door and almost fell over her where she lay in a heap. "Hattie! What ... " He lifted her from the floor.

Smith's shock turned to horror. She was burnin' up! He grabbed the quilt off his bed, wrapped it around Hattie, and with her in his arms, hurried through the rain back to the house. Stumbling through the house in the darkness, he found the bed and gently laid her on it. He lit the lamp and, finding enough covers for a pallet, he ran to the front room and made a bed for

Dulcie. He carried her in, laid her down, and went back for Jackie in his cradle. After making sure they were still asleep, he went back to Hattie. Her skin was alabaster against her dark hair. She was so white, she looked almost ghostly. *Don't you die on me, Hattie. Don't you dare die! We got things to do, you and me. I got plans for us. You hear me.* He put his hand against her forehead; she was on fire.

As fast as he could, he went to the kitchen and brought the water bucket to the bedroom. He soaked a hand towel in the cold water and laid it across her forehead. Then he took another towel and bathed her hands and her feet. There was blood on her nightgown! Slowly he raised it to her knees. Carefully he bathed the bloody wounds. *You'd be fit to be tied if you knew what I was doin'. That's okay, Darlin'. You get mad, good and mad, then wake up and holler at me. Come on, Hattie.*

All through the night Smith did everything he knew to bring Hattie's fever down. He tried trickling water down her throat, but it just ran off her chin and wet her nightgown. Finally, he soaked a bedsheet in a bucket of water he'd just drawn from the well and draped the cold, wet cloth over her nightgowned body. Nothing worked. What was he going to do? Smith knew if he didn't get help Hattie would die.

Shortly before dawn, Smith scurried from room to room. He took all the chairs from the dining room and placed three across the connecting door to the front room where Dulcie was sleeping. Then he did the same at the bedroom door to the front room. He was going to have to go for help and somehow had to keep Dulcie from getting up and climbing in bed with Hattie, or worse, trying to follow him.

"Dulcie, wake up, Honey. You and me are gonna play a game. Wanna play?"

"Uh huh." came the sleepy reply.

"Listen, Sugar. I'm gonna run up the hill to Annie's and fetch somethin'. I want you to stay in the front room and count all the red things you see. Then I want you to count the blue things, and after that the green things. Can you do that?"

This was a game he'd been playing with Dulcie when they were outside together. "How many bluebirds do you see?" or "How many toadstools do you see on that stump?" She was fast learning her numbers.

"Uh huh. Den can I come out?"

"Oh, no. This is your castle, and you're a princess. An evil troll cast a spell on you, and you can't come out 'til the handsome prince gives you a kiss. Okay?"

"'Kay. You gonna be da pwince?"

"You bet I am! If you go back to sleep, remember not to come out when you wake up, okay?"

"'Kay."

Smith dashed back to Hattie and stripped the now-warmed sheet off of her to resoak it before he left. Her wet nightgown was nearly transparent. *"Lord, she is beautiful. Please don't let her die. I ... I love her."*

As he raced across the porch, he snatched Jack's old slicker off of a hook and fastened it as he ran through the mud up the hill to town. It was slow and tortuous but he knew he'd never get the truck through. Once he slipped to his knees and fell forward, cutting his forehead on a rock in the mud. With blood pouring down his cheek, he struggled forward—nearly out of his mind with worry for Hattie and the children. *Please Lord, don't let there be a fire. They'll be trapped in the house. Please let me get help in time. Please don't let Dulcie try to come after me. Oh, please, Lord, look after my family!*

Tears began to mix with the blood and the rain beating down on his face as he labored on. Smith suddenly realized that he'd said, "my family". When had he come to think of them that way? He didn't know.

Finally he began to see the lights of Drakesboro. He ran on. He ran past several houses until he saw the light on at Radburn's store where he knew there was a phone. He pounded on the door until Annie came in her wrapper to let him in.

"Smith, what'sa matter? What's wrong? You look 'bout done in!"

"It's ... It's ... " He gulped air. "It's Hattie. I think she's got the influenza. She's been burnin' up all night. Can you call Doc Wadkins?"

"He ain't home. Him and the other doctor was called to the hospital 'cause so many of the sick is bein' carried over there. I might be able to get Ma Richards. She's most as good as any doctor I know. Oh, my! Poor Hattie. Let me try Ma and then I'll call Carrie." Annie stopped. "Smith, if I can get Ma as far as here, how you gonna get her down to Hattie's?"

"I'll carry her down if I have to. Just get her, will you?"

Once again, as she had so many times during a small town crisis, Annie Radburn made emergency use of her telephone for another family.

"Well, Ma'll come. You're in luck. Miz Baggett was spendin' the night with her, and she said she'd drive her this far. But she won't go no futher through that quagmire called a road—and Mr. Radburn's car battery is dead."

"Fine."

Smith felt like he was dying as moment after moment crawled by. Annie made him a cup of hot coffee, and then she washed and dressed the wound on his forehead.

"Quit frettin'. It ain't doin' you or Hattie a bit a good."

"I can't help it, Annie. I ... I ain't never seen nobody taken so bad with the fever. Even all them with jungle fever in the Philippines. It weren't like this. I ... you'll prob'ly just laugh, but I prayed, Annie. I prayed all night long. You don't think God would take Hattie to punish me, do you? He wouldn't do that, right? I mean, my sins is *my* sins. Ain't that right?"

"Oh, Smith, 'course He wouldn't. If Hattie dies, it's 'cause, well ... it's just because. It ain't nothin' you did." Annie had tears in her eyes. "You got it real bad for her don't you, cousin?"

101

"I reckon I do. I realized on my way here that I was praying for 'my family'. Ain't that somethin'? Like she'd ever think to see me that way. You were right when you said she was too good for me. She's way better'n anyone I've ever known. And she ain't *that far* from death's door." He held his forefinger and thumb a hairsbreadth apart.

Smith laid his head down on the counter, and great racking sobs shook his exhausted body. Harwell came to the door, but Annie waved him back. A man had his pride. Smith wouldn't want anyone ever knowing he'd taken on so over Hattie.

By the time the little bell over the door announced the arrival of Ma Richards he was calm again—calm and determined. He and Annie had worked out a plan to get Ma down to Hattie's.

"Ma'am, if I give you this slicker, you reckon you could ride down to Hattie's on Annie's mule, Buster? I'll lead him, but it'll still be a ride you won't be enjoyin' much. It'll be wet and cold, but I'm scared Hattie's gonna die if you don't help her. Annie says you're 'most good as a doctor. If that's true, I'd be awful obliged for your help."

"*Almost* as good as a doctor? Son, I'm *better'n* most. Now if you think you can lead me, I think I can ride. But I ain'ta takin' your slicker; I brung my own."

She unfurled a huge voluminous slicker from a canvas bag slung over her shoulder. "This here was my Daddy's. It's the onliest thing I wanted when he died. It's kept me high and dry in worse storms than this!"

If it hadn't been a life-and-death situation, Annie and Harwell would probably have laughed at the sight of dignified Ma Richards draped in the folds of the slicker and clinging to Buster's back like a baby possum to its mama.

They headed out into the rain, and once again Smith broke into a run, tugging Buster into a trot.

"Wait, boy! You gonna go down like a mule steppin' in a rabbit hole and break your leg. I ain't got my long rifle along to shoot you with, and I don't feel like ridin' the rest of the way

102

alone. Slow down to a steady pace, and I believe we'll get there just as fast."

Smith did as he was told, but his mind raced ahead to the house at the end of the lane. *Hang on Hattie. I'm comin'. I'm bringin' help just like I said I would. You hang on Darlin' just a little longer.* On and on in his mind he reassured Hattie he was coming back.

The return trip was wearing him out. He could barely lift one foot and put it back down and then repeat the motions with the other leg. Buster jerked on the lead rope and almost yanked his arm out of the socket. He slipped into a near hypnotic state of pain and exhaustion.

On and on they went. From the top of the hill he could hear Dulcie and the baby crying. Finally he could see the light in the window. "I'm coming, Dulcie. Rock the cradle for Jackie," he called in a voice barely above a whisper. "I'm comin'."

Up the drive he staggered. They had arrived! Smith almost dropped Ma Richards in his haste to get her off the mule so he could get to the children. *Check them first. That's what Hattie'd want.*

"Hey, Darlin'. How many blue things did you count?"

"Six," the little girl sobbed. "You was gone a wong, wong time, an' you said you'd be wight baaaaaaack." The sobs changed to a long wail. "I cwied and cwied, and Mama didn't come!"

Smith knocked the chairs aside, dropped to his knees and held her to him. "I know I was gone a long time, and you were my good big girl to wait right here in your castle. Now, I'm gonna be your prince and give you a kiss." He kissed her forehead. "Better, Princess?"

"Yes! ... but I hungwy!"

"Okay, Sweet Thing. You come on out to the kitchen with me. I'll get you some cold jelly biscuits. How's that?"

"Wif milk?"

"You bet. First, though, we got to find what your mama feeds Jackie. All right?"

"I know, I know!" Dulcie hopped up and down. "She feeds him her!"

"Oh." Smith knew he was out of his league. "Ma Richards, I'm gonna need your help with this 'un," he called into the bedroom.

She told him how to make a sugar teat to tide the baby over until she could warm diluted milk sweetened with sugar. Smith tended the children, and she tended Hattie. When Jackie went down for a mid-morning nap and Dulcie was quietly drawing a picture, Smith finally slipped into the bedroom.

"She's bad-off, boy. I don't think I've seen anyone worse. I've already give her two cups of my willow bark tea, and the fever ain't breakin'. It ain't even comin' down none that I can tell. You the one who wrapped her in the wet sheet?"

"Yes, ma'am."

"Well, she'd be pluckin' a harp by now if you hadn't did that. If she lives, she can thank you for savin' her."

If she lives ... The words rang in Smith's ears. *If she lives. If she lives* ...

"Boy, you're lookin' mighty poorly yourself. Did ya get any sleep last night?"

"No ma'am, I come down here to help Hattie and ... "

"How'd you know she needed help? She holler?"

"No, ma'am. I heard a poundin' on the porch. She'd got up there to the smokehouse somehow. By the looks of her knees I think she musta crawled most of the way."

"Well, I swan! Bless her little heart, she musta felt it comin' on. I'd hate to think what woulda happened if she hadn't made it to you. She'd a-died out there in the rain, as sure as I'm standin' here."

"Ma'am, ain't there nothin' more you can do for her? Ain't you got no powders or tonic you could give her?"

"Powders and tonics is for snake oil salesmen. I'm a midwife and a healer, not a sideshow act! The onliest thing I can do for Hattie now is pray, and that's just what I been doin'. From what I've heard about you, you could use some prayin', too."

"Beggin' your pardon? What are you talkin' about?"

"Well, sir. I heard it from Mamie Dunford who heard it from Eunice Crowe that you been in some trouble with the law. That so?"

"Not bad trouble." Smith dropped his eyes.

"Did ya shoot up the poolhall at Beech Creek? Did ya shoot Sheriff Westerfield off a ladder when he was lookin' for moonshine? You been fired from pert near every mine in the county, ain't you, for fightin'? And you like your liquor, I hear tell."

"Yes, ma'am, I done all that and prob'ly more, but ... "

"Good for you. You got spunk, boy. I like that. But you gotta learn to put reins on it. Hattie needs a man with spunk! I thought Jack Crowe was a nice enough youngster, but he didn't have that kinda spunk. I'm glad you got yourself a plateful!"

"Yes, ma'am. Thank you, ma'am."

"Now, why don't you get in there and lay down on that couch in yonder before you fall on your face and split open the other side of your head. I'll wake you if there's a change."

Smith did as he was told. In a moment his tired body fell into an exhausted sleep, and he dreamed of holding Hattie in his arms.

He awoke when he heard Hattie cry out, "Jack! Jack! Here I am! I'm comin', Jack. Wait for me. What're you doin', Jack? You been to town? Whyn't you wait for me?" Her head thrashed back and forth on the pillow. Her arms fought the air. "Jack? Where you goin'? Wait. I wanna go, too."

Smith ran to the bedroom.

Ma Richard's bathed Hattie's forehead with a cold cloth, and then chafed her wrists. "Talk to her, Son. The other one's heavy on her heart. You got to give her somethin' to live for."

Ma Richards' voice cracked with emotion, "She's gonna follow her Jack if'n you don't call her back."

"Hattie, it's me, Smith. You come back here, you hear me? Your babies need you. I need you! I ain't lettin' you go. What would Dulcie do if you wasn't here to teach her to make thimble biscuits. Who'd be her mama? Who'd take up where you left off. Nobody could do it like you. You gonna let Eunice Crowe get 'em, Hattie? You gonna let Ferd be their 'daddy'? Is that what you want? Fight, Darlin'. You fight. You can do it, Hattie. You listening? I'm talkin' to you, woman! You come back, y'hear? I ... I love you Hattie. Please don't die. Please! I ain't had a chance to tell you yet, but I love you so much it pure pains me. Come back, Hattie. I even been prayin' for you, Hattie. Me. Ain't that somethin'? You done that. You showed me it was the right way. You did. I need you to teach me more. I can't go on without you." Smith sank down on his knees by the bed and snatched up Hattie's thrashing hand. "Hattie. Please, Darlin'. Fight. Fight. You got to fight."

Slowly, ever so slowly, Hattie calmed down. She still raved on for awhile, but softer, quieter.

"Is she dyin', Ma?" Tears shone in Smith's eyes.

"It's too soon to tell. She's either dyin' or she's comin' back. Only the Lord knows which way she's goin' at this point."

On and on through the afternoon and evening and into the darkest hours of the night, Hattie cried out for Jack, and Smith called her back. He begged and pleaded with her not to leave him and the children.

At dawn the next morning, Hattie's body suddenly convulsed in great shaking heaves. The force of the spasms raised her up off the bed. Smith grabbed her by the shoulders and hung on. Hattie's unfocused eyes flew open, and ropes of mucus poured from her mouth. She vomited until Smith didn't think she could possibly vomit again, but she did. When the spasms were over, she sank back against Smith. Still. So very still.

"Well, that's it then. She'll be comin' round soon."

That was a good sign? A hopeful sign? Smith looked at Ma Richards as if she were ready for the asylum. "You mean that was good?"

"Yes sirree, that was a good sign! She's tryin' to throw off the poison in her body. I b'lieve she'll live now. Help me get her cleaned up."

Smith was shocked. Ma Richard's believed Hattie would live! *Hallelujah. Thank you Lord. Oh, thank you for savin' my Hattie!*

"You gonna stand there lookin' like a dunce, or you gonna help me? Get them sheets off the bed. Take 'em out in the yard and leave 'em. We'll burn 'em later. The quilts we'll soak in lye soap. Where's the clean ones? You know where she puts her night clothes?"

"No idea. I'd never been in the bedroom 'til night before last."

"Well, dig around 'til you find a nightgown and bring it here."

A moment later he held out a soft, flannel gown.

"Yep, that'll do. You lift her while I change the sheets. She ain't bigger'n a minute. Good. Just let me get this last corner on. There. Now, hold her up."

Smith had no idea what the granny woman was going to do next. By the time he realized her intent, it was too late. Ma whipped the soiled nightgown off Hattie. His hands were on her bare torso. He felt like his fingers were about to burn right off, and not because of her fever! Quickly, he averted his eyes. Ma smiled a near toothless grin as she gently pulled the clean nightgown over Hattie's head and smoothed it down the length of her body.

"Now, lay her down real easy like. I want to look at her legs. You're right about her crawlin'. Look at them knees. Mm mmm! That's just a shame! Gimme my bag. I got some salve in there somewhere ... "

Together they made Hattie clean and comfortable and then left her to rest.

"You're gonna have to listen real close. If you hear her chokin', you get yourself back in there and raise her up. She may still have poisonin' in her. Now, if you can handle things for a bit, I'm gonna fix us somethin' to eat, and then I'm gonna lay down for a while. I was bringin' a baby durin' the night and I ain't had no sleep neither."

Smith was stunned. This dear old woman seemed to have the energy of six grown men. She'd gone without sleep so that he could rest!

"Ma, I just wanna thank you for what you done. I don't reckon Hattie would have lived if'n you hadn't come when you did."

"I didn't do it for you. I done it for her. But ... you're welcome. You be good to her. Hear me? And I tell you what I'll do. I'll start tellin' folk around here what I know of you—that you're a good'un. That'll settle Eunice Crowe's hash. If'n I say it's so, they'll believe me over her."

"Thank you again. I don't rightly know what to say."

"Then don't say nothin'. There ain't nothin' I like less than idle talk."

Ma was back to her usual brusque self, but Smith knew they'd formed a special relationship.

He grinned and went to bring in fresh water from the box-well and a bucket of coal for the stove. When Ma called, he and Dulcie ate the food she'd prepared. She left him feeding Jackie in the rocking chair and took Dulcie into the front room with her to nap. When the baby was full and sleepy, Smith quietly carried him in and laid him in the cradle. Ma's blanket had slipped to the floor. He picked it up and gently covered her.

She's one of a kind, ain't she, Lord?

About 7:30 that night the rain finally stopped for the day. Ma Richards was restless. She couldn't abide idleness, and there was nothing left for her to do. She longed for a way to get home to her little house.

108

She'd told Smith what was needed to take care of Hattie. She even parceled out some of her willow bark tea with strict instructions on how it was made. She watched him make it to be certain he did it right. She'd had him kill a chicken and made broth to spoon feed Hattie when she awoke. Everything was done, and she was getting antsy.

"Boy, you reckon you could get your truck up that hill out there?"

"I might could, but I'd hate to try. I'd have to leave Hattie to take you home. I know you're ready to go, but I just can't see my way clear to leavin' her again. And, I'm thinkin' if the road was passable, some of the Stoneworths would be here by now. I 'magine they're 'bout sick with frettin' that they can't get down here."

"I s'pose you're right. I'll just have to be content to stay, then, but I ain't likin' it much!"

"No, ma'am. I'm sure you ain't." Smith grinned.

In the silence of the night, Hattie stirred and slowly opened her eyes. It took awhile for her eyes to focus. Then, in the dim light she made out Smith's form dozing in the rocking chair beside the bed. *Smith's here. Yes, that's right. I remember ... Smith's here. Good,* she thought, *everything'll be all right now. Smith's here.* She slipped away again into a healing sleep.

8

Early the next morning, Gene Beckwith eased the nose of his car over the crest of the hill. Ever so slowly he fought his way down the slope, sliding and gaining a grip, slipping and catching again, until he got to the bottom.

Carrie flew from the car to the house. Gene followed a little more slowly, pausing to wipe the sweat from his forehead. It had been a nerve-racking drive. Most of the county roads were flooded; some of them were swept away completely. Under the flood waters you couldn't see whether the road was there or not. Few people ventured out on the roads.

"I musta woke up stupid this mornin'!" muttered Gene to himself for the hundredth time since they'd left their house. Then he added, "I can't believe I let you talk me into this, Carrie." Carrie was already in the house so he followed behind her.

Smith rose to greet him. "Gene, you have a bad time gettin' down here?"

"Never seen the roads worse than they are right now. Earl Brewer said he rowed uptown yesterday, and the water was so high he could almost touch the stoplight. How's Hattie?"

"She's fair. Still fightin'. That's the good news. Ma says she'll live."

"Some folks in town are callin' you a hero."

"Me? What for?"

"Everybody's talkin' about how you run to town and packed Ma Richards in here on that mule to save Hattie. 'Course there's some sayin' since you ain't brought Ma back, you're only half a hero."

Smith laughed. "That sounds like Forrest Stoneworth. Am I right?"

"Yup. He's the one what said it."

Gene and Smith sat in companionable silence and listened to the women talking quietly in the bedroom.

"When I got here she was wrapped in a wet sheet," said Ma Richards. "She'd a died certain sure if he hadn't thought to do that. He done blocked off the doors to the front room and told Dulcie it was a game and to stay there 'til he got back, then he run up that hill and come got me and brung me back. That child waited like a little angel. She minded him like he was her daddy. He's a fine man, Carrie."

"I can see that. I'm just so thankful Hattie's gonna live. She ... she still looks awful bad, Ma."

"Honey, she looks fresher'n new-mown hay compared to what she looked like two days ago. I ain't never seen nobody look so dead that weren't! It like to broke my heart."

"Carrie?" Hattie's voice sounded weak. "You here? I was hopin' you'd come." She opened her eyes.

"'Course I did, Honey. Gene brought me an' he's in the kitchen with Smith. We had to check on our girl. You liked to scared us half to death, Honey. We knew you were sick, but the roads were so bad with the rain and all ... "

"Is it still rainin'?"

"Yes, Honey. Forrest's talkin' bout buildin' him an ark for Vida and Clifford."

Vida had delivered a healthy boy three weeks after Hattie had Jackie. "He just dotes on that boy, you know."

A slight smile played at the corners of Hattie's mouth. "He does. I knew he'd be a good daddy because he was always so good to us kids. Is everybody all right? The family, I mean. Was anyone else took with the influenza 'sides me?"

"Eldon, Rose Ellen, and two of their younguns were sick—and Willa, too, but they're comin' along. I think you got it the worst. Eldon's coughin' some, but he was doin' that 'fore he took sick. We been real fortunate, Hattie. Lotta folks died. Lou Ann Knott passed away yesterday; and the littlest McPherson girl. She was such a sweet little thing ... "

Hattie pictured chubby little Katie McPherson. She had been in Dulcie's Sunday school class.

"Bertie McPherson must be heartbroke."

"I heard tell she's takin' it real hard. Annie said she's blamin' God for takin' her baby. She just carried on over the casket somethin' awful, and wouldn't even let Brother Fenton preach a funeral. Said she didn't believe in no God that would kill her baby."

"Oh, Carrie, what a shame! She oughta be lettin' Him comfort her 'stead of *blamin'* Him. He didn't kill her baby. He's there to carry her through if she'll just let Him."

"I know, but she was raised up in one of them churches that teaches, good or bad, God done it and you got to live with it. Guess it's not surprisin' she'd hold Him responsible."

Hattie was tiring. Ma Richards stepped to the bed and laid her hand on Hattie's forehead. "You're still feverish, girl. You rest a bit. I'm gonna take your sister in the kitchen, and we're gonna have us a visit. I ain't had no fresh faces to look at for awhile."

Carrie leaned over and kissed Hattie's forehead. "I'll be here when you wake up, Honey."

Hattie's eyes were already closed.

Gene was alone in the kitchen since Smith had gone out to check the animals.

"You two come in the dinin' room. I don't want Hattie to hear what I'm gonna say." Ma said as she led the way. When they were seated she said, "Eunice Crow's been spreadin' trash about that man out there. She's tryin' to raise up the town against him. I ain't sure, but I'm thinkin' she might be makin' some headway with it, too. I've had several folks askin' me questions. Now, I know Hattie, and I know she's a good girl, but folks like havin' someone to sneer at. If it's a good person they

113

can tear down, that makes it all the better. I'm afeared Eunice is just bidin' her time afore she pulls somethin' big. Word's gonna get out that Smith was here alone with Hattie when she first took sick. I reckon that'll be all Eunice needs to fan the flames."

"But, Ma, you said yourself that Hattie would've died if Smith hadn't stayed with her."

"Carrie, Honey, I been around a long time. Some folks might say too long. One thing I've learned in all my years is that when times are hard, folks need someone to hate. It gives 'em a place to put their frustrations. I ain't wantin' to see that place bein' Hattie's doorstep, but I'm thinkin' that's where it's comin'."

"But, Ma, that don't make no sense ... "

"No, Carrie," Gene cut her off. "Miz Richards is right. I seen it up at the mines. There's been more drinkin' and fightin' up there in the last three weeks than I ever seen. Them boys are all about desperate tryin' to keep body and soul together. They're worried about their jobs and feedin' their kids, and instead of gettin' together and helpin' each other, they're tearing each other apart. Not all of 'em, of course, but a good number anyway. I know Eldon's been tryin' to stay out of it and so do most of our folks, but there's a long winter comin' and no relief in sight. I reckon it's gonna get worse 'afore it gets better."

Ma Richards continued, "It don't help none that in the past Smith's raised more cane than a sugar farm, neither. Now, I've spent the last two days with him, and he's about as fine a man as I've seen, and in case you don't know it yet, he's in love with Hattie. I hate to see either one of 'em get hurt."

"But Ma, don't you think that things'll settle down once the rains stop? I mean, won't families pull together for each other? We ain't got a lot neither, but when one of us is hurtin', we take care of each other."

"You ain't like most folks. I don't mean to say there ain't good folks around here. Most of 'em are, but folks is runnin' scared. Nothin' hurts a man's heart worse than watchin' his babies starve and his woman cry. 'Ignorance breeds ignorance'

114

my Mama used to say, and that's a fact! Look at those feuds back east. Don't nobody even remember why they hate each other no more, but they hate anyway just 'cause their daddy did, and their granddaddy, and so on back up the line. It don't make sense, but it's the truth."

"Miz Richards, the way I see it we gotta stop folks talkin' against Smith. How you reckon we can do that?" Gene asked.

"Well now, I been thinkin' on that, and what I decided is we got to make Smith out to be the biggest hero since George Washington. I'll be tellin' folks he saved Hattie's life and that'll help, but he can't get in no more trouble. He's got to be clean as a preacher's shirt from now on. Either that or he's got to marry up with Hattie the minute she's well enough to get up the hill to the church-house."

"Hattie'd never agree to that, Ma. It's too soon. She's still grievin' for Jack. We sure ain't gonna force a weddin' on her!" Carrie cried.

"She may not have a choice in the matter. Eunice's got blood in her eye over Smith bein' here. I ain't never knowed a woman so spiteful as she is. She's had Ferd runnin' all over the county diggin' into Smith's past. Anything that boy's done since he was in short pants is fuel for her fire. And he's got a past to talk about! Taken one at a time, them stories 'bout him are funny, but all wrapped up in one package, it don't sound too good. Hattie's gonna have folks lookin' at her crossways. The more I think about it, seems like her marryin' Smith might be the best way to quiet the talk. He won't mind, and I think she'll learn to love him in time."

"No, Miz Richards," Gene also insisted, "Carrie and I won't have no part pressurin' Hattie to marry. She's more like our daughter than a sister. There's got to be another way. The folks in town are already talkin' about how Smith fetched you down here to Hattie. The ones I heard sounded real proud of him. Don't you think that'll be enough?"

"Might be, if the rains stop and the mines open. If they don't ... The ones who're talkin' bad ain't gonna say nothin' to your face, Gene. The Stoneworth name carries a lot a weight in this county, but that's also what makes Hattie such a prime target. Nothin's better than a 'good girl gone bad' story."

"But she *ain't* gone bad, Ma!" Carrie was crying now. "That ain't fair. You know it ain't."

"Honey, whoever told you life was fair lied to you," Ma said simply. "Like I said, I been around a long time, an' I've seen the ugliest of folks and the best. Somehow the ugly ones seem to shout with the loudest voices."

The screen door squeaked opened, and they heard Smith stamping the mud off his shoes on the mat inside the door. Next came thudding sounds as he pulled them off and dropped them to the floor.

Carrie wiped her eyes and blew her nose. She rose to greet him as he came into the dining room. "You better sit down, Smith. We got us a problem."

Smith sat down and listened while Ma Richards summarized the conversation she'd just had with Gene and Carrie. When she finished he leaned forward on his elbows and rubbed his hands over his face. "I reckon I brung this on Hattie. I'm real sorry. I told her I wouldn't do nothin' to bring shame on her or hers, but I reckon that's just what I done. I'll clear out if that's what y'all want me to do."

"It ain't," Gene said. "If you run off, it's gonna look worse than it already does. It'll look like you're guilty of somethin' whether you are or not. 'Sides, Hattie still needs your help. You leave, and we'll have to find someone else. There's a lot of men out of work that'd be happy for the job, but I don't know 'em, and I wouldn't trust 'em like I do you."

"Thank you, Gene. That means a whole lot comin' from you. What are we gonna do?" asked Smith.

"I reckon we'll have to let things lie for the time bein' and make the best of whatever comes. Listen though, Ma's right

116

when she says you can't get in no more trouble. You got to toe the line," Gene emphasized.

Smith grinned. "I'll be a lily white saint if that's what it takes."

Ma snorted, "Humph! That's a lie if I ever heard one. You just do your best."

Smith thought for a minute, then he said, "If Hattie won't marry me, and y'all don't want me to leave, I got a sister, Zonie, that never married. What if I brought her down here to stay with Hattie 'til she's up and around again? Would that help?"

"Couldn't hurt. Might be just the thing to take the pressure off. Willa could come, too, but she's been 'most as sick as Hattie," Carrie said.

"Gene, if I write Zonie a note, you reckon you could get to Old Hebron and fetch her? I know the roads are still bad."

"I s'pose I'll die tryin', since Carrie won't give me no peace if I don't."

Carrie ran to find paper and pencil, and Smith quickly wrote the note. Gene gathered his rain gear, kissed Carrie goodbye, and headed for the car. They watched from the front window as he took a running start at the hill. The car made it half way up, fishtailed, and slid back down. Again and again he raced up the hill only to slide back. Finally, gunning the engine for all it was worth, Gene made it to the crest and over.

"Y'all realize it's gonna drive Eunice Crowe near to dyin' when she hears there's another woman down here and it ain't her," Ma said.

"I know. I thought of that, too," Carrie replied. "I guess I don't care if it does. I know it ain't my place to judge another, but ... "

"Then don't. I don't like what she's doin' either, but I know some things about Eunice that another soul on earth don't know. I'm only gonna tell you 'cause you need to understand what makes her the way she is. Eunice's daddy was the meanest man I ever laid eyes on. He was a drunk, a mean drunk. Well, I don't know what all he did to her for sure 'cept beat her everytime he got drunk, but I do know he sold her to Big Jack Crowe for a five dollar gold piece when she was twelve years old."

"What?" Carrie dropped the window curtain she was holding back and turned toward Ma.

"He sold her when she was just a baby. Big Jack was a good man. He married her, but she weren't never right in the head. She was the purtiest baby you ever did see, but bein' treated the way she was wears a body down. By the time Big Jack got her she was a sad sight. He cleaned her up, and they got on purty good 'til he died. As long as he was livin', she did fine most of the time, but she's got the meanness in her from her daddy. I saw her tear into her son, Jack, with a razor strap one time. She whipped him so hard I thought she was gonna cripple him. It took me and Big Jack to pull her off him."

Smith moved closer to the woman. "Why do you think she's so all fired determined to move in on Hattie?"

"Well, partly 'cause she's lonely and partly 'cause she thinks it's her right. But mostly, I reckon, 'cause she ain't never had nothin' she could call her own. That house she calls hers, ain't. It belongs to Big Jack's cousin Marthy and her man. They let her live there 'cause they like it up in Cincinnati. Don't nobody know that but me, and I ain't tellin' no one else. I'm trustin' you not to, either. Maybe if she coulda had more younguns she woulda softened, but she didn't. She lost four babies in the womb and had a stillborn. I think that's what finally pushed her over the edge."

Ma moved her hand in an all-encompassing sweep. "Seeing you so close and havin' so much more than she does pert near makes her crazy. I think she believes in her heart that if she moved in down here she'd finally have the family she's always dreamed of. What she don't understand is that if she'd just asked Hattie 'stead of tellin' her, Hattie probably woulda let her come. She's like a starvin' soul, graspin' and grabbin' for what she can get."

118

"Ma," said Carrie, "I ain't never heard nothin' so awful. Poor Eunice. I'm so ashamed I could die."

Ma's sharp eyes honed in on Carrie's stricken face. "Well, now, don't be feelin' too sorry for her. She's brought a lot of them bad feelin's on herself. There's plenty of folks been through pain that didn't grow up ugly. They chose to go on and be decent. She chose to push and bully. It were a choice she made. Don't be thinkin' otherwise."

Smith shook his head, then asked, "Where was her Ma when all that was goin' on."

"She was dead. Buck Barnett beat her to death. I was called in to dress the body—ain't never seen nothin' like it in my life. They couldn't prove he done it, and he said she'd fallen off the roof. I don't know any woman'd go up on a roof, but that's what he said, and they couldn't prove otherwise."

"So Eunice didn't have nobody to take up for her?" Carrie asked.

"Well now, I don't know about that. I think Ferd tried. When he was a boy, he was smart as a whip, but he took so many beatin's I think it addled him. He ain't the same as he was then. I know he tried to hide Eunice from Buck from time to time."

"Whatever happened to Buck Barnett?" asked Carrie.

"One night he got real liquored up, loaded his shotgun, and blew his own head off. Some folks said 'good riddance', but that man was sick. He was sick in his mind as bad as Hattie's sick in her body. Someday folks are gonna realize that people that do the kinds of things Buck Barnett did have a sickness."

"Yeah, sick in their heads," Carrie said.

"No, Carrie. They ain't just crazy or mean. Oh, I ain't sayin' there ain't real wickedness in the world, but there's mind sickness, too. Otherwise, I don't believe a parent could do to a child the things he done to Eunice."

Smith thought about that for a moment. "You may be right about that, Ma, but it don't make me feel better about it. Whether it's mind sickness or meanness, the mistreated younguns suffer no matter what caused it."

"Yes, they do. That's a fact. That's why I told y'all about Eunice. She's suffered, and she's seen more'n a body oughta have to see. It's a real shame."

Carrie considered what Ma had said, then asked, "You reckon if Hattie'd let Eunice move in she woulda been happy here?"

"No ma'am, I don't," Ma said. "I've thought on this a lot since that day when Hattie had the baby. I believe it might've made things worse. Eunice would always be an outsider. It still wouldn't be her house, and she wouldn't be its mistress. She'd just be livin'-in. She'd come to realize that real fast. I'm afeared she might take out her meanness on Dulcie. She'd know better than try it with Hattie, but the babies ... I'm tellin you true, it scares me to think about it. That's why it's important for you to be here, Smith, and why you got to make sure Eunice don't get a toehold!"

Zonie Delaney's eyes crinkled with laugh lines. She was plump and comfortable. Dulcie loved her the minute she laid eyes on her. 'Aunt Zonie' became a household favorite from the time she stepped over the threshold. Smith was relieved to hand over baby duty to her.

Gene loaded Carrie into the car and once again fought his way up the hill. This time Ma went with them. Smith was going to miss the feisty old lady. She'd become a true friend in the two days she'd been there.

When supper was over and the babies put to bed, Smith and Zonie finally had time to talk.

"It's bad up home, too, Smith. Folks are droppin' like flies. Granny's been goin' from place to place tryin' to help. I don't know where she finds the strength, but she just keeps on. She rides that mule like he was a white charger from a storybook! I wasn't sure if I should leave her, but Colt and Virginia said

120

they'd look in on her. I'm glad they're just up the road. Colt said he'd send John down to stay with her at night. He's turnin' out to be a fine boy."

"Prob'ly the fine example his daddy and I set for him." Smith chuckled. "Don't you reckon?"

"Fiddlesticks! If y'all were the onliest examples he'd ever seen, he'd be a convict by now! Granny and me and Virginia's switch is what's kept him on the straight and narrow. You was the orneriest boy I ever saw. I think Mama 'bout give up on you."

"Did not! I was her favorite."

"Ha! Favorite headache maybe. Anyway, you seem to be gettin' along purty good now. You likin' it here?"

"I am. Wait 'til you meet Hattie. She's a doll, Zonie. She's so little and fine, like a china doll."

"Her little girl's sure good. She must be a good mama."

"She is. You shoulda seen her. I come to the kitchen door with a bucket of coal one mornin' and she had Dulcie up on a stool at the counter. She gave her a ball of dough and helped her roll it out. Dulcie was cutting it into tiny biscuits with a thimble while Hattie made the real ones. That youngun was covered in flour and sticky all over. Hattie just helped her put them little bitty things in a tin and baked 'em in the oven right along with hers. Dulcie was so proud she pert near burst when they come out! Who'd of thought to teach a little girl to do that? It ain't just that though. Hattie knows the name of every tree and bush. She can name 'em all. Bugs, too. I never knowed nobody that knows as much about nature as she does. When she takes Dulcie outside, she points out this or that and tells her what it is. That child can name more plants than I can."

"Hattie sounds like a good woman, Smith."

"When I almost lost her, I 'bout died myself. I don't think I coulda stood it if she'd died."

"You got it bad, boy, real bad. She know how you feel?"

"I don't think so. I ain't wantin' to put her off, her bein' a new widow and all. Her husband died in April. It ain't been that long."

"Well, bide your time. If she's the woman God's holding for you, He'll let you know when the time is right."

"That's kinda how I'm figurin' it. She's worth waitin' for, Zonie."

They settled down for the night with Smith taking the first shift sitting with Hattie. She'd been awake for a little while earlier in the evening and had met Zonie. They seemed comfortable with each other.

Smith sat in the rocker and watched Hattie's sleeping face. She still looked mighty sick. She was a little restless tonight, and as he reached up to straighten the covers, Hattie woke up.

"Hi. I didn't mean to wake you."

"That's all right. I been wakin' up off and on anyway. I can't seem to get comfortable tonight. Guess I been in this bed too long."

"You want to try to sit in the rocker for just a little bit?"

"I don't know. I'm still purty weak."

"Tell you what, I'll wrap you in the quilt and hold you on my lap." Smith moved before Hattie could stop him. He carefully sat down with Hattie and pushed her head down on his shoulder.

"How's that? Better?"

"Heavenly! It feels so good to be up. Even if you have to hold me like a baby."

Smith gently rubbed her tired back. She snuggled a little closer and closed her eyes.

Sweet torture, that's what this is. I'm holdin' her in my arms, and she's lettin' me! Oh, Hattie, how I love you, Darlin'.

Smith held her as she slept. When Zonie came to relieve him, they were still there. Both of them were sound asleep. His cheek was pressed against her hair.

9

The first week of November Smith drove Hattie to Eldon's house. The house was one of many in a row that were built exactly alike. Small, poorly built, rectangular shotgun cabins that housed the miners and their families. Some were pitiful—no curtains in the windows, trash around the doors. Others were bright and cheery, where the ladies had done their best to make the crude shacks into homes. Eldon's was one of those.

Eldon wasn't doing well. He'd never fully recovered from the influenza, though he was certainly better than he had been. Rose Ellen was worried sick. That's why Hattie had insisted on going for the visit.

"He's my oldest brother, Smith. Carrie likes to think that she's the head of this family 'cause she's the oldest, and the bossiest, but it's really Eldon. Nothin' seems to rattle him. He just keeps on doing what he's always done. Workin' hard. Playin' fair. Treatin' others like he wants to be treated. I just want to see for myself that he's all right. Can't you understand that?"

"Yeah, I understand it, but Hattie you ain't been outa bed long yourself. Ma Richards said you might go down sick again if you was to get wore out too quickly. I think she'd have my head if she knew I was bringin' you out in this weather."

"I'm a grown woman. I can make my own decisions. 'Sides, I'm wrapped up good, and when I get tired, I'll tell you, and you can take me home. All right?"

"I reckon. Glad we left the kids with Zonie, though. I don't like bringin' you into Coaltown, much less them younguns."

"Don't talk nonsense. People raise their kids in these Company neighborhoods all the time. They ain't that bad. I'll grant you the Company could have put more time and money into the houses, but the folks here, they're just like everyone else."

"'Cept right now, they're hungry. A hungry man's an angry man. I don't like it one bit. If'n I was up here by myself, well, that'd be different, but bringin' you up here sticks in my craw."

"There's the house. Now straighten up and quit fussin' at me." She climbed out of the truck and headed for the door with Smith hot on her heels, glancing back over his shoulder into the shadows.

"Hello? It's Hattie. I brought Smith, too." Hattie opened the door and went in with Smith right behind her.

Eldon rose slowly from his chair. "Hey, Least'un. What are you doin' comin' out here like this? You still lookin' mighty peaked."

"Ha! Have you checked your ol' mug in the lookin' glass lately? You look worse'n I do. Sit back down before you fall down. Rose Ellen, you been feedin' this miner?"

"Whenever he'll eat. Most the time he don't. Says it don't sit right. I been 'bout at my wits end tryin' to think of things he might like."

"You had the doctor in?"

"No, he won't let me. Says he's doin' better and that's all that matters. He's just an old mule!"

"Let's go see if we can find something to feed him," Hattie suggested. "I'll help you."

Smith sat down with Eldon.

"I ain't seen you around here since they let you go at the mine, Smith. Why'd you bring Hattie?"

"She said if I didn't bring her, she'd get Carrie to. I figured if it was me, at least I can protect her if things get ugly."

"I s'pose that's right. It's got real bad up here the last few weeks. If I had anywhere to send Rose Ellen and the kids, I'd do it."

126

"Eldon, you know Hattie'd take 'em in if you asked her."

"Rose Ellen won't go. She says as long as I stay, she's stayin', too—and she calls me a mule!"

"I heard they're gonna open a couple of the workin's in a few days. That true?"

"Who knows? I hope so. The men got to have work. Most of us'll have to work all winter to pay off what we owe to the Company store. It's gonna be real tight."

"Would you be willin' to take help? I don't mean from the dole—from a friend?"

"No. I ain't gonna start that unless there ain't no other way out. But, thanks for askin'."

They continued to talk about the mine, the unrest and the Depression until Hattie came back from the kitchen.

"Smith, I left that plate of cookies in the truck. Would you get it for me?"

"Sure, Hattie. 'Scuse me, Eldon. I'll be right back."

Smith walked toward the truck in the moonlight and was just reaching for the door handle when someone grabbed his shoulder and spun him around.

"Well, well, well, if it ain't the great trouble maker, up here stirrin' things up again."

Jeb Sawyer's potbelly seemed to have swollen since the last time Smith had seen him.

"Yeah, that's right. Can't you read the picket sign I'm wavin'? What'sa matter, Sawyer, your goons take the night off? You havin' to walk patrol by yourself? Ya ain't afraid some of them hungry women are gonna burn you out, are you? Don't worry, old boy, if I see one comin' with her rollin' pin cocked, I'll protect you." Smith truly disliked this man. He knew Sawyer for the coward and bully he was.

"I don't need no protection, not from the likes of you. You're nothin' but trash, Delaney. Always was, always will be. You an' all your kin."

Smith saw red. He could take a personal insult, but to insult his family was another thing.

"Heard you got yourself some kinda white trash woman down in Mondray. She'd have to be to crawl between the sheets with the likes of you!"

Smith swung. He connected with Sawyer's nose. Blood flew. Sawyer staggered back, then roaring like a bull, launched himself at the smaller man. Blow after blow landed. They went down with the massive Sawyer almost smothering Smith. Twisting his wiry body, Smith rolled from under Sawyer. Still clinging, clawing, and flailing, the men staggered to their feet. Sawyer landed a punch to Smith's midsection, knocking the wind out of him. Bent and gasping, Smith circled while recovering, then closed in, powerful arms moving with the speed and force of a jackhammer. His blur of blows soon took their toll.

Smith was not a large man, but he'd swung the pick for years. Sawyer was management. Physical labor was far in the past. He used cronies to bully and intimidate. It wasn't long before Smith had the upper hand.

"You're ... gonna ... eat ... them ... words ... " Each word Smith spoke was punctuated with a blow to Sawyer's body or face. "You ... ain't ... fit ... to ... breathe ... the ... same ... air ... as that ... woman." He punished Sawyer until the larger man slumped to the ground again and rolled onto his fat belly, trying to cover his head with his arms. Even then, Smith didn't quit. He tugged Sawyer to his feet. "Take it back you miserable excuse for a man ... " A right uppercut to the jaw sent Sawyer reeling backward. Smith moved in again.

"Smith! No!" Hattie grabbed his swinging arm and hung on for dear life. The momentum of his intended blow yanked her forward and almost threw her to the ground. "Quit! You got to quit it! Please!" She was crying now. She wrapped her arms around him to keep him from hitting the large, whining man, who was on his knees in the mud. "Stop it!" she ordered him in her best 'this-is-your-mama-talkin'-and-I-mean-it' voice. It always worked with Dulcie and it worked for Smith, too. He stood still.

She grabbed his face between her hands and looked hard into his eyes. "Don't you move from this spot. You hear me?"

He nodded and leaned down to rest his hands on his knees, sucking air.

Hattie hurried to the man on the ground. He was getting up slowly. "Mister, I don't know what happened here," she said, "but you better clear out. Go on. Git! No, don't say nothin', just git!" Hattie put her hand in the small of his back and gave him a shove down the street. "Now, just go on and cool your head. He ain't gonna hit you any more. I won't let him."

Sawyer turned back. He glared out of the eye that wasn't blackening and waved a bloody finger at Smith. "This ain't over, Delaney! It ain't over, you hear me? I'm gonna take care of you, one way or the other." He brushed the back of his hand against his split lip, turned and stumbled away.

Hattie hurried back to Smith. "You hurt, Smith?—Smith, I asked if you was hurt."

Smith raised his head. "No ma'am. I ain't. Not bad enough to talk about." Slowly he straightened up and walked with Hattie back to the house. Rose Ellen and Eldon stood in moon-lit door-way.

"Can't think of one man who needed his behind kicked more than Sawyer," said Eldon. "Just a little surprised you done it again. Come in here and let the women look at you."

Rose Ellen brought a basin of water and a clean wash cloth, and Hattie bathed Smith's wounds. The cut he'd gotten when he fell while running up the hill to get Ma Richards for Hattie had split open again. His nose was bleeding, and his lip was cut. Other than that, he was fine. He knew he'd be sore in the morning, but he didn't care. Except ... Gene's words rang in his ears, "*You can't get in no more trouble ...* "

"Hattie, I'm sorry. I shouldn't a done that. I just plain forgot myself. I'm hopin' you don't think poorly of me."

"Right now, Smith Delaney, I don't know what I think of you. You oughta be ashamed of yourself. You were beatin' that man into the ground. I want to know what possessed you to fight him. And you're gonna tell me *right now*!"

Smith had never seen Hattie in a temper fit before. She was kinda cute all riled up like that, tapping her foot, with her hands on her hips.

Smith hesitated. "I had just cause. More'n just cause. That's all I'm sayin'." He wasn't about to tell Hattie what had been said out there. She would be horrified. "You'll have to believe me when I tell you I had cause." He looked straight into her eyes, willing her, begging her, to trust him.

"Just take me home. I'm so sorry, Eldon, Rose Ellen. I can't tell you how ashamed I am. Please don't think badly of Smith. He says he had just cause, and I ain't never known him to lie. Y'all come see us soon, and bring the kids."

Hattie hugged them and turned to the door.

"Don't open that door yet. I want to look out first." Eldon blew out the light and waited for his eyes to adjust. He moved to the window and eased the curtain open a crack. He looked one way, then the other, and back again. "I don't see nobody movin' out there. Hattie, Smith's gonna go to the truck by way of the back door. When I see him get in, I'll send you out the front door. When I open the door you run as fast as you can and get in. Smith, you gun it out of here. Sawyer ain't gonna take this lyin' down. Watch your back."

Smith nodded and followed Rose Ellen through the kitchen to the back door. He glanced around and then slid into the shadows.

Eldon watched for Smith to round the edge of the house and climb into the truck. When the engine caught, he squeezed Hattie's hand and opened the door.

"NOW!"

Hattie ran. Smith leaned across the seat and threw the door open. She clambered in as quickly as she could. Smith took off.

130

He didn't turn the headlights on—just drove quietly in the moon-light through Coaltown. A mile or so down the road, he leaned down and switched on the lights.

Hattie hadn't spoken a word since she'd run from the house. She was scared to death. "Why'd we have to leave like that? Who was that man? Eldon said 'Sawyer' ... " Realization dawned. Eyes huge, she turned to Smith. "He didn't mean the Strawboss. Not *that* Sawyer! What have you done?"

Smith grinned. "That's the one. I ain't gonna tell you what he said, Hattie, but he earned everything he got. You can either trust me or not. It's up to you."

"Smith, I *do* trust *you*. It's *him* I don't trust. Everybody knows not to cross him. I'd never seen him before, but I've heard about him ever since I was a kid. He is nobody to be messin' with!" She was shivering so hard her teeth chattered. "I'm scared. He could send his men after you. He could have you bushwhacked. He could ... "

"Hattie, come here," Smith ordered in a quiet voice. He pulled her close. "Listen here, he could do a whole lot of things, but he ain't gonna do nothin'. He's a coward. I whipped him good. He won't be comin' back for more of the same."

She cares about what happens to me, thought Smith. *Yes, she does! That's a first step ...* Smith almost burst into song. He was *so* happy. "Now, look. I'll lay low for awhile, stay outa sight at your place for a few days, and it'll all blow over. You wait and see if it don't."

Hattie wasn't convinced, but she felt better now that he had his arm around her—much better. They rode that way the rest of the way home.

"Hattie, that's Ferd's truck, ain't it?" It was pulled up next to the house. Her hands flew to her face. Smith parked beside the truck and came around to open Hattie's door. "Take a deep breath. Now, relax. Miz Crowe don't have no power over you. You're a woman with her own mind, and it's a good one. She can't make you do nothin' you don't want to do. All right?"

"All right." Hattie held her head up and walked into the house. Smith followed behind her, much as he'd done at Eldon's.

Ferd sat at the kitchen table drinking a cup of coffee. "Folks are in the front room."

Zonie sat tightlipped on the couch, hands clenched in her lap. Eunice was in the rocking chair. Baby Jackie was on a quilt on the floor. "Mother Crowe, this is a surprise. You haven't been down for a while."

"Seems you got plenty of company. You ain't needed mine. Heard you was bad sick with the influenza and come to see if you was doin' all right, but you look fine to me if you're out runnin' around the county with the likes of him," she sneered.

"That's real kind of you. I hope you haven't been waitin' long."

"Long enough. I come down here to say some things to you and I'm aimin' to say 'em 'fore I leave. I think you should ask your *hired man* and his *sister* to leave us in private."

Hattie hesitated, "Mother Crowe, Mr. Delaney and Zonie have been good friends to me. I think I'd like 'em to stay."

Eunice's face reddened. "Suit yourself. It makes no nevermind to me!" She pointed a gnarled finger at Smith. "That man you're harborin' is a common criminal. He's been in more brawls than a dog has ticks. He tried to shoot a man at Beech Creek. He shot at Sheriff Westerfield, too. The sheriff told me so hisself. He's suspected of bootleggin' and havin' a still. He's known for bein' a hard drinker. He's even said to have run a gamblin' room. I've been hearin' all kinds of things about him. You're keepin' a dangerous criminal on your property. I just thought it was my Christian duty to tell you. He's violent, and I don't see him bein' good for the younguns to be around. Now if you have the sense of a cricket, you'll do the right thing and run him off afore he murders you in your bed, or worse."

"Yes, ma'am. I know all about his past. Mr. Delaney told me. It doesn't make any difference to me. He's here to stay until he decides to go. Was there anything else you wanted to say?"

Eunice looked stunned. "You mean to tell me you knew about him and you're lettin' him stay on! Why, look at him. It looks like he's been in another fight. He's all beat up."

"I know. I was there."

"You was there! But ... "

"He had just cause for what he did."

"Have you lost your mind? He's a ... "

Smith interrupted, "Zonie, where's Dulcie?"

"She's in the closet under the stairs," Zonie looked ready to cry. "Miz Crowe put her in there."

Smith was gone. He ran to the closet and yanked the door open. Dulcie was huddled in a heap in the corner, whimpering.

"Come to Smith, Darlin'. It's all right. Come on out now."

"I can't. She said ... she said ... " Dulcie gulped, "I's a wicked bad girl. I got to stay in here, or da Devil's gonna get me."

"Oh, Honey. She's your grandma, but she's wrong. You ain't wicked. Let me take you out of there."

"I'm weeeeeet!" Dulcie sobbed.

Smith reached in and picked her up. "Sugar, I don't care if you're wet. You'll dry, won't you?"

Hattie reached up and took Dulcie from Smith. "It's all right, Dulcie. Remember? I told you, sometimes even big girls have accidents? We won't worry about it."

"But she saiiiiiiiiiid ... "

"Shush now. Zonie, will you get her cleaned up? I got some things to say to Eunice."

Zonie took the frightened little girl and helped her take off her wet panties. She washed her, changed her into her night-gown, then tucked her into bed. She sat by Dulcie, rubbing her back, until she went to sleep. Her little body shuddered every few minutes from crying so hard. Smith had never in his whole life seen Zonie so angry!

Hattie marched into the living room. "What gave you the right to punish my child?"

"Well, she was back-talkin' me." Eunice wouldn't meet her eyes.

"You put her in a dark closet for backtalk? She's only four years old! Isn't that a little harsh? Did she use a bad word?"

"No, 'course not. She wouldn't do what I told her to do. She needed to go, and when I said she was big enough to go to the outhouse, she refused."

"She refused 'cause Miz Crowe wouldn't let me go with her." Zonie stood in the doorway. "She told Dulcie she was a crybaby, and when Dulcie said 'No, I'm not,' Miz Crowe slapped her face. Then she dragged her into the bedroom and latched her in the closet."

"Eunice, you get outa my house. Don't you come back." Hattie was beside herself. "I'll load the shotgun and shoot you myself if you do!" She could take Eunice picking on her, but she was infuriated at the thought of her abusing Dulcie. "Get out!"

Eunice went completely white. She backed out of the dining room and ran through the kitchen and out the door.

Ferd was standin' at the back door. "She shouldn't a hit your little girl, Hattie. I'm real sorry I couldn't stop her in time. If it makes you feel any better, I was whispering to Dulcie through the door so she wouldn't be all alone."

"Thank you, Ferd. Take your sister off my land. And don't never bring her back. I mean it."

"Yes'm."

Smith escorted him to the truck and watched until they were gone. When he walked back into the kitchen, Hattie was pacing. Zonie was telling her what had happened.

"First off, when she got here, she ordered me up to the smokehouse. I told her I lived here, not at the smokehouse, and I guess that made her mad. She didn't like it one bit. Dulcie tried to show Eunice her doll, but she practically knocked it out of her hands. When Dulcie tried to tell her why she named the doll 'Hat,' Miz Crowe told Dulcie to be quiet and sit down.

"Well, you know how it is with a little one. When they got to go they get all squirmy. Dulcie was squirmin', and Miz Crowe told her to sit still. I asked her if she needed the chamber pot, and Miz Crowe said she could go to the outhouse, that it was foolish for Dulcie to use the chamber pot when she wasn't big enough to empty it by herself. Dulcie said she'd go to the outhouse if I would take her. Miz Crowe wouldn't have none of that. She tried to make her go out by herself, and Dulcie kept sayin' how she's afraid of the dark. She started to cry. Miz Crowe, she just hauled off and slapped her a good one."

Zonie twisted the handkerchief she clutched in her hands.

"Oh, Zonie!" said Hattie.

"It scared Dulcie so bad, she wet herself. Miz Crowe started screamin' that Dulcie'd done it on purpose just to make her mad, that Dulcie was a wicked, hateful child who ought to be whipped. I told her if she hit her again, I'd call the law on her. That stopped the hittin', but she dragged Dulcie in there and locked the door and kept screamin' at her. It ... it was just awful. I kept tellin' her to stop. She said I weren't family here. But she was. It was her duty to discipline her grandchildren. She just plain come unhinged!"

Smith stood with arms crossed and fury in his eyes. "Ma Richards was right. She ain't right in the head. That woman's a menace to you, Hattie, and your younguns. You done the right thing throwin' her out. If you hadn't done it, I was about to. You just beat me to the punch."

"Hattie, I can't tell you how sorry I am," Zonie said. "I tried to stop her. I really did. But she ... "

"I know, Zonie. I'm not faultin' you for what she did. I just feel like I been gut punched is all. I ain't never threatened to kill no one before." Hattie was shaking again. "I got to sit down. I'm feelin' awful wrung out."

"It's the shock," Smith reached for Hattie's arm. "First you wade into my fight, then you run off ol' Sawyer, and when you finally get home, you have to threaten to take after Eunice with a shotgun. It's been a mighty tough day."

Smith walked with her into the front room and sat next to her on the couch. "Put your head down right here on my shoulder. I'm gonna just sit here next to you and keep you company."

Hattie hesitated, then leaned into him. "I've never said nothin' so awful in my life. I hate to think what my Mama would say."

"Let's see, I believe she'd say, 'Well, girl, you protected a friend, and you stood up for your youngun. You done good.' That's what my Mama'd a said."

Hattie laughed softly. "I don't think so. My Mama would have said. 'Hattie girl, you lost your temper. You need to talk to the Lord about it and make it right.' That's what my Mama would've said."

"Is that what you want to do? Pray? We can do that Hattie. I'll pray for you if you want me to."

Hattie raised her big brown eyes to meet his blue ones. "I'd be proud for you to pray for me, Smith."

"Here, take my hand." When Hattie placed her small white hand in his large tanned one, he bowed his head. "Lord, it's me, Smith, again. I brung Hattie with me this time. We ain't done our best for You today and we just want You to know we're sorry. Help us to do better tomorrow. Thank You and Amen."

It was during the simple prayer that Hattie realized she could love this "wild" man, if she let herself.

10

"Under dat one over dere," Dulcie said. She pointed underneath a bush at the edge of the yard. "It just wunned under dere, an' I couldn't catch it."

Smith leaned over to look for the runaway rubber ball. "I don't see it, Sugar. You sure this is where it went?"

"Uh huh. I saw it. It just wunned and wunned down da yard 'til it hid under da bush, and I couldn't see it anymore."

"Okay, I'll see if I can find it." Smith got down on his hands and knees and peered under the thick foliage. "There it is. I see it. Hang on, I'll get it."

As he raised back up, a branch caught the edge of his flat cap. It flipped off his head and onto the ground. Dulcie picked it up and plopped it on her own head.

"I'm Smiff! I'm Smiff!" She strutted around him in a circle, snapping imaginary suspenders.

"You're a mess, that's what you are. You're sweet enough to eat and I'm gonna eat you up!" He growled deep in his throat and chased the delighted child through the yard to the porch swing and around it. He grabbed her from behind and pretended to bite her neck.

"No, Mr. Big Bad Wolf! Don't eat me! My childwen will cwy and cwy if I don't come home."

Smith laughed, "Oh, all right, but next time you come into my woods ... " He chomped her neck again as a warning. "You warm enough, Honey? It's a bit cool this mornin' and your cheeks are mighty rosy."

"I could get warmer if I sat in your lap."

"C'mere, you little con man. We'll swing for a few minutes, then you got to go in. Okay?"

"Kay. What's a con man?"

Smith sat down on the swing and pulled Dulcie up on his lap. He opened his jacket and pulled her inside its warmth. Then he set the swing rocking. Back and forth they went.

"A con man is a someone who tricks folks to get his own way. Like maybe he says he's got some fine land for sale. He might even have a picture to show, but the truth is, the land he's sellin' is just a big ol' swamp. Or maybe he says the medicine he's sellin' will cure anything that ails you, but it's really just turpentine and castor oil."

"Yuck! dat's a wie, ain't it?"

"In my book it's a lie—it sure is."

Dulcie tipped her head back to look at him. "Smiff, will you tell me a story? A good one wike you told me da other day?"

"A story? Well, did I ever tell you how to catch a monkey?"

"No, sir."

"A long time ago when I was a lot younger, I got sent to a country called the Philippines. That's a long, long way from here."

"How come you had to go there?"

"Well, there's this country called Spain. The United States of America, where we live, and Spain had a war. We won, so some of the places that had belonged to Spain became our property. We had to go take care of 'em. I was in the Army, so they sent me and some other boys to be part of the occupation force. That's what they called us.

"Anyway, when I was in the Philippines, a buddy of mine said he knew how to catch a monkey. We all laughed at him 'cause they were feisty little things. They wouldn't even let us get close to 'em."

"Why?"

"I reckon 'cause they was scared. We were a lot bigger'n them. So, this buddy of mine says, 'So you don't believe me, huh? I'll show you slackers!' He went out and got a coconut. Know what that is?"

"Uh huh."

"Good. He takes his knife outa his pocket, and he starts boring him a hole. He tips it up and drinks all the coconut milk. Then he turns it over and makes two littler holes. He gets him a piece of wire and sticks it in one of the little holes and out the other. He twists the wire into a loop and takes it outside. He walks over to a tree and ties a rope to that loop of wire he made. Then he tied the rope around the tree. Next he digs in his pocket and pulls out a shiny brass key. He drops that key into the big hole and sets the coconut on the ground, and he walks back into the hut where we lived.

"We peeked out and watched that coconut." Smith shaded his eyes with his right hand and looked from under it as though watching something. "In just a minute or two a little monkey come down out of that tree. He sniffed the rope. He sniffed the coconut. He looked around real quick to see if anyone was comin'. When he saw the coast was clear, he picked up the coconut. He shook it. It rattled. He dropped it and scampered about halfway up the tree. Nothin' happened. *Slooooowly,* he came back down and snuck up on the coconut and gave it a push. He jumped back. Nothing happened. So ... " Smith paused dramatically.

"So, wha' happened?"

"So, he went back to the coconut and picked it up again. This time he turned it over in his little hands and saw the hole. He looked in it, and he saw somethin' shiny lookin' back at him."

"Da key! Da key!"

"That's right. Well, monkeys are curious critters. He'd never seen a key before, and he wanted it, so he put his hand in the hole and *grabbed* it! Then, he couldn't get his hand back out of the hole. He was caught!"

"But he got his hand in da hole. How come it wouldn't come back out?" asked Dulcie.

"When he put his hand in, his fingers were straight out like this, see?" Smith showed her with her own hand. "Then when he grabbed the key he had to make a fist so he could hang on to it." He curled her little hand into a ball. "Look at the difference."

"Oooooh!"

"We had caught us a monkey. We just ran right up to that tree and got him. Ain't that somethin?"

"But, why didn't he jus' dwop da key and wun away? Weren't he scared no more?"

"Oh, yeah! He was scared. He was tremblin' and shakin', jumpin' up and down, screechin' an' makin' an awful racket, but he wanted that shiny brass key more than he wanted to get away. And that's how you catch a monkey."

"Hmmmm. I don't tink you caught dat monkey. Your buddy didn't neither."

"Sure did, Honey. I was there and seen it with my own eyes."

"Uh uh. Y'all didn't do it. Dat monkey catched hisself!"

Smith stared down at Dulcie in amazement and then burst out laughing. "I guess you're right. That monkey did catch hisself. How'd you get so smart, Little Britches?"

"God made me dat way!" Dulcie grinned and hopped down. As she skipped into the house, Smith rose and followed, shaking his head.

"Hattie, that youngun's about as smart as they come."

"She is at that. Sometimes I don't know how I'll stay ahead of her. She's always makin' me think. What'd she say this time?"

Smith told the story to Hattie and Zonie. When he finished, Hattie laughed. "I'd never have thought of that, but she's right."

"Me neither, and I was there when the monkey caught hisself." Smith was tickled all over again. "You're gonna have your hands full with that one!"

140

"Don't I know it? I'm thankful every day her disposition's so sweet. If she was that smart, and a willful child, she'd be pert near impossible to live with."

"Mama, can I have a cookie?" Dulcie ran in from the other room. "I'm hungwy."

"Well, look at you," said Zonie. "What're you doin' with Smith's cap on your head, you little darlin? Ain't she a sight in that cap?" Zonie was delighted. "You look like one of them boys on the cover of Horatio Alger's books—those newspaper boys. You know, the ones that yell, 'Extra, Extra, Read All About It' in New York City?"

Dulcie's face dimpled. She crawled up on a stool at the table with the cookie her mother had given her.

"Why'd dey yell dat?"

"Because they want folks to buy the papers. They holler real loud to get 'em to notice. When there's an 'extra' edition, that means it's real important news, like when the Big War was finally over," Zonie explained.

"Smiff was in a war. It was in Philippians."

"No, Honey," Hattie corrected. "It was in the Philippines. Philippians is a book in the Bible."

"Oh. Was da Philippines war da same as da Big War?"

"No. The Big War was different," answered Smith.

"Why didn't you go to da big one, 'stead of da little one?"

"First off, when I was in the Philippines, the little one was already over. I was just helping out there. Second, I *was* in the big one."

"How come you got to go to boff?"

'Cause, like an idiot, I got sot drunk with Colt and woke up reenlisted, thought Smith, but he said, "Seemed like the right thing to do at the time."

"Dulcie, run on. You're askin' too many questions. Give Smith his cap back, Honey," Hattie said.

"Let her keep it, Hattie. I got another one. She looks so cute in it."

141

"Smith ... " Hattie cautioned.

"Is it my birfday?"

"What? No, Honey. Your birthday was in September. That's when you turned four, remember?"

"Den I have to swap you for it," said Dulcie, turning from her mother to Smith.

"You do?"

"Uh huh. Mama says we don't take charity. If'n it's your birfday you can take a pwesent, or Chwistmas. But for evewyday, it's better to swap."

"Is that right?"

"Uh huh. Mama says."

"Well, what do you have to swap?"

"Ummmm… I got a cats-eye marble and a steelie, and a whisthle."

"Better show me."

"'Kay. Be wight back…" Dulcie ducked into the bedroom and came back with a small pasteboard box. Inside the box were the two marbles, the whistle, a penny, and a rock with shiny flecks.

"Can't have my fool's gold. Daddy got it for me when I was little."

Smith, Hattie and Zonie exchanged smiles over the serious little tyke busily poking through her treasures.

"Can't swap you my cats-eye marble, neither."

"Can't, huh?"

"Nope. Gotta keep it fowever, 'cause Fatty Harper gived it to me."

"You're kiddin'? He did, sure 'nuff?" Smith looked up at Hattie for confirmation. When she nodded, his eyebrows shot up.

"Yup. Me an' Daddy was at the ten-cent store in Central City an' I wadn't 'posed to wun, an' I forgot. I wunned awound da corner and wunned smack into Fatty Harper. An' it hurted me so I cwied. Mr. Harper said, 'Don't cwy little girl.' He gived

142

me dats cats-eye marble so I'd feel better. Pulled it wight out'a his pocket and said it was for me."

"That sure was awful nice of him," Smith said.

'Yup, and know what? He said I was cute as a button!"

"You are, Little Britches."

"And my daddy said I gots to keep dat marble for always, 'cause Mr. Harper's da bestest marble shooter in da whole wide world."

"That's right. I read that in the paper. He won the world champion marble shootin' contest."

"So, I can't swap you my catseye marble. How 'bout if'n I buy da cap with my penny?"

"Honey, it's not worth a penny. That there whistle work?"

"Uh huh, it's real loud. Mama won't let me blow it in da house. Wanna swap for it?"

"I reckon so. But if you ever need the whistle you let me know. I'll keep it in my pocket so you can borrow it anytime you want to."

"Kay. You can borrow my cap, too. Shake on it?"

Solemnly they shook hands to seal the bargain.

Dulcie smiled, and scampered out of the kitchen, the cap cocked over one eye.

"She drives a hard bargain. You sure you don't mind about this, Hattie?"

"No, it's her whistle. If she's happy with the swap, I'm fine about it. You know the story about the marble? She was too little when it happened to remember it, but Jack told her about it over and over, and now the story is her own special treasure."

"It's a great story. I hope she does keep it. It's one of those, what do you call 'em? … Keepsakes," Zonie said.

Smith pinched a chunk off of a cold biscuit, then casually said to Hattie, "I'm going to Greenville in a little bit. You want to ride along?"

"Oh, I'd love to go, but I need to do the ironing. I guess I'd better not."

Zonie interjected, "I'll do it. I don't mind. I'll even keep the kids. 'Cept for goin' to church you ain't been outa the house since you went to your brother's. If you want to go, go on. This is the first nice day we've had in a long time."

Zonie was right. The rains had stopped, but it had been cold, too cold to want to be out for any length of time. The sky had been overcast, but today the sun was shining. That's why Dulcie had been allowed to play outside.

"Are you sure, Zonie?"

"Yes, I'm sure. Now go change your dress and get ready. Go on!"

Hattie grabbed Zonie in a hug, then ran to the bedroom. "I'll just be a minute. Wait for me." She quickly unbuttoned the brown dress she had on, let it drop to the floor and pulled her second best over her head. It was blue, the perfect complement to her coloring. She grabbed her brush and pulled it through her hair. Snatching up pins, she pushed the heavy mass up and pinned it into place. "I'm coming," she called as she found her purse and raced for the door.

"Slow down, rabbit. Sure and steady wins the race," Zonie laughed as Hattie scooted past her and out the door.

Smith was leaning on the hood of his truck, waiting. "My, don't you look nice," he said as he straightened up.

"Thank you, sir. I reckon I'm passable."

Smith laughed. "I reckon."

As they rode down the road, Hattie turned to Smith. "You sure get along good with Dulcie."

"That youngun's a pleasure to spend time with."

Hattie felt a warm glow inside as she thought of her little girl. "She's a treasure, all right. And I sure do want to thank you for the fine gift you gave her this morning."

Smith chuckled. "Yep, that old cap was some fine gift. Some fine, fine, gift!—Naw, it wasn't even a gift, remember? It was a trade."

144

"I'm not talkin' about the cap, Smith. I'm talkin' about your spendin' time with her. I don't believe big folks realize how they bless little'uns when they take time for them and really pay attention to them."

"Like I said, Dulcie's a pleasure to spend time with."

"An that story you told her—why it was full of gifts. Think of all the things you fed her little mind. Now she'll be all full of thoughts and pictures and questions. You gave her monkeys, coconuts, and palm trees. She learned about the Philippines, the Big War, and the Little War, —and you taught her a mighty important lesson about a monkey that got hisself caught by bein' selfish and holdin' onto somethin' he didn't even need."

"Well that last part you got a little confused. She actually learned me about how that monkey caught hisself."

"Well, anyway, you gave her a mighty fine gift. Interest in nature, and history, and geography—and, mostly, you helped her know she's important, 'cause you took time with her, and I sure thank you."

Smith nodded. They rode in silence for a while, then he said, "Hattie, I been thinkin'—as a mama, you beat anything I've ever seen. I don't guess I've ever been around a woman so patient with her kids. My Mama's a good woman, but she could flat lift the roof off the house when she was hollerin' at me."

Hattie laughed. "You prob'ly needed it. Zonie's been tellin' me stories 'bout you and Colt. If they'd yelled at you as loud as you deserved, it prob'ly woulda deafened everybody at Mud River!"

"Now, don't you go listenin' to her. She ain't to be trusted. I know. I lived with her." His eyes twinkled. "She ever tell you 'bout the time she and Janie snuck off to the dance at Dunmor? My mama 'bout skinned her alive! See, you can't believe nothin' she tells you. I ain't the only child in that family with a past."

"I don't think sneakin' off to a dance is in the same league as shootin' Sheriff Westerfield off'n a ladder!"

"I didn't hit him, just put the fear of God into him. He was pokin' his nose where it didn't belong. He didn't get hurt. Just shook him up a little."

"Even so ... "

They rode along the old road that led from Drakesboro to Greenville past Ebenezer Baptist Church and on past Pond Creek, the lowlands that had flooded so badly earlier in the fall.

"I always like Pond Creek in the spring when the pussy willows are comin' out. That and Mama's crocuses are what tells me it's really springtime."

"How come you know so much about plants and birds, Hattie?"

"I don't know. I guess 'cause my mama used to read these books by a woman named Gene Stratton Porter. I still got 'em. Anyway, she'd read 'em out loud to us kids. They were just full of nature stuff, and I fell in love with the stories. Miz Porter wrote about livin' on the edge of a swamp and how the butterflies and moths looked. And she wrote about the trees. The people in her books seemed so real! It was like gettin' to know a friend. I was always a little sorry when Mama'd finish a book 'cause it seemed like my new friend had gone away. I saved all those books, and I'm gonna start' readin' 'em to Dulcie."

"Are they children's books?"

"No, they're grown up books, but children can understand 'em. They're good stories about regular folks that are just tryin' to live right and make the best of their circumstances. My favorite is called 'A Girl of the Limberlost'. It's about this young girl whose mama doesn't love her. I cried like a baby when Mama read that book."

"How come her mama don't love her?"

Hattie laughed out loud. "You sounded just like Dulcie when you said that! Her mama doesn't love her 'cause she thinks the little girl kept her from savin' her husband's life when he was drownin' in quicksand in the swamp. So, she's mean to her.

She feeds her and clothes her, but that's about all. She just hurts that little girl's feelin's somethin' awful."

"That ain't right. So she didn't have nobody to love her?"

"Well, she had the neighbors. They loved her and helped when they could, and she loved them, too. They were real good to her, and that made a big difference. She'd catch moths and butterflies and gather up different kinds of plants and sell 'em in the city so she could buy books and go to school. She was hungry for learnin'."

"It still ain't right."

"No, it's not, and the mama finds out it's not, but it takes a long time before she comes to it. When she does, the mother feels real bad about it and tries to make it right, but there's a lot a hurtin' between 'em by then."

"So does the girl go off on her own and cut her mama off without a look? That's what most folks would do."

"I don't think I'm gonna tell you any more. You'll have to wait and listen when I read it to Dulcie. There's a lot more than that. The girl falls in love with a man, and he loves her, but he's got a secret ... Never mind! You got me tellin' again after I said I wouldn't! I guess I got pert near twenty books by Miz Porter. They're each as good as the last, but that one's my favorite." Hattie chuckled. "I even wanted to name Dulcie 'Elnora' after the girl in the book, but Jack wouldn't let me. Said it was a good book, but he couldn't abide the name. I made him let me read it to him the first winter we were married. Guess he didn't love it like I did."

"Ain't that somethin'. I never did take to books much when I was a kid. You make me think I orta got started readin' sooner myself. I don't reckon I read a whole book all the way through 'til I was in the army. On the troop ship that carried us to Europe there was this feller who couldn't read. He'd beg us to read to him. We sorta took turns. Everything from books or magazines to letters from his Mama. At first I felt kinda foolish readin' out loud to a grown man, but 'fore long, I was like a sponge. Couldn't seem to get enough."

"What did you have to read on the ship?" asked Hattie.

"Some of the men had a book or two with 'em. They all swapped 'em around, so I read whatever they had. Then I went up to the ship's lounge and read through the military books they had up there. One man had a book on the great cities of Europe." Smith laughed out loud. "You shoulda heard me tryin' to pronounce some of them names, *Chartres, Notre Dame, Neuschwanstein*. By the time I got to France, I knowed where I was goin'. This old boy from Old Hebron, Kentucky was the one that pointed out the Arc de Triumphe to the rest of them guys. That was a proud day for me. Now, I'll read just about anything I can get my hands on."

"I'll be jiggered, Smith! But you didn't read at home?"

"No. Weren't a lot of readin' at my house, I guess, 'ceptin' the Bible."

"Oh, my Mama read the Bible, too. Jonah and the Whale, Noah and the Ark, Daniel and the Lion's Den. We heard 'em all."

"Yeah, so did we. Don't know how I turned out so feisty when Mama tried so hard to teach me right."

"She did teach you right, Smith. You know the difference between right and wrong. You just sorta took off on the wrong road is all. I reckon that happens sometimes. I've never seen you do anything wrong, 'cept fightin' with Mr. Sawyer."

"Didn't your brothers and sisters ever cut up like me an' mine?"

Hattie thought about that a moment, "No, but that doesn't mean they didn't think about it. There was some mischief, but somethin' 'bout not lettin' down Mama and Daddy kept us from goin' too far, I reckon. Them and God."

"Like not wantin' to burn for all eternity?"

"Well, there's that," Hattie grinned, "but it's more than that, too. Our Daddy was so good to us. He and Mama had somethin'

148

special. It was a pleasure to see how much they loved each other, and us." Hattie watched the scenery whizzing past as she continued, "Mama always called God our 'Father in Heaven'. I guess we all thought that with our flesh Daddy bein' so special, the Heavenly One must be just beyond words, *He's so* special."

"I reckon I never thought of it that way." Smith looked thoughtful as he negotiated a curve in the road. "I guess I always believed in God 'cause I was afraid *not* to believe in him. That burnin' for all eternity business, an' all."

"But that's not the right way to look at God! Look, you love Dulcie, right? If you were her daddy an' she made a mistake, like when she wet herself, you wouldn't punish her for bein' bad. I know. I saw you. You picked her up and loved her. That's how a lovin' father deals with his children. Now, if she was really naughty, you might have to teach her not to do it again, but you wouldn't hurt her, now would you?"

"No, 'course not."

"She might have to sit on a chair, or if it was a really bad thing she did, like playin' with the stove or hittin' the baby, maybe you'd even have to spank her. But it wouldn't be outa anger, it'd be outa love, to teach her not to do it again. Right?"

"Well, yeah, but ... "

"There's no buts about it. That's how a lovin' father teaches his children to do the right thing. He doesn't threaten to put 'em in a dark closet like Eunice did! Now, I believe in hell— don't get me wrong—but that's only for the folks who rebel against God. They aren't sorry for what they've done, don't try to make it right, and won't let God help 'em."

"I guess that makes sense, when you say it like that."

"'Course it does, an' that's what the Bible says. Jesus said, 'Abba, Father.' Brother Fenton said that means the same as 'daddy' in the language they talked. And he says we can call God 'Abba,' too. That's humblin', don't you think? It's right in the New Testament in Mark, Chapter Fourteen, verse thirty-six, and in Romans, Chapter Eight, verses fifteen and sixteen."

Smith didn't know what to say. He'd never thought of God quite that way. He'd always seen Him as a figure who sat in judgment of what he'd done, not as someone who loved him the way he loved Dulcie.

"So, what you're sayin' is, if a man was truly sorry he'd taken that wrong fork in the road, then God would love him anyway."

"That's right! In fact, God loves us, period. And that love isn't gonna run out. You're not plannin' to stop lovin' Dulcie are you?"

"Not likely. I think she could set the barn on fire, and when I was done fussin' about it, I'd love her anyway."

"All right, then. And if she was sorry? Would you forgive her?"

"Yes, but I'd want her to promise not to do it again."

"That's just how God is. If we fall down, He picks us up and keeps on lovin' us. Sometimes we pull a stunt and we got to take what's comin' to us, but He doesn't beat us to death. He loves us and stands ready to help us to do better the next time."

"Like I'd do with Dulcie."

"Just like that. Sounds to me like *you're* gonna be a pretty good daddy, someday."

"Well, I've always liked young'uns. Annie was always one of my favorites."

"Annie Radburn?"

"Yep, I even use to send her stuff when I was overseas. Just little things, but I think she kept most of 'em. At the store the other day, I even seen one of the shells I sent her from the Philippines."

Hattie's eyes grew large. "The big pink one?"

"That very one."

"Smith! I listened to the ocean in that shell from the time I was little girl in pigtails."

"You mean it?"

"Sure did. I never knew who that 'cousin' was, but I've heard about you all my life. See, remembering to send a shell to a little girl—thoughtful little things like are what would make you a good daddy."

"Huh! I ain't likely to find a good woman willin' to take this ol' sinner on, so I don't reckon we'll ever know. I'm almost forty. I 'magine if there was one out there willin' to try, she'da found me by now."

"I reckon she's out there. She just hasn't got around to tellin' you yet. Maybe you just need to give her a little more time. She might be a little, well, scared to say how she feels." Hattie stammered, "Maybe she doesn't think she's ready to love anoth ... a man, right yet."

Smith glanced away from the road to Hattie's pinkened cheeks and back again. "Maybe so. Well, I reckon I can wait a little longer if'n there's a chance she might be thinkin' in my direction."

"I s'pose there's always a chance."

"Don't figure you'd tell me if you knew who she might be? No, course not. That'd be gossip. You ain't one to speak out of hand," Smith teased.

"No, I wouldn't! And if you don't straighten up, I'm gonna tell her all them bad stories 'bout you and scare her off. Then you'll die all alone in your wickedness!" Hattie teased back.

11

Hattie and Smith drove past the cemetery and on into Greenville to the courthouse square where they parked the truck.

"I'm runnin' into Cohen's Hardware for that new pulley I told you we need for the well," said Smith. " Where you gonna go?"

"I'm lookin' at the dry goods. I need embroidery silk. I'm making a hankie for Zonie for Christmas and need some yellow to finish it up. And I want to look at material for Dulcie and Jackie. That baby's growin' like a weed! He's gettin' too big for everything already. I need to run into the drugstore, too. Where do you want to meet?"

"Let's see. How 'bout I give you an hour, and then we'll meet at Cotton's Corner Restaurant kitty-cornered across from the courthouse. Will that give you enough time?"

"I think so."

They parted, with Smith heading toward the hardware store and Hattie to the dry goods store. Hattie loved to look at the cloth. The silks and satins, the calico and broadcloth. Even the plain cottons felt good between her fingers. She carefully examined each piece to determine its weight and strength, then she chose a pretty pink for Dulcie and soft green for baby Jackie. She looked through the rainbow of embroidery floss for just the right shade of yellow and finally chose the one she wanted.

Viola Brooks and Flora Montgomery were in the next aisle. She greeted them and didn't think much of it when both ladies were less than friendly in their responses. She didn't know them well, since they were town folk.

After she'd paid for her purchases, Hattie made her way to the drugstore and wandered the aisles looking at this and that. She really only needed toothpowder, so she saved that for last. Coming to town was such a treat she didn't want to miss anything!

As she stood in front of a display case of glassware, admiring a small glass bird, she overheard two ladies on the other side of the stand.

"Eunice said if it were up to her, she'd take those children and not let Hattie see 'em no more. She said the way Hattie and that Delaney man carry on is just shameful!"

"Why, I'm pert near shocked to death, Viola. I can't believe Hattie Stoneworth would be so cheap. Why, her mama, if she was alive, would flat lay down and die, she'd be so mortified! I guess it's true what they say about still waters runnin' deep."

"I'm tellin' you true, Flora. I reckon what bothers me the most is the way she keeps on goin' to church. Eunice said she just acts like nothin's goin' on, and she's got a right to be there. And him drivin' her to every service. It makes me sick. You'd think their preacher'd say somethin' 'bout it, but he don't seem to notice."

"It's a cryin' shame. It is! She's just a Jezebel, and that Delaney, he's ... well, I don't know what to say about him. I always figured he'd come to nothin' good, and I guess that's just what he's done."

"All the ladies are talkin' about it. It's just the saddest thing. And her havin' those kids down there with 'em. I think Eunice is right. She oughta go get 'em and take 'em outa there."

"Ain't it the truth ... "

Hattie's cheeks burned as the older ladies walked out of earshot. They must have followed the same path she had and come in after she did. Surely they hadn't seen her. *Jezebel.* They were calling her *Jezebel!* Tears stung her eyes as she turned and rushed from the store. She hurried down the sidewalk looking neither left nor right. She climbed into Smith's truck and laid her head back on the seat. She shut her eyes to block out the sight of the people walking by. Were they all looking at her? Did they all think she was cheap? How had it come to this? *Eunice.* She should have known Eunice wouldn't take being ordered out of her house lying down. Now she was spreading lies.

No matter how it'd happened, Hattie'd shamed her family name. Oh, how would she face the town! How would she face the family? They'd believe her and stand by her. She knew that, but still ... She'd never be able to hold her head up, again. Someone would always remember what had been said about her.

Hattie thought of the conversation she'd had with Smith on the way to Greenville. She'd been so happy! She knew she was crazy to have feelings for Smith, but she did. A few times in the last weeks she'd lain awake at night just thinking about her feelings for him. Sometimes she felt guilty because Jack had only been gone six months, and she'd truly loved him, but it had been different. Young love was so exciting—that first look, those shy glances. She'd loved Jack Crowe since she was fourteen years old, and he an older seventeen. It'd been exciting to the point of exhaustion when he'd walk her home from school, carrying her books, telling her all his plans for the future. Her heart had pounded hard the first time he'd casually reached out and taken her hand in his. It was glorious.

Carrie and Gene had been cautious about the relationship but had accepted it. They'd given Hattie a lovely wedding at the little church. Everyone came. It was the social event of the season. Hattie'd looked like a dream in her pretty white dress with orange blossoms in her dark hair. Carrie'd had those flowers shipped in by train all the way from Georgia. She'd been so happy and so scared! Jack's palms were so sweaty he almost dropped the simple gold band he slipped on her finger. It was a day out of a fairytale.

Jack had been good to her, too. He'd worked hard to make the old Stoneworth house everything it had once been. He'd been so proud when it was ready, and when Dulcie came along he'd been beside himself with delight. Now ... Hattie just wanted to cry. *What am I gonna do? Lord, you gotta help me. I'm so hurt I could just die. I know I haven't done nothin' wrong, but if folks are talking. ... Help me. I just can't stand it! Help me to know what to do. I'm not sure I can even get back outa this truck to go meet Smith. Oh, please Lord. Give me strength ...*

Hattie heard a metallic thunk as Smith dropped the pulley into the bed of the truck.

He tapped on the window. "Hey, what're you doin? I thought we were gonna meet at ... What's wrong? What's happened?"

She motioned him into the truck. When he'd walked around to the other side and gotten in, she told him what had taken place at the drug store.

"I can't stand it. It's not *true*! They were tellin' it like it was the gospel! Like there weren't any room to question," Hattie sobbed. "Take me home. Please take me home."

"Hattie, I ain't your daddy, and I ain't your brother. I got no right to do this, but you're gonna get outa this truck and walk over there to Cotton's Corner with me. We're gonna sit us down and have us a dish of ice cream before we head back home. Now, get out!"

"I am not! I'm not about to give these folks nothin' else to talk about! I'm goin' home, an' you're gonna take me!"

"No, I ain't. I'm tellin' you, those ladies want to see you runnin' scared. That's what Eunice wants. Don't you get it? If she can shame you into hidin', then she can say, 'See she can't even show her face around here?' You gonna let her do that to you? 'Course not. You're bigger'n that. Get out. We're goin' to get some ice cream."

"But ... "

Smith walked around the side of the truck and opened her door. "Let's go. Hold your head up and walk down the sidewalk like you own it. Do it, Hattie." He took her by the elbow and gave a gentle tug. "Come on. We're goin' if I have to carry you, and that *will* raise a stink."

156

"I'll never forgive you for this, Smith Delaney. You're makin' it worse!"

"I reckon I'll just have to live with it then. Now look. We were gonna meet at Cotton's Corner anyway. I don't see how it's gonna make things any worse, just 'cause we know what a bunch of old hen's are cluckin' about. 'How do, Mr. Jessup, Miz Jessup.'" Smith tipped his cap in greeting to a couple as they walked past. "Try smilin', Hattie. You look like you just kissed a porcupine's nose."

Hattie pasted a smile on her face and nodded at the people walking by on the sidewalk. "Smith, I'm gonna flay you when we get home!" she whispered.

Smith marched her down the sidewalk, just as he'd said, as if they owned it. They looked like anyone else in town for the day. Maybe Hattie looked a little strained, but he appeared as relaxed as a well-petted cat.

"Here we are. Keep that smile on your face." He opened the door and held it for her as she walked through. Inside he escorted her to a table and held her chair as she sat down.

The waitress came over to take their order and after she'd left, Smith leaned his elbows on the table. "Now look, as long as I work for you, there's gonna be talk. We knew Eunice wasn't gonna dry up and blow away just 'cause you hollered at her, right?"

She nodded a little doubtfully.

"So she's spreadin' lies. Is that really such a surprise? You know how she is. Most folks know how she is. Sure there's gonna be some that believe her, but most folks won't. Them old women are always gettin' themselves twisted up about somethin'. This time it just happens to be you. I know that 'bout binds you up, but they gotta have somethin' to do with their flappin' lips 'sides eat."

Smith leaned back as the waitress brought their order, then continued when she'd gone.

"Now, what're you gonna do? Hide? That ain't like you. You ain't one to back down from a fight any more'n I am. I still get tickled when I think about you shovin' Sawyer down the street, tellin' the ol' strawboss hisself to 'git'!"

Hattie felt herself start to relax a little. Smith was right. She wasn't going to allow herself to be run out of town on a rail because of lies.

"Okay, but it's still a problem."

"Yeah, but not a big one. They'll move on to somethin' else if you act like everything's fine. And everything *is* fine, so ... "

"All right, all right. I guess I just let myself get upset over nothin', but it hurts to be called a Jezebel! I've lived my whole life so folks would know I'm a Christian. It just breaks my heart that they'd judge me so harshly!"

"That's just the nature of folks, Hattie. You've spent most of your life with decent folk who'd give you the shirt off their backs if you needed 'em to. I've spent more time with the other kind. They'd as soon steal the shirt off your back as ask for it. You got to stand up to that kind of folks or find yourself shirtless! That ain't what you want, is it?"

Hattie blushed at the thought, and Smith grinned.

"Hey, Smith. Mind if I join you?" A small, wiry man in the flat cap of a miner walked up to the table.

"Hey, Mahlon. How you doin'? I ain't seen you in a coon's age! Pull up a chair. Hattie, this is Mahlon Hennings. He's a buddy of mine from way back."

"How d'you do, Miz Crowe? Don't know if you remember me or not, but I worked with Jack at Coaltown. He was a fine man."

"Yes, of course, Mr. Hennings. Yes, he was, thank you."

"I heard you'd put this ol' ring-tailed tooter to work. Good for you, ma'am. He needed some direction in his life," Mahlon said.

Hattie liked the friendly openness of Mr. Hennings. It was obvious he had real affection for Smith.

158

"How's things at Coaltown?" Smith asked.

"Some better now that they've reopened for some work. It's awful wet underground though. Some of the works are still flooded, and you can't get at the face without wadin' through water."

"That doesn't sound very safe," Hattie said, thinking of Eldon and his son, Ben.

"No ma'am, it ain't, but a man's gotta work. If'n we waited 'til it was safe ... " Mahlon paused. "There's a lot of folks hungry, ma'am. And the mine don't wait."

"There's a rumor that at Graham, Mr. Duncan is paying his men half-wages to wait," Smith said. "He ain't opened up yet and says he won't 'til he's certain it'll be safe for the miners."

"I heard that, too. I doubt it, but Duncan ain't like the rest. Nobody else is waitin'. Not Peanut Mine, nor Black Diamond in Drakesboro, nor Browder, neither. None of 'em, 'cept Graham-Skibo, and maybe Luzerne, though most of the rest waited a little longer than Coaltown 'fore they sent men down the cages. They's all opened up now, except Elk Valley. It's so full of water it may never open."

Smith lowered his voice. "What's happened with the strike? I was hearin' some talk of one."

Mahlon replied just as quietly, "Well, sir, what's happened is, Obie Perkins and that bunch of foolishness he hangs out with says they're gonna strike for better wages and conditions as soon as the mine's runnin' full up again. Then if management brings in scabs, they're gonna bust up the place. He's gonna bring in outsiders to do the dirty work. I think he's nuts, and so do most of the fellers, but times is hard ... an' they don't look to get no better if we don't do somethin'."

Hattie was horrified! Hired thugs, flooded rooms, strikes. What was the world coming to?

"When you reckon Coaltown'll be back up to full operatin'?" Smith asked.

"Maybe another week or two. There was pretty bad damage done to the cage riggin' during the rains. But they're workin' on it. I reckon there's already forty or fifty men underground. It won't be long 'fore they'll all be back at it."

"My brother's at Coaltown," said Hattie. "He's Eldon Stoneworth. Him and his boy Ben both mine. D'you know if he's one of them that's workin'?"

"Yes ma'am. He sure is. He was one of the first ones down. His boy, too. They went down with the first shift. I got to tell you, he ain't lookin' too good these days."

"No, he's been sick all fall. We been mighty concerned. I know he's been frettin' over not bein' able to work. It bothered him somethin' awful. But with him bein' sick and all, I just worry he'll get worse if he's standin' in water all day."

"Well, there's that, but ma'am, Eldon's one of the finest underground men I ever seen. He can swing a pick better'n anybody, and he always seems to know what to do if there's trouble. He don't panic over nothin'. It's like he's got a sixth sense or somethin'. I wouldn't worry yourself too much over him. Where he's workin' at ain't as wet as some. He's got what it takes to make it down there. I don't guess there's another man in the mine knows what he's doin' more than Eldon."

"He's right, Hattie. Eldon's a good man to have next to you in a bad situation. He don't know the word 'quit'."

"Yes, but he ain't well. If somethin' happened, ... " Hattie faltered.

"Shoot, Miz Crowe. Ain't nothin' gonna happen. We all watch out for each other down there. It's a strange thing, but it's like a brotherhood. We all pay attention to the roof and the walls, and if anybody gets a little sleepy or stupid, we yank 'em out faster'n you can say 'Jack Robinson' and get the fans blowin' so the gases get pushed out 'fore we go back in. Eldon'll be all right. His boy'll be watchin', too. He's got a good head on his shoulders. What is he, eighteen, nineteen?"

"Sixteen. He's Eldon's oldest."

160

Mahlon leaned his chair back and balanced on the back two legs, "Sixteen! Is that right? I'd a never thought it. He's almost as levelheaded as his daddy! Looks like his mama, though, with them blue eyes."

"Yes, he does." Hattie answered.

"My girl, Nell, sure thinks he's the limit. She's been sweet on him since she was a little thing. Says he's the onliest boy on the hill worth lookin' at twice. Can't even get her to talk about no one else. My Junie's 'bout to make herself sick worryin' over that girl. When I tell her how young Ben is, it'll relieve her mind some. We been thinkin' he might be gonna rob the cradle, but they's only a couple of years between 'em if he's just six-teen."

"Rose Ellen'd have a fit if she knew Ben was carryin' on with a girl!"

"No ma'am, he ain't. We ain't lettin' Nell see boys yet. I know some that do, but it ain't for our girl. She'll wait 'til she's sixteen like her mama done. No," he repeated, "they're just makin' calves eyes at each other."

"How old were you, Mr. Hennings? When Mrs. Hennings was sixteen, I mean," asked Hattie.

"I was ... let's see ... " He counted on his fingers, "never was much good at cipherin'. Musta been nigh on to twenty-eight or twenty-nine. That must be right. Junie figgered it out one time an' tol' me there was thirteen years between us."

"How come you care, then, if Ben's sixteen or seventeen?" asked Smith, glancing at the clock on the restaurant wall.

"Don't think I do, much, but Junie, she's got some highfalutin' ideas. Now, me, I think a man oughta be at least ten years older'n his woman. That gives him plenty a time to sow his wild oats, if'n he's a mind to. An' then when he's ready, he looks around an' takes his time to pick the best of the litter comin' up. He's ready to be a husband and a father. That's what I think. Junie, now, she says a bride don't need another daddy. She needs a partner. Not that she's complainin' none. She just wants somethin' different for our girls. She's gonna have her work cut out for her, 'cause we got eleven younguns, every one of 'em girls. I keep tellin' her she might have to sing a different tune to find husbands for all of 'em, but she says the Lord will provide. I reckon He will, too. She and the Lord know each other purty good."

Hattie and Smith laughed at the good-natured miner. He was a sweet man and it was obvious he thought the world of his wife and daughters.

The little bell over the restaurant door tinkled, and Hattie glanced over to see Forrest come in. She waved him over.

"Hey! What are you slackers doin' hangin' round here? Hi, Little Sister. You're lookin' better than the last time I saw you."

Another chair scraped across the floor as Forrest dragged it over and plopped himself down. "I saw Smith's truck and wondered if I'd run into you today. Whatcha been doin'? Christmas shoppin' for me, right? Hey, Honey, how 'bout a cup a coffee for this tired ol' miner?"

The waitress grinned and waved. She, like almost everyone else around, knew the outgoing Forrest Stoneworth. She gathered up a cup and saucer and brought them to him. "Can I get you folks anything else? Pie?"

Smith shook his head, "No, thanks, I'm fine. How 'bout you, Hattie. Want anything?"

"Coffee sounds good, if we're gonna be here a little longer."

"Bring this girl a cup. 'Course you're gonna be here a while," said Forrest. "Now you got me to talk to, you ain't gonna want to leave." He was his usual teasing self.

When the waitress brought the coffee to the table and set it before Hattie, Forrest looked around the small room and leaned forward. "So, Smith, you heard the strike talk?"

"Yeah, me and Mahlon was talkin' about it a little bit ago. You think it'll happen?"

"It'll happen. Don't rightly know when. Things are awful. Somethin' needs to be done, but Obie don't have the sense of a

162

chicken in heat. He's gonna make trouble whether we need it or not. Him and that buncha goons he calls friends are stirrin' things up somethin' fierce. I wish he'd leave it lie, but he won't."

"Why don't he just go to another mine if he don't like Coaltown?" Hattie asked.

"He says Coaltown's the worst, an' if they can change it, they can change 'em all."

Mahlon Hennings pushed his hand through his hair. "Yeah, I heard that, too. Once Obie gits the fidgets, he don't leave nothin' alone."

"Smith, what'll happen if they strike? I mean, will all the miners get involved or just some of 'em?" Hattie bit her lip.

"Well, I reckon to be effective, they'd need most all of 'em to walk out. I don't guess it'd work too good if only a handful was involved."

Forrest took a drink of coffee and said thoughtfully, "A lot of 'em are ready. If the ones that ain't try to keep workin', they'll run into bad trouble, I'm thinkin'. Them hired thugs is gonna be watchin' who's willin' to work and who ain't. That's why they brought 'em in. Strikebreakers, from what I hear, ain't gonna be tolerated."

"But that ain't right," Hattie set her cup on the table.

"Well, I don't know whether it's right or not, Sis. If we're gonna change things we got to be unified. Them that's willin' to work in spite of the strike will be goin' against what we're tryin' to do. We've taken bein' treated little better'n animals 'bout as long as we're gonna."

"You don't mean you're gonna strike, too!" said Hattie.

"Don't see how I can keep from it, Sis. We got to do somethin'. Eldon don't see it the same way, but I guess if it comes down to it, I'll walk the line with the rest of 'em."

"You'll be supportin' Obie and his thugs! You can't do that."

"No, I ain't. I don't think nothin' good of him or them goons. They're about as lowdown as they come, but if it comes to a strike I got to do what I think's right."

163

"What will Eldon do? You said he don't see it the same way." Smith tugged at his chin.

"I don't know. We ain't had a whole lot to say to each other since I told him how I feel about it. He don't approve. Says if I don't like Coaltown to move on, but seems to me the whole industry needs changin', not just Coaltown. I reckon that's where I do agree with Obie."

Hattie couldn't believe what she was hearing. Forrest and Eldon not speaking. Why she'd never thought she'd live to see the day when any of them would get that far apart. Sure, they'd had differences—but this, this was inconceivable.

"Hattie, we better head back." Smith glanced toward the door. Men were running down the sidewalk, jumping into cars, and squealing tires around the courthouse square heading out of town toward Drakesboro.

"What's going on?" Smith went out and grabbed a man running by. "Hey, where's the fire?"

"Explosion at Coaltown Mine! Some killed, some badly hurt, a bunch trapped or missin'," came the reply.

12

Smith slowly wove his truck through the crowd that was making its way up the narrow road leading to the Coaltown Mine. Word traveled fast in the face of disaster. People were converging on the site on foot, on horseback, and in slow-moving vehicles. Forrest and Mahlon Hennings were right behind Smith and Hattie.

"Hattie, I ain't seen this many people together in Muhlenberg County since the Centennial in '98. I was just a little kid."

"It must be awful bad. Just look at their faces. You can almost tell which folks have men workin' this shift. I ... I'm almost certain Eldon and Ben were."

Smith glanced at Hattie's troubled expression. "Now, don't you go gettin' upset 'til you know you have reason to. Even if they was workin', that don't mean they were at the place where the explosion happened." Seeing a man he recognized, Smith called out the window, "Hey Clem, what happened? Jump up on the runnin' board, and tell us what you know about it!"

The miner grabbed hold and stepped up beside Smith, hanging on as they bumped along. Others, seeing the truck take on a rider, climbed over the back and into the bed to ride up the steep hill.

"Howdy, Delaney. Miz Crowe, ma'am. Best I heard, Ferguson's crew set off a blast in the Central South Entry an' musta hit a pocket of fire damp. That gas erupted in a powerful blast just as I was steppin' off the cage. The wind from it hit so hard it throwed me plumb back against the wall!"

"Ferguson and them others?"

"Never had a chance. I seen the Mohon brothers and Mac Drucker draggin' Eb Pickens. He was dead and they're in bad shape. Lum Mohon said the blast flung 'em around like they was rag dolls. The cage is barely workin' on account of the lines gettin' fouled somethin' fierce in the blast. Messed up the phone, too. I just run down to Peanut Mine to call and get the word out. I thank you for the ride back."

"How bad you reckon it is down in the mine?" asked Smith, shifting to low gear as the truck crept through the crowd on the rough road.

"Tank Beadnell said the brittle roof of Right South Entry collapsed. Said he was at the junction of Central and Right South Entry when the air from the explosion in Central knocked him flat. He heard the Right South Entry roof cave in right where he was headin'. Told me he took a deep breath, held it and scampered outa there fast as he could. Said white damp was settlin' in fast. The gas had 'im coughin', and chokin' somethin' awful when he staggered out to the shaft and signaled for 'em to drop the cage to him. It's a wonder he ain't dead!"

"Other survivors?"

"Well, sir, them from the North Entry is comin' out and them from the Left South Entry. The cage is movin' slow, but they're comin' out."

"But none from Right South Entry?"

The miner shook his head. "You know how it is, Delaney. Ain't likely nobody back there survived it. Eldon Stoneworth and his crew was workin' back there. I don't think they coulda ... " Clem swallowed the rest of the sentence as he saw the horror on Hattie's face. Her hands flew up to cover her mouth. "Miz Crowe, pardon me, ma'am, I plumb forgot you was—you are Eldon's sister. Maybe I ain't right about what happened, maybe they ... " His voice trailed off to awkward silence.

Smith pulled the truck to the edge of the crowd gathered around Coaltown Mine shaft and tipple. The tipple was the superstructure extending from above the shaft. It contained much

166

of the mine's equipment, including that which separated coal into huge hoppers of various size lumps. The riders jumped off the truck and headed into the crowd.

Smith reached over and took Hattie's cold hand. "Honey, we don't know nothin' yet. You got to hang onto that powerful faith of yours. Yonder's Rose Ellen and the rest of the family. You go join 'em. I'll be there when I find out what's goin' on." She sat in silence, staring at the milling throng.

Smith hurried around the truck, opened the door, and took her hand as she stepped down from the truck. Hattie was unresponsive when he pulled her rigid body into a hug. She tried to compose herself, brushing her hair back with her hand. Just then Forrest hurried up from behind them, where he and Mahlon Henning had parked. He slipped his arm around his sister.

"Thanks, Smith," he said over his shoulder, as arm in arm he and Hattie made their way through the crowd to their family.

Earlier that morning, deep in the bowels of the earth in the Right South Entry of the Coaltown Mine, Eldon Stoneworth was struggling. He paused to try to draw a deep breath. Ben, swinging a pick beside him, stopped when he saw his father remove his hat, wipe the sweat from his brow with his sleeve and cough hard into his handkerchief.

"You okay, Daddy?"

"I reckon. The air's sorta heavy today, ain't it son?"

Before Ben could reply, they felt the rumble and heard the dull thud of the explosion in Central. Those standing upright when the compressed air thundered into the room were knocked to the floor or slammed against the face of coal they had been digging. The carbide lights went out, plunging them into darkness. In pitch blackness they heard the nightmarish sound of the passage between them and the outside world collapsing. They were entombed.

Hattie, Rose Ellen, Gene, Carrie, and Forrest stood together with their friends and neighbors. They'd watched in horror as Quince Bidewell's body was brought out of the cage. He'd never had a chance. His widow stood silently watching, her white face almost expressionless until another of the women came to lead her away. Then slowly, one tear trickled down her cheek. She didn't weep or sway, as Madge Foley had when her husband's body was carried out. She didn't cry, just let them take her away to a waiting car. It was as though she was no longer there, just a walking body, with no one left inside.

Hattie, watching, took a deep breath as memories came flooding back. She bit her lip and fought her fears—and her tears. Now was not the time for the Stoneworths to weep. They knew nothing other than that Eldon and Ben were down there somewhere. *But God knows, and He cares,* she thought. Hattie looked at Rose Ellen huddled in the middle of the family. They stood guard around her, ready to protect her from whatever might come as the day went on. The children were silent; they'd seen similar scenes before.

Smith walked into Razz Morgan's office with two other miners. He'd always gotten along with Mr. Morgan and knew if he could just talk to him, the owner might listen.

"Sir, I know this here is your mine. I know you call the shots as to whether there's gonna be a rescue attempt to go after survivors. I've also heard that Sawyer there is saying nobody coulda survived," Smith said as he nodded at the big man sitting in a chair to the owner's left. The miners stood facing them.

"You're right on all counts," Mr. Morgan replied.

"I reckon you know better?" Sawyer added sarcastically.

"Mr. Morgan, Beadnell said the roof collapsed close to the junction with Central. Ain't one chance in a million that passage caved in all the way back to the face where the Stoneworth crew was workin'. Eldon's got a cool head. I'm thinkin' he barricaded off that area the minute the cave-in stopped and sealed it so no gas could get to 'em. He's been a miner since he was younger'n that boy of his down there with him. He'd know exactly what to do."

"Well, Smith, if they survived the initial blast, they're sitting there in a small pocket of air that's going to run out quick," replied Morgan, drumming his fingers impatiently. "They're not going to be able to dig their way out. We're not going to be able to dig our way in. The best we can do is draw up final paperwork to give the families, along with our condolences. "Even if they're still alive—and let's face it, that's a mighty big 'if'—we just can't reach those men in time."

"Only an idiot would even try." Sawyer sneered.

"Maybe so, in your eyes, Sawyer, but since I ain't never seen you show the slightest respect for the life of a miner, or even any animal for that matter, it don't surprise me none," said Smith. "Now, Mr. Morgan, if you'll just give me a minute to explain, I'll tell you what I was thinkin'. Me, Brother Fenton, and Amos got a plan."

Razz Morgan jumped to his feet. "Delaney," he shouted, then dropped his voice and said intensely, "before you get all worked up, I'll tell *you* something: There is no plan that will work! If I send men to almost certain death, the unionizers will add that to their claims that management's insensitive to danger. I'd be held liable. There is absolutely no way, under any circumstances, I'll even consider sending a crew down ... "

There was a knock on the office door. Before Sawyer could trouble himself to rise from his chair to answer it, the door burst open and a small, excited, self-assured man strode in. His eyes swept the room. He held out his hand to the mine owner and said, "Mr. Morgan, I'm Skeet Davis, of the *Louisville Courier-Journal*. Sir, I was covering a bank robbery up in Owensboro, heard about the accident, and boarded the next train. I'll give you full and fair coverage of every aspect ... " Spotting Fenton, he paused mid-sentence, grabbed the minister's hand, and began to pump it. "Fenton, you rascal! I haven't seen you since, well, since the Floyd Collins incident, God rest his soul."

"Hello, Skeet," Fenton said warmly, then turned to the mine owner. "Mr. Morgan, you couldn't have a better reporter to cover the events here than Skeet Davis. He even won the Pulitzer Prize for his coverage of Floyd Collins being trapped in that cave. Don't know when I've been more proud than I was for you, Skeet. Oh, pardon me for not introducin' you around. This is Smith Delaney. That's Amos Frazier, and over there's Jeb Sawyer. He's one of Mr. Morgan's foremen. Gentlemen, this is Skeet Davis. He's a friend of mine." The men shook hands all around.

Mr. Morgan took his seat, stuck his thumbs behind his suspenders, pulled his shoulders back and said, "Davis, we're proud to have a man of your reputation here to cover this disaster, which was certainly beyond our ability to prevent. We'll be glad to fill you in on the details later, but when you came in we were discussing a strategy to save some of our possibly trapped miners. I want you to know it's far beyond what is normally done. They may well be dead, but we feel we must exhaust every effort, if there is the slightest shred of hope they can be rescued. Mr. Delaney, please proceed."

Smith pursed his lips to keep from grinning. The mine owner's whole attitude had changed with the pressure brought by the presence of a noted reporter there to quote his every word.

"Sir, before I got fired for that run in I had with Sawyer over him beatin' a bank mule, we were workin' a section that branches off about half way down Central South Entry toward Right South Entry where the miners are trapped."

"Or dead," muttered Sawyer.

Skeet Davis, writing pad in hand, was scribbling shorthand at a furious pace.

"Be quiet, Sawyer," said Morgan. "Go on, Delaney."

170

"That passage is sealed off, and we can't get to it right now because of the white damp fillin' up the passage leadin' to it."

"What's white damp?" the reporter asked.

Fenton, standing next to him, answered, "Carbon monoxide and smoke—left behind by the explosion. Doesn't take much in a man's lungs to kill him."

Smith continued, "The way that abandoned passage was sealed off probably kept the white damp out of it. And there's not much danger of fire damp, though there's likely some black damp."

Fenton whispered to Davis, "Fire damp—that's the name miners give methane. Forms in coal sometimes. Highly explosive. Caused today's accident. Black damp is carbon dioxide and nitrogen mixed, or air depleted of oxygen. It's not explosive but will kill a man if he breathes enough of it."

"What are you getting at, Delaney?" asked Morgan.

"For some distance those old works run right alongside Right South Entry. Back when we barricaded and sealed it off, we talked about how when Right South Entry was finished, we'd cut through the wall of coal separating them and rob the coal from the support pillars and from between the two workin's."

"Yeah, still plan to do that," said Morgan, drumming his fingers on his desk.

"It's likely that from the left side of the old entry, the three of us could dig through the six to twelve feet of coal to where the men are trapped."

"That's the dumbfoolest thing I ever heard of!" sputtered Sawyer, leaning forward, his clenched fists on his ample thighs.

"Delaney," said Morgan, "there's no way we can get you in there to dig through in time. I figure they've got no more than a day and a half of air, if that. It's going to take somewhere between one and three days to get the fans up and running just to clear the gas out enough for you to get in there. We'd have to open the seal to the old passage, get air in there, then get you in and let you dig. There's not enough time, and besides ... "

"Sir," interrupted Smith, as he walked over to the window and looked at the growing crowd around the shaft and tipple. "I don't mean to be disrespectful, but we're wastin' valuable time discussin' this. Mr. Morgan, there are several small air ducts runnin' down to the old works. Two-thirds of the way to the end of that passage there's one we could go down. It goes out the ceiling up to the top of the hill. Remember?"

"Sure, I remember, but that's insane! It's too small for a man to go down."

"No, sir, it's not. Before I came in here I ran up there and looked. There's a grate and a screen, but they'll come off. The openin' is about fourteen inches by twenty-four inches. I can make it. I asked the crowd for volunteers and most of 'em raised their hands. I told 'em the odds were slim they'd make it back out. They stepped forward anyway. I picked Brother Fenton and Amos here to go in with me."

"What'd you do, look for the runts of the litter?" grunted Sawyer.

"They gotta be small! Weren't you listening?" snapped Delaney. "You couldn't get one leg down that air duct, Sawyer, even if you had the guts to try. I gotta take men with strong chest and back muscles and powerful arms. First, to get down the duct, then we ain't gonna have the luxury of diggin' a standin' trench through the coal. We're gonna have to lie on our sides or bellies to scrounge a cut through to them trapped men. The cut'll be just big enough for the largest man in there to get out."

"You sure did a great job plannin' this out!" sneered Sawyer, crossing his flabby, massive arms on his chest. "Look at your choices. Fenton's a preacher, likely soft. And Amos! Well, he's a colored!"

Fire flashed in Smith's eyes. He clenched and released his fists and moved his jaw from side to side as he forced himself to breathe deeply. "Mr. Morgan, I'd like you to ask Sawyer to get out of this meetin'. Brother Fenton is in the pulpit on

Sundays, but every other day of the week he's in these mines. I happen to know that God's Word is in that lunch pail he carries every day. He's as fine a miner as I ever swung a pick with.

"He's got pluck, too—ask Mr. Davis. It was Eli Fenton who crawled with him deep into that cavern down near Cave City where Floyd Collins lay trapped. Time and time again they crawled in there. Took food and water and comfort to Collins. Didn't give up on him 'til Collins was dead. Davis and Fenton are men of courage. And havin' Brother Fenton along will give me something else. I'll have a man down in that mine who's on far better speakin' terms with the Father above than this way-ward son of His happens to be."

Smith stepped to the side of the small, muscular black miner and put his hand on his shoulder. "As for Amos Frazier, I don't know a finer man. The medal our government hung around his neck for bravery durin' the Big War oughta tell the kinda person he is better than anything I could say." Smith whirled toward his old enemy. "Sawyer, you lousy excuse for a man, don't you let me catch you outside this office spoutin' off remarks about these men. I'll ... " Smith took a step toward the big man who jumped to his feet and stumbled backward out of Delaney's reach.

Eli Fenton moved between Smith and the big foreman, but Morgan rose from his desk and said, "Sawyer, get outa here. You've done enough for one day."

"But they're just ... "

"Jeb, you may be my brother-in-law, but you're getting on my nerves. Get out!"

Sawyer promised retribution with a glare at Smith and stormed out of the office.

"Go on Delaney," said Razz Morgan, "but I have to tell you, this is pretty far-fetched."

Smith took a deep breath to calm his temper, then explained, "All right. Me and Brother Fenton and Amos will shinny down that air duct one at a time. The angle is enough that our weight

173

should carry us down with us holdin' ourselves back a little or nudgin' and squeezin' ourselves along if we need to. We'll need one long-handled pick to use at first and a short-handled pick the rest of the way. And we'll also need a shovel and a short-handled rake. Take the heads off the tools, and we'll divide 'em up and put 'em in three tow sacks."

Smith paced, thinking on his feet, alternately rubbing his hands on his thighs or through his graying, auburn hair as he gave instructions. Morgan jotted down the items he asked for, and Skeet Davis wrote frantically.

"I need a hat and a carbide light. Fenton and Frazier have theirs with 'em. I want three back-up lights and a small can of carbide. One of us at a time will work hunkered down in the little tunnel we'll be makin'. The other two will shut off our lights so the flames don't eat up the air. We'll wait by the air duct where the air's the best, so's to get ready for our turn to dig. One will dig for five minutes, diggin' and draggin' the coal back as best he can. The next will head in at five minutes, rake out any loose coal remainin', and dig 'til he's relieved. He'll head back out to the duct, grab a few lungs full of air and rest. We got to take short turns 'cause of the chance of bad air back there, and to save energy so each can work fast and furious when it's his turn. Eldon Stoneworth's lungs ain't good. We got to get to 'em as quick as we can. Oh, and we'll need food. Miners comin' up for the next shift should have some they can spare us since they won't be workin'."

Smith paused in his pacing and leaned both hands on the desk. His pale blue eyes peered into the face of the owner. He spoke softly. "Mr. Morgan, I'm askin' you, man to man, don't spare your money or man-power gettin' those fans runnin'. If I can get to them men and bypass the cave-in through the old passage, you got to clear Central South Entry of gases so we can get 'em out. I can't take 'em back up the air duct. They got to come out Central. Now, my plan will work *if* you get the gas cleared out and get your men to unseal the old passage into

174

Central by noon tomorrow. But if you ain't there, and the gases are still down there when we break through, we'll all die. Will you do it, sir?"

"What do you figure are the odds?"

"The odds for them men is *zero* if we don't do something!"

"But you don't even know they're alive do you?" asked Skeet Davis.

Smith turned to the reporter. "More important, we don't know they're dead! 'Til we know they are, and we ain't likely to find out 'til we dig through to 'em, we're assumin' they're alive. If they're dead, we'll bring their bodies home to their families."

"Delaney, you didn't answer my question," Mr. Morgan spoke. "What are the odds of you making it and getting the men out, if they are alive?"

"That depends. My guess is about one in three. That's what I told the men who volunteered. But Brother Fenton says 'with God, all things are possible.' And 'all things are possible to them that believes' or somethin' like that. Ain't that right, Brother Fenton?"

"That's right, Smith."

"Amen, brother!" came the rich bass voice of Amos Frazier.

"But I also heard him quote another scripture," Smith continued. "'Faith without works is dead.' So, I guess that unless we do our part, God may well wash His hands of the whole matter. It's time we acted. Mr. Morgan, you never answered my question neither. I told you the supplies we need. I asked you to get the fans runnin' and the cage operatin'. I asked you to promise a team to get Central cleared of gasses and unsealed by noon tomorrow. I'm further askin' that you have a field hospital set up, and short of an emergency elsewhere, have Doc Wadkins and Doc Wilson standin' by."

Smith again walked to the window and looked at the milling crowd. He continued, "Sir, the management of this mine's been gettin' a lot of bad talk. John L. Lewis is bringin' in his Yankee thugs to help dissatisfied miners unionize and put management

175

in its place. They're makin' the most of every mistake y'all make. They're sayin' you shoulda had more fans runnin' to clear the gases. They're sayin' you shoulda had more airshafts for ventilation. They're sayin' this accident coulda been avoided if y'all cared for anything except the profit you're makin' off the backs of your workers—the men who put themselves in danger every time they ride down the cage into that mine."

Smith walked to the front of the manager's desk and looked directly at him. "You got the opportunity to show 'em they're wrong in what they're sayin' about you and others in management. Get behind us, Mr. Morgan. Skeet here is gonna pass the word to the world that you did everything you could to save those men. Or, he's gonna say you wrote 'em off as a lost cause without even tryin'. It's your choice Mr. Morgan. I'm goin' down that shaft. You gonna meet me when we come out at the other end?"

Morgan didn't speak. The clock on the shelf behind his head beat a slow rhythm. His fingers, which had been drumming the blotter, stopped. Sweat bathed his brow. He stared at the desktop.

Smith broke the silence. "Morgan, I just made the longest speech of my life. I'm through speechifyin'. I ain't a man of words. I'm a man of action. I'm gonna take some kind of action, right now. I'm expecting you to get up off your backside, sir, and tell me whether we can depend on you. I'm waitin' for your answer. But I ain't waitin' long."

Except for the ticking of the clock, stone quiet filled the office. Amos Frazier walked to Smith's side. Then Eli Fenton. Then Skeet Davis.

Morgan didn't look up. He slid his hands, palms down, forward on the desk, took a deep breath, let it out, leaned forward, pressed down and slowly raised himself. He stood erect, locked his eyes with Smith's, stuck out his hand and said, "You got yourself a deal."

Three more bodies were brought up in the cage. The heart-broken widows and children of Jake Shannon, Abner Earle and Finis Walker were led away by loved ones, friends, and neighbors. Still no word came to the families whose men were in Right South Entry. Somewhere in that darkness, a brother, a father, a husband, a son waited to be brought to the surface. Would they be found? Would they be alive? Those questions hung in the air.

Rose Ellen was seated on an old wooden crate. The family still stood sentinel, though Forrest and Gene had left for a time to try and gather news. Carrie had somehow managed to bring Rose Ellen a cup of coffee from one of the nearby tarpaper houses. Now, they waited.

In the mine office, Smith was speaking. "Everything's gonna depend on timin' and teamwork," he told the men gathered around. "If anybody comes up short it'll mean the ruination of this rescue. So do your part, and do it right."

Fenton and Frazier left to get supplies, change clothes, and meet briefly with their families.

Skeet Davis continued to take notes while Smith instructed the men who would head separate parts of the operation. Morgan had called in his six top men—only Sawyer was excluded.

Smith spoke a few final words and went to check the equipment Morgan had requested for his use.

Razz Morgan wasn't used to playing second fiddle to an uneducated miner, but he realized Smith knew more about the hands-on, day-to-day workings of the mine than he did. He could only take satisfaction in the fact that the reporter was seeing his full cooperation, in fact—his participation—in the rescue effort.

"Men," he said, " briefly outline your responsibilities as laid out for you by Mr. Delaney. Gill, you first."

"Sir, my crew will get the cage pulleys lined up, the frayed cables replaced, and the cage to workin' right. Deadline: midnight."

"Roberson"

"I'm gettin' a blower fan of some sort to the top of the hill at the air duct. Should have it ready by an hour and a half from now. Gotta get the grate and screen off'n the duct and clear the area around it. With your permission, sir, I'm leavin' right now to get at it."

Morgan gave him a curt nod of dismissal, and Roberson pushed his way out.

"Thompson?"

"As fire-boss, I'm getting' me a crack team together, ready to head into Central, make sure the air's clear, and open the barridade to the old passage. We'll be standin' by to help bring 'em out, if... well, when they ... " Thompson mopped his brow and swallowed hard. "Don't you worry, Mr. Morgan, we'll be there to he'p 'em to the cage when they come out."

Morgan turned to a massive blond man and uttered one word, "DeKoven?"

"Ve're gonna set up dat hospital dat Mr. Delaney vants. Gonna get dem supplies he asked for, and I'll go after da Doctor mine own self, Mr. Morgan. Gonna find a place for da *gut* preachers, so da families vhat's lost der mens can be talkin' to dem preachers, somewhat. Don't you t'ink so, Ja? Ve gonna find a good quiet place for dem Men of Gott and dose hurtin' folks." The huge Dutchman blinked what looked suspiciously like tears from his clear blue eyes.

"You can use my office for that, DeKoven," said Morgan. He glanced toward Skeet Davis so quickly that most of those gathered there didn't seem to notice. "Heltsley?"

"Well sir, I'm gonna get the main blower system up and operatin', with backups wherever I can. Focus on clearin' the gas out of Central. Deadline: midnight. Sooner if I can."

178

Morgan looked at each man and stated, "All right, get it done. Let me know if there's anything you need. I'll make phone calls to the other mines for help, if there's anything we can't supply. You're dismissed. Get outta here and make it happen."

When the last of his men left, Morgan turned to Skeet Davis. "Well, as you can see, this mine's management is doing all it can to take care of its own."

"You certainly seem to be, sir. You do seem to be," replied the reporter, though his expression said otherwise. As he closed the door behind him and walked away, he said under his breath, "That's not all I've seen. I've seen a man roll up his sleeves, take on management, whip it into doing the right thing whether it wanted to or not, organize a massive effort involving scores of workers and equipment as well as hand pick two fine men to head into a possible death trap. In Smith Delaney, I think I've just seen genius and courage walking upright on two legs. What a story."

13

"MINE DISASTER RIVETS NATION'S ATTEN-
TION" So read the headline of a lead article in the *Louisville
Courier-Journal*. The column detailed the tragedy. Another article by the same reporter gave factual coverage of the rescue
efforts underway, and on the editorial page, Skeet Davis re-
vealed his personal reaction to the drama unfolding in Coaltown.

There is so much going on here at Coaltown,
site of the mining disaster. You must see beyond the opportunists hawking souvenirs, drinks
and cold bologna sandwiches to the huge crowd.
You must get beyond the giddy laughter of excited curiosity seekers. You must witness the
empty, vacant horror of families of the deceased miners. And the coal-dust covered, sweat
and tear-streaked faces of survivors who now
refuse to leave the shaft side. They wait. With
friends and family and strangers they wait.
They await the next arrival of the trembling
cage/elevator from the bowels of darkness to
see if it will bring to the surface a coal-
digging comrade, a neighbor, or brother, or
son, or father. And to see if they are alive,
injured, maimed—or dead. Of the latter, there
are seven now.

But I saw another scene enacted here at
Coaltown Mine. I saw management wrestle with
what to do about a group of miners possibly
trapped in "Right South Entry." That's their
designation for a section of the labyrinth of

rooms, "breakthroughs" and "workings" that honeycomb the beds of coal that underlie Muhlenberg County—one of the nation's richest coal-producing counties.

I saw Coaltown Mine's owner/manager, Razz Morgan, sweat and fidget under the pressure of a small, wiry, steel-eyed coal miner by the name of Smith Delaney. Delaney outlined a plan where he and two others will try to bring out the trapped men, dead or alive.

Well might Morgan sweat. Odds are good that he is sending these men to their death. The United Mine Workers organization, under John L. Lewis, is trying to completely unionize the mines in this county. They insist the explosion would not have happened had management not forced men to work in dangerous, inhumane conditions. If no effort is made to save the trapped miners, the union will say management is without heart. If they allow these men to make this effort and they die, the union will say management has no judgment. The passages of the mine are filled with poisonous gases— the miners refer to them as fire damp, white damp, and black damp. The first is explosive methane, the likely cause of Tuesday's tragedy; the second is a deadly combination that kills almost instantly; the third kills too, but more slowly. The mine's equipment that is needed to disperse the gases was damaged in the explosion. It is barely functioning.

Delaney proposed that he and his companions squeeze into a tiny air duct and work their way down hundreds of feet to an abandoned, sealed-off passage. They will follow it to where their passage parallels the pocket at the end of Right South Entry where they believe the miners are entombed. Using only hand tools they will tunnel an opening large enough for the men to escape through. They will then make their way to the barricade that seals it off and await its being opened from the Central South Entry. For that to happen, management will have to get the cage repaired and the blowers fully functioning to clear the passage of noxious gases.

Odds of success, according to Smith Delaney are one in three, maybe one in four. Delaney pressured Morgan to throw money and manpower behind the slim-odds effort to give five of his otherwise doomed men a chance to live, or, if oxygen has run out in their underground vault, the opportunity for their families to honor them with a proper burial.

I watched Morgan struggle with this life-or-death decision. Then he got to his feet and extended his hand to Delaney with the words, "You've got yourself a deal, Smith."

At 5:07 p.m., I saw Smith Delaney test his carbide light, turn it off "to save air," and put it back on his miner's hat. He shoved into a small air duct a sack of supplies tied to his right ankle by a short length of rope. He followed, feet first, into the duct to his armpits. His compact body filled the opening. He raised his hands over his head, rounded his shoulders and slid down and out of sight. His two companions, each with a sack of supplies tied to his ankle, waited their turns.

I started to leave to dispatch this message. As I approached my car, I stopped. From the top of the hill came a sound—the voices of miners, wives, sweethearts, neighbors, and strangers. They were singing "Amazing Grace." They sang about grace "that *saves* ... " I could not leave. Then came, "Rock of Ages, Cleft for Me."

How appropriate the words of that beloved old hymn. "Cleft," that word, as a verb, means "open." Perhaps that rock will open to free those trapped men—and the ones valiantly trying to reach them.

May I suggest that you pray, America? Yes, *pray*! By the time you read this as you drink tomorrow's coffee and enjoy your breakfast, Smith Delaney, Amos Frazier, and Brother Eli Fenton—if they survive—will be digging a tiny tunnel, inch by inch, toward the trapped men. Maybe they've dug through by now. Pray the men they find are alive. Pray Coaltown management's teams will have done their part. Pray that, sometime before nightfall tomorrow, the repaired cage at Coaltown Mine will bring to the surface five rescued men. Pray that with them will be three men of valor who stared death in the face to reach them. Pray that all will be alive and well. Pray America. Please pray.

The events mentioned in the feature story by Skeet Davis happened at dusk. Smith Delaney looked back at the crowd following him, as he, Fenton, and Frazier made their way to the air duct on the top of the hill. With him came the Stoneworth family. Rose Ellen, Chloe, Carrie, Marva, Lalie, Hattie, Forrest and the rest left their place of vigil by the cage shaft to walk with him. They were near the front of the crowd swarming toward the tiny ventilation shaft that led to the abandoned workings far below.

The three men reached the duct and began final preparations to descend into it. Roberson's pickup truck had wound its way through the woods to the site. Now it powered a makeshift fan blowing down the duct.

"Mr. Delaney," said Amos Frazier, "that there duct slopes at a purty good angle. You gonna slide in bottom-side down like on a slidin' board, or are you gonna be facin' down like you wuz crawlin'? Onliest thing is, sir, there ain't room 'nuff to crawl."

Smith checked his carbide light. "Amos, I figger we better slide in feet first, backside down, hands over our heads. There won't be room to reach down past our bodies, but with our hands up we can press against the sides to hold back a little if we need to. The tricky part will be about ten feet before we get to the old mine where the chute makes an almost right turn. But we'll be sittin' right to make the turn and scoot the rest of the way flat on our backs. I'll go first.

"Tie your supply bag to your leg," said Smith. As they checked the equipment, he continued, "That way we won't have to be fightin' the sack to keep it from slidin' down on us or have it cut off good air from above. We can't take a chance of turnin' it loose and slidin' it down ahead of us—or after us, for that matter. If the tools get caught and we can't get to them or past them, we'll sure 'nuff be up a creek. This way we can shove 'em and poke 'em along with our feet if we need to.

"Y'all keep that fan blowin down the chute," he said to Roberson. "Give me twenty minutes to get to the bottom. Then shut the fan down for about ten seconds and listen for my signal that I made it. I got a purty good little whistle—it's a loud un." A smile broke over his face, and then he gave the whistle a loud toot. "When they shut the fan off, I'll feel the fresh air let up, and I'll whistle to signal you that I made it. Have somebody with good hearin' stick his head down and listen. If y'all don't hear my whistle, keep turnin' the fan off every five minutes, till I signal you. But don't leave the blowers off for more'n half a minute. When I signal, turn the blowers on and off a couple of times to let me know you heard me, then leave 'em on for about five minutes. Then, Amos, you scoot on down. But if I don't

185

signal in an hour, you'll know the gases got me and not to follow me down."

"Yes, sir! I'll be right behind you, Mr. Delaney, feet first, backside down. My missus says that's my favorite position— backside down."

Smith chuckled, so did Fenton, who said, "Amos, we've seen you work. You're not one to sit around on the job. We're mighty proud to have you teaming up with us."

Smith, tightening the knot in the rope that attached his supply sack to his leg, said, "While you're workin' your way down, I'll check out the air and see if I can figure the best place to tunnel through. Brother Fenton, we'll use the same signal for you. Meantime, I'll start diggin', and when you get down, we'll go to takin' turns."

Skeet Davis, hurrying through the crowd gathering around, approached the men and said, "Fenton, I'm sorry Delaney won't let me go down with you. I know I could make it, but Smith says one more man would mean using up that much more good air. And I guess my experience with a pencil doesn't mean I'd be much good with a pick and shovel."

"He's right, Skeet," said his friend.

"At least promise me that when you come out, you won't let the *Banner* or *Tennesseean* or *Star* get a scoop on me, okay?"

"It's a deal."

Foreman Roberson's workers lifted the fan back from the duct. A few of the men and boys from the crowd of spectators climbed trees to see over the throng. Stragglers continued to arrive. Smith walked over to the Stoneworth family. He held under his left arm the cloth sack of supplies tied to his leg. "Rose Ellen, ladies, Forrest, fellows, Eldon's a good man. Ben's a fine youngster. We're gonna do our dead-level best, God bein' our helper, to get them and the others outta there. We'll make it. Just keep trustin'. Brother Fenton says this is one of the times that calls for everbody to 'watch and pray'."

186

He shook Forrest's hand, nodded at the rest, took both of Rose Ellen's hands in his own and said, "Try not to worry too much, ma'am. We'll get to 'em." Then, to the woman he adored, he said, "Hattie... Hattie, please tell Zonie I love her. And... Dulcie," his voice broke a bit, "and Jackie. I'll be back..." Words failed him when he saw her soft smile and the tears welling up in her eyes. He swallowed hard, turned, and walked back to the duct. There he paused. His companions joined him by the opening. The crowd hushed and waited.

Eli Fenton took his miner's hat from his head and said, "Folks, Brother Edwards from First Baptist in Drakesboro will lead us in prayer."

The sounds of people shuffling to their feet, men removing their hats, and a few nervous coughs combined for a moment. Then there was silence except for the sounds of nature and the resonant voice of Brother Edwards. He prayed for Divine intervention on behalf of the trapped men, the team seeking to reach them, their families, the deceased, the bereaved, and those waiting. His "Amen" was joined by a multitude of voices.

Smith Delaney glanced at Hattie, tipped his head slightly toward her, then slipped into the shaft feet first. The sack of supplies preceded him into the darkness. As his head disappeared into the tube, he heard a gasp or two and sobbing. Immediately Roberson's crew moved the fan back into place to force life-giving air into the duct. Over its dull hum Smith heard a sweet soprano voice singing, "Amazing grace ... " The voice was unsteady at first, then stronger. *It's Hattie!* he said to himself. Then he heard Marva's contralto, Forrest's tenor. Then he thought, *Listen to that barnyard bass beltin' it out. That's Amos...and him the next 'un comin' down. He oughta be savin' his lungs. Just listen to 'em... that whole bunch is singin! Lord, I'm expectin' to get out of here, but if I don't, well, I reckon there ain't many folks privileged to hear such fine singin' at their own funeral.* Smith chuckled at his own joke.

The friction of his body against the walls of the narrow shaft kept him from descending rapidly. Occasionally he had to squirm a bit or push with his hands to keep moving. At first, by tipping his head back slightly, he could see the duct opening above him grow smaller and smaller as he wormed his way down.

He made good progress for some time, then the passage tightened, and he stopped completely. He was wedged in a narrow neck. He tensed his body, took a couple of deep breaths, and relaxed as much as possible. Emptying his lungs to narrow his chest, he rounded his shoulders, and pulled with the toes of his shoes, pushing with his hands as best he could. His upraised arms ached from being over his head, his hands tingled from lack of blood flow. *Dear Lord,* he prayed silently, *please help me make it. For the sake of them trapped men, and them folks out there, and—yes, Lord, for me, too—please help me get through here.* Slowly his body inched downward a bit, and then, like a cork out of a bottle, he was past the bottleneck. He could breathe. *Oh, Lord, I sure do thank You!*

Smith inched downward. *I'm glad Amos and Fenton ain't no bigger'n me. And I sure am glad this here's a one-way trip. No way a man could go up it. Shouldn't be much farther to the bend.* After another ten minutes or so of wriggling along, he felt the tug of the rope tied to his ankle let up. Then his foot hit the sack of supplies. It was resting at the point where the duct turned and became almost horizontal. He was only a dozen feet or so from the abandoned mine passage.

His heart rose in his throat and began pounding. The air blowing down the duct had stopped! In a panic, he thought, *Did the blower break down? I have to have air! Wait! Slow down! Take it easy. They turned off the fan to listen for my signal. It must be takin' longer than I thought it would to get to the bottom. Just breathe slow. Breathe slow.* He felt the air begin moving again. The fan was back on.

He took a deep breath. With his left foot, he probed to get a sense of how the joint intersected. Then he hooked the toe of

188

his right shoe under the bag, moved it to the center of the duct and pushed it with both feet. Soon he was in a sitting position, legs along the horizontal passage, chest, head, and arms still upright in the air duct. Gradually scooting down, he slid feet first until he was lying on his back. *Well, I guess I know how a crawdad feels when you flop 'im on his back—only I ain't got room to turn myself back over. Just a few more feet. Just a few more feet.*

Without gravity pulling him along, progress was torturous. Once again, he shoved the sack of supplies with his foot, squirmed along on his back, pulling with his heels as best he could. Another kick of the sack and the line went taut and yanked his foot. The sack had dropped into the abandoned mine – he'd made it! A few more seconds of wriggling forward, then twisting over onto his stomach, he lowered himself into the five-foot high passage.

In the blackness of the small room where Eldon and Ben waited with their co-workers, all was quiet. In the seconds after the explosion they had instinctively crawled away from the horrible sound of the slate roof collapsing its way toward them. It stopped, and their frantic, fear-filled scrambling ceased, too. They sat and lay, choking and coughing the smoke and coal dust that filled the air. Finally a man, gasped out, "Oh, Lord! Oh my Lord!" It was more a prayer than an oath.

There was a pop and a flash as Eldon Stoneworth re-lit his carbide light. "Ezra," he said, "light your lamp. Rest of you hold off for a minute. We're gonna need to save ever bit of air we can. Ezra, you and Ben, go check to see if we need to seal off this room, or if the cave-in did it for us."

Ezra and Ben returned very quickly. "We don't need to seal it off, Daddy. It looks like no gas is gonna get through to us. From the way it sounded and the way it looks, the breakdown sealed us off real tight."

189

"That's good, son. We won't have to use up any air, or our strength, tryin' to close it off."

"This wuz s'posed to be my last shift workin' the mine," said Thaddeus Carver. "Looks like it will be. Worked twenty-five years in this here mine. Seems a shame to go out this away."

One man sobbed. Another put a hand on his shoulder.

Smith scooted feet-first out of the air duct and lowered his legs. He heard his supply sack softly splat when it hit, and a second later he landed ankle-deep in water and muck. He snatched the bag up before it got soaked through. *Mighta knowed there'd be water* ... He pulled his shoulders back, rolled them, stretched his legs and leaned over, shaking blood back down his numb arms to his hands. He twisted his neck, then body, to get the kinks out, and paused to sniff the air. A faint breeze flowed from the duct now that his body no longer plugged it. He stepped away from it, smelled and tasted the familiar dank, acrid, mine atmosphere. He filled his lungs, emptied them, filled them again, and waited. *Seems okay. Don't feel any light-headedness. Air seems a little heavy. Prob'ly a bit short on oxygen, but I should be able to handle it for a while.*

He knew he was at a critical point. If fire damp were present, he wouldn't be able to smell the explosive gas. It was odorless. *There's only one way to find out. Light my lamp. If there's fire damp, it'll be over in a second. I'll never know it.*

He took the carbide lamp from his miner's hat, turned the control by feel to allow water from the lamp's upper chamber to drip onto the lump carbide in the lower chamber to release flammable gas. He cupped his right palm over the reflector to create a pocket to capture gas spewing from the small nozzle in the center. He prepared to sweep his hand quickly to the right across the flint wheel. This would throw a spark that would light an open flame… and set off a deadly explosion if fire damp was in the still air.

Smith held his hand in place, bowed his head, and closed his eyes, even though in pitch-blackness. *Lord, please be with me. I want to live and I want to be able to get those trapped men out. Please be with them. I... I want a life, Lord. One You'll be proud to see. Someday, I want to make a life with Hattie, Lord. I want to live... You know I ain't good at this prayin' business, but in the name of the Lord Jesus, I pray. Amen.* Smith took a deep breath, flipped his hand across the flint wheel and saw a beautiful two-inch flame shoot out from the center of the reflector on his small carbide light. Thanking the Lord above, he adjusted the control to reduce the flame.

The air was suddenly close and still. He fumbled for the whistle in his shirt pocket as he splashed back to the air duct, stuck his head in and blew the whistle as hard as he could. He waited, felt the airflow start, stop, start again, stop, then start and stay on. They'd heard him. Standing near the air duct, Smith hammered his pickhead back on its shortened handle. *They're gonna let the fresh air blow for a while, then Amos will be heading' down. That gives me a half-hour or more to go find the place to dig through.*

Deep in the pocket at the end of Right South Entry, time crept. Eldon and his crew slept in fits and dozes. Eldon ordered the lights be kept off to keep from using the gradually depleting air supply. Talk dwindled, and halted, then sporadically broke out. Then faded again. The hours crawled by. Once in while Eldon let them light a carbide lamp and check the time. How could time drag so? Occasionally a man would eat something from his lunch pail or drink from his water jar.

Late in the evening, Billy Scarbrough became hysterical. Screaming and crying, he hunted for his pick to attack the break-down. Before he located it, Eldon, gasping for air, caught him and slapped him across the face with his open palm. The frightened man collapsed in tears.

"Men," said the wheezing foreman, "don't be foolish by using up the air trying to dig out. The situation don't look good. If you *was* able to break through the cave-in, which you couldn't in a year, you'd be sealin' your fate and ours, too. There's gotta be gas in the passage. While your mind's workin' right, ... " he paused, shut his eyes, and took a few shallow breaths, ... "while you can, if there's anything you need to talk to your Maker about, you'd better do it." He paused again. "He parted the sea for Moses. He can part the earth for us. Ain't sayin' He will. Don't know how He'll do it, but somehow I b'lieve He will. We all got family out there prayin' for us and pushin' for management to send a party in. We got to have faith, knowin' they're comin' for us. Now ... I gotta rest." He sat down on the floor and put his head between his knees. Then he raised his head to try to breathe.

Ben reached down and took his father's arm. "Come on, Daddy. Let's go over to the breakdown. I saw a big flat piece of slate you can lie down on. It's up high and the air's better there."

The father-son team made their way to where the coal and slate had crashed down and sealed them in. Ben helped Eldon climb up onto the slate shelf. Soon the others had found places near the haggard foreman. They slept the fitful sleep of the hopeless.

Smith could tell by the decrease in airflow from the duct that Amos was on the way down, his body was blocking the movement of fresh air. Smith slogged down the passage till he came to the point where he felt sure it paralleled Right South Entry. With his pick he tapped three times on the wall, then three times on the ceiling. Maybe the men trapped behind the thick wall of coal would hear him and signal back. He thought the slate roof might carry sound better than the coal, but he couldn't be certain.

He moved a couple of strides and repeated the process. After an eighth of a mile, he thought, *Maybe my Dulcie's whistle will carry through the wall.* So he began blowing it before each move to a new location. He knew that if he should never get a response, he would simply have to guess and start digging. *I'll shore be a prayin' for a good guess!* Time ran out before anyone responded to his knocks. *Gotta get back. Wouldn't want Amos to come to my place for a visit and not have a welcomin' party.* He left his pick to mark the place where he'd stopped and headed back to the air duct.

Once he got back, Smith didn't have long to wait before he heard Amos trying to negotiate the turn in the tube. Sticking his head into the opening, he yelled, "That you, Amos?" He heard a muffled response.

"No, sir! It's Santa Claus, 'n he's stuck in the chimney!"

"C'mon, Amos, you ain't stuck. You best not be takin' a nap! Get yourself outa there. We got work to do. Poke that bag of toys out here," he joked.

Soon he saw the supply sack slide toward him in the duct—but still out of reach. Scooting, groaning, and straining, Frazier squirmed toward him, feet first, and kicked the bag closer. Smith stretched forward.

"Got it, Amos! You just relax, and I'll drag you outta there by the rope."

"I'm ready for relaxin', so pull away, Mr. Delaney, but gentle like, if you please."

Smith pulled on the rope, and his friend slid toward him. When he could, he grabbed Amos' ankles and gently tugged. Soon Amos squirmed out of the duct and stood, ankle deep, in the water beside him.

"Oh, man," said Amos, filling his lungs and stretching, "that there turn wuz somethin'. But it wasn't as bad as the squeeze up a ways. I was stuck tight! Thought for a minute I wasn't gonna budge up or down. Then 'pop' I was past it."

"Yeah, like to got me, too. Think Brother Fenton will have a problem with it?"

"Don't b'lieve so. I looked 'im over good. Ain't big as neither one of us. He'll make it fine, just fine."

The air rushing out of the duct stopped.

"They're stoppin' for the signal!" said Smith. He snatched the whistle, leaned into the duct and gave three shrill blasts. Before the ringing in his ears stopped, he felt the fan make intermittent stops and starts to indicate the crew on top heard his signal.

"Amos, you stay here, work out your kinks, eat a bite, and put the handles back on your tools. Oh, and check out your lights. I'm goin' back to see if I can find where to tunnel through. Wait for Brother Fenton. When he gets to the corner, you help him out like I did you. Leave him here to get his breath, and you come huntin' for me. I hope I'll be diggin' away."

"That'll be fine, Mister Delaney. I'll wait for 'im."

Smith clamped Amos Frazier's shoulder with his left hand and extended his right for a handshake. "You're some kinda fine man, Amos. We're gonna get those men out, with some help from the Maker."

Amos nodded. "Amen. God bein' our helper."

Smith turned back down the passage to where he had left his coal pick. When he found it, he resumed his practice of striking the pick against the coal on the left wall three times, then on the slate ceiling three times. After each three blows with the pick he blew Dulcie's whistle.

Finally, when no response came in return to his rhythmic tapping, Smith decided that the wall of coal was too thick for sound to penetrate. *I reckon it was a longshot,* he thought, *but it sure would have made my job easier. Well, Lord, I believe this is the right spot to start diggin'. I'm gonna do like Hattie says and step out in faith that this is the place. If it ain't, we're gonna be wastin' a lot of time and a lot of air. Would you just let me know somehow if I'm wrong?* Silence hung in the eerie light of the carbide lamp. Smith grinned. He didn't know what he'd been expecting God to say or do. Maybe point a glowing, divine finger at the very place where he was supposed to dig. *Well, You give me a brain, and it's tellin' me this here's the place. I'm havin' faith You're with me, Lord.*

With practiced eye and experienced motion, Smith Delaney adjusted his grip on the shortened pick handle and spread his legs. He poised his body for maximum efficiency and began the powerful, rhythmic strokes that had made him a valued worker, as long as he could stay out of trouble, for every mine he had worked in.

After about ten minutes of non-stop digging down and dragging out the coal, he began mumbling to himself. *Wall looks funny—all wavy-like. What's wrong with my eyes?* A sound like rushing water, or the buzzing of insects, filled his ears as a wave of dizziness threw him off balance. Smith danced backward unsteadily until he hit a wall and slid down to the floor of the room. *Gotta rest a minute,* he thought. He shook his head to clear the cobwebs and realized he'd been away from the air duct too long.

There was not enough oxygen in the old passage for the extended time he'd spent there. Slowly he pulled one foot up under him and pushed himself upright. He staggered back along the passage toward a faint bobbing light. *Stupid! Stupid! Stupid! 'Bout let yourself get took for bein' stupid! If you'd died for bein' stupid how do think you'd have faced them folks up there waitin'?*

He staggered on, bouncing off the wall once as he forced himself to move toward the strange dancing orb ahead of him in the passage. He berated himself for staying in the noxious, oxygen-poor air too long. *How you gonna explain it to Hattie?*

195

Huh? Stupid! She ain't gonna wanna marry a stupid man. 'Specially if he's dead. Again and again he shook his head to clear it.

"You all right, Mr. Delaney, sir? You all right?"

"Th...that you, Amos?"

"Yes, sir! It shore is. Ain't much choice as to who you keepin' company with tonight, sir! 'Cept, Brother Fenton just arrived on the Eight O'clock Special, lookin' fit as a fiddle! I b'lieve that man..." he stopped as he saw Smith weave on his feet. "Whoa, steady there, Mr. Delaney. You ain't alookin' too good!"

Amos Frazier took a strong grip on Smith's arm and helped him wade through the passage back toward the air duct. The closer they got, the clearer Smith's head became. A short way from the duct, Smith turned to Amos.

"I'm all right now. Much obliged for your help. Listen, there ain't much air back there—black damp's purty heavy. I can make it back to the duct on my own now, but when you get to where I started diggin', work just as hard as you can. But only for five minutes, Amos. Work hard, work fast, but just work five minutes."

Smith staggered through the darkness toward the air duct. A short time later he found Fenton examining his lights and other equipment.

For the next six hours the three men took five-minute turns. Five minutes at the duct, five minutes to walk to and from the excavation, and five minutes of furious digging. Smith ended each of his turns at the wall by blowing intermittently on Dulcie's whistle. Surely, if they were in the right place, the men inside, if alive, would soon hear either the blows of the pick or perhaps the whistle and know that help was coming. The tight tunnel allowed no great swinging motions of the arms and throwing of weight into the blows. Biceps and other muscles of the arms and wrists powered the blur of short but powerful blows that ground away the black mineral that separated the trio of tiring workers from the desperate men a few feet away.

196

In the dark, air-constricted room where Eldon and the others lay sleeping, the silence was shattered by a scream. It was Scarbrough. "I can't get the door open. I can't find it in the dark. I finally find it, but it's locked!" he whimpered. "Someone just keeps knockin' and knockin', and I can't get the door open!" His sobs echoed in the hollow chamber.

"It was just a nightmare, Billy, that's all," said Ben. "You probably heard slate crackin' or fallin' in your sleep. That's what it was."

"They knocked and knocked. I called to them, but I couldn't get to 'em. The door wouldn't open. It just wouldn't. All I could think about was gettin' out to my Mary. We got our first baby comin..." Billy Scarbrough's voice trailed off, and his body began to shake with shuddering sobs.

Eldon's raspy voice came out of the eerie darkness, "Wait, Ben! Listen, I heard it just now!"

The men sat up. All was quiet. Then, a dull, "thump, thump, thump."

"There *is* someone knocking!" They heard it again.

The men were now standing, gasping, leaning toward the sound, then staggering toward it.

"What's that other noise," asked Ben, stopping in his tracks.

"What other noise?"

"After the knocks, there's another sound. Listen!"

As the next knocks came, the men held their breaths—and heard a shrill, high noise barely making its way thorough the wall of coal.

"Ben! Ben!" wheezed Eldon, "That's a whistle! I bet it's the one Smith Delaney carries in his pocket. Ben, Smith Delaney's out there! Sure as the world, Smith's come for us! Go answer 'em. Knock on the wall. I ain't feelin' so ... " Ben grabbed his father as Eldon slumped, unconscious, to the floor.

14

Skeet Davis watched Morgan's team execute the plans for the rescue. About three hours after Fenton disappeared into the duct, a truckload of machinery pulled in near the big shaft.

Davis approached Rodney Heltsley, who was signaling the driver backing the truck into position for unloading.

"What are they bringing in, Mr. Heltsley?"

"A blower and extra parts from Black Diamond mine in Drakesboro."

His team immediately began its installation and continued repairs of other parts of the system needed to get the gases out of the mine and the fresh air in. Only when this was done could a rescue team enter the mine to open the seal to the abandoned section where Smith and his team would be trying to bring out the trapped men.

Skeet Davis jotted notes as he watched Eb Gill's team, like monkeys in a tree, scale parts of the rigging above the shaft to replace frayed cable.

"Everything going well, Mr. Gill?" asked the reporter.

"We got one big problem, but we think we can solve it. The main wheel was off center and the torque burned out the bearings. We think we got one comin' from Gibraltar Coal Company. If not, we might get one from Luzerne Mine."

"Are you going to have the cage running on deadline by midnight?"

"Can't say for certain. Don't look good, but we're sure tryin', and we shouldn't be too far behind if we get the parts in time."

Skeet visited the six-cot field hospital being set up. "DeKoven General" they were calling it after the gentle, big foreman bulldogging the arrangements. Next Davis stopped by the food station the Radburns had arranged for the miners and their families. Everywhere, people were doing their part. "Sure is amazing how a tragedy pulls people together and brings out the best in folks. Maybe I ought to write an editorial about that," said Skeet to himself.

"Stop, men!" yelled young Ben Stoneworth at the three trapped miners, screaming and pounding on the thick wall of coal that separated them from Smith Delaney.

"Stop!" he shouted again. They paused. "One of you try to figure out the closest place to where they're comin' in. Hit it with a pick. Do a four count, and hit it again. That way Smith can home in on it. That racket's gonna echo all through the mine. He don't need a bunch of confusion to aim for." The men began a steady thump against the wall.

Ben turned his back on his companions and went to check on Eldon. He had just reached the slab of shale that had become his father's bed when he heard a commotion and turned to see Billy Scarbrough frantically digging at the wall to try to reach Smith and the rescue party.

"Scarbrough, stop!" yelled Ben as he stumbled toward the crazed man.

Billy Scarbrough turned with a snarl, "Don't you boss me, you young pup! You ain't no foreman. I'm gonna dig my way out." The man was panting for breath.

"Billy, please. We don't have the strength to dig. Not enough air. If we use up our energy – use up the air in here – we won't last 'til Smith gets here. My dad's unconscious over yonder. He's a goner if we use up the air. Please, Billy, fellers, just sit real still and wait. The Lord's sent someone to rescue us. Let's let 'im do it. Please," the boy begged.

"You heard 'im men," said old Thaddeus Carver as he put an arm around Ben's shoulder. "This youngun's got a head on his shoulders, cut outta the same cloth as Eldon. C'mon, son, let's go see if we can help your daddy."

Billy Scarbrough dropped his pick and sat down by the wall of coal.

On the other side of the wall progress continued, but at a slower pace. Hours passed as the tunnel lengthened and speed diminished. It was necessary for each worker to dig a bit, then dig back out, raking with him the coal just dug down. He would crawl back in and repeat the process. At least the air was some better since a little of the flow from the duct was beginning to reach the area. Fenton backed out of the hole, raking coal behind him out onto the floor of the large passage just as Smith arrived to relieve him.

"I think you might break through, Smith. We gotta be getting' close. I'm almost sure I heard muffled talkin', unless the air's worse than I thought and it addled my brain."

"Good. Go on back to the duct. Tell Amos to wait just a couple of minutes and then get on down here. You get yourself some good air and be ready to come on back."

Hattie rubbed her hands along her arms to take the chill off a little. The sun would be coming up in an hour or so. They'd waited through the long, dark night. Still, the crowd was immense. They stood in clusters and small groups of families. Those without families stood alone until someone would draw them into their group. Rose Ellen had taken her smallest children back to the house hours before and put them to bed. She'd returned to stand in wait with the rest of them at the shaft.

Sobs punctuated the early morning hours. Now and again a voice would break out of the noise created by the crowd. Miners were angry; women were frightened; children were quiet.

Hattie couldn't help but think of the day she'd waited by the shaft for them to bring Jack out. It was too soon to do it again. Of course, it would always be too soon. No one should have to stand vigil by a shaft that plunged down into darkness, to wait for a loved one to be brought out. It was too hard. She was trying to sort out her feelings about Smith, but one thing she knew. She didn't want him to die. Not now. Not this way. Eldon or Ben, either. None of the others, for that matter.

She'd seen young Mary Scarbrough who was only seventeen and expecting her first baby. Her mother had stood and wept with her. Would she be a widow tonight? At seventeen? She wouldn't be the first.

A voice spoke, "Girl, what are you doin?"

Hattie jumped. "Ma Richards! You like to scared me half to death. I was woolgatherin', I guess. I never was real good at waitin'. How're you?"

"I'm just about as fine as a ninety-three year old can be, I reckon. Don't s'pose you'd like to tell me what you was thinkin' on?"

Hattie gazed into the darkness. "I ... I was rememberin' when Jack was hurt. That time it was just him. There wasn't a crowd or nothin'. I think I liked it better that way. I'm 'bout wore out with the carryin' on." Hattie shook her head, "I guess that's not real charitable ... "

"Ever'body grieves in their own way. Some folk need to holler and shout. Some folks need to be alone. I seen grief from every side. It ain't never easy, and it ain't never the same."

"No, I s'pose you're right. Reckon I'm just one of those folks that in the midst of the hullabaloo needs to find a peaceful place."

"Well now, I reckon I'm sorta like that myself. Ain't real big on carryin' on. How's Rose Ellen holdin' up?"

Hattie expelled a breath. "She's doin' as well as can be expected. I think it was easier when she had the little'uns around to distract her. Just sittin' there waitin's mighty hard on all of us."

"Annie Radburn said for me to tell you to come get a bite to eat. She's fixed up a real nice place back yonder by the trees. Her and Mr. Radburn brung their tables and chairs and set up a stove. She's got coffee and food for whoever's hungry."

"I don't think I could eat anything, Ma. I'll walk over after while and see if I can help out, though."

"No, you won't neither. You stay with your family. There's plenty of folks up here ain't waitin' for nobody. They're just spectatin'. They can go help out if help is needed. You're helpin' just by bein' here for Rose Ellen. 'Sides, I think you got feelin's that ain't so brotherly for one of them men down there. You need your family as much as they need you."

At 8:30 a.m. a sleepless Skeet Davis ran into an equally sleep-less Razz Morgan having a cup of coffee at "Miz Radburn's Paradise Café," a makeshift collection of tables and benches under a stretched tarpaulin roof. There the Radburns were run-ning a twenty-four-hour free food service for the miners and their families, management, and the press.

"Things going well, Mr. Morgan?"

"Amazingly well, Davis, as best we can tell. Delaney, Fenton, and Frazier all made it into the mine. They all signaled that they did. Of course, we haven't heard from them since. Gill got the pulleys fixed, put new cables in place, and replaced the main wheel, thanks to Gibraltar Mine in Central City, so the cage is operating smoothly. Heltsley's crew has the blower sys-tem fully operational. We owe Black Diamond and Mr. Bridges a lot for their help with that. There was some delay, but it's been working full power since about one o'clock this morn-ing."

"How soon will men be going down?"

"Fire-boss Nat Thompson's crew is ready. You know what a 'fire-boss' is?"

"I think so. He goes in first, when there's a possibility of danger?"

"That's right. Anyway, him and his crew are supposed to be comin' in at nine o'clock. I sent 'em home last night to get some sleep before they head into the mine, but I've seen most of 'em milling around here already. Thompson's goin' down to test the air. Then he'll send in Eb Mallory and Hank Addison. They'll test all the way back to the barricade to old passage if they can. Then they'll come back to report on conditions. If they give the all clear, the rest of the crew will head in and open the barricade– and hope for the best. The old passage behind the seal may have a little gas in it, but Delaney will have checked that out pretty thoroughly before he signals the other fellows to come down."

"You have a lot of confidence in Delaney, don't you?"

"It depends. When he's not drunk or angry, he's got one of the fastest and best minds I've ever encountered. He's cool in the face of danger, and he's a worker! He and Will Brumley, before Will got into management, set a record of the amount of coal hand dug and loaded. Never been equaled, as far as I know – probably never will be. Coal's not mined that way now. Anyway, he's a fine worker who has absolutely no tolerance for injustice. Can't stand to see a child or an animal mistreated. Takes sides in every dispute. If somebody tries to cheat him, you'd think you'd thrown match in a keg of black powder. He's got a chip on his shoulder and a short fuse—a bad combination. But he's a kind man underneath it all. And if he's on your side, there's nothing he won't do for you."

Before Davis could comment or inquire further, Nat Thompson hurried to them. "Sir, Addison and Mallory are ready to go down and make the tests. Got your go ahead?"

"Make sure they're fully equipped, Thompson."

"They are, sir."

Within the hour Davis jotted on his note pad that the test crew found residues of gases but reported fresh air was moving well within the passages. They should be able to get in safely and open the barricade and unseal the old passage.

Skeet Davis slipped into a deserted tool room, dressed in borrowed clothes and put on a miners hat. He stopped at a coal chute to wipe coal dust on his face and hands. A little later he slipped in among the crew that climbed into the cage for the trip down the shaft to open the seal to the abandoned passage. If anyone noticed the well-liked reporter, they chose to ignore him. He *would* have a scoop.

Ben was rubbing his father's hands and talking softly to the unconscious man when the exultant men cried, "He's coming through!"

"He's here, Dad. Smith's here," Ben whispered to his father. "I'll be right back." He clambered across the breakdown to his companions. A small portion of the coal wall burst into the chamber as Delaney's pick struck from within the tunnel. An interminable long two minutes later, Smith's head stuck through. His coal-blackened face broke into a huge grin. "Howdy, boys!"

His head disappeared back into the narrow tunnel, and the head of his pick blasted the last of the coal that blocked his way from climbing into the chamber. Then his wiry body wriggled into the room of excited, exhausted miners. Scarbrough rushed toward the hole as Smith got to his feet.

"Hold on there!" said Smith, grabbing the panicked miner by the shoulder. "I know you wanna get outa here, but here's how we'll do it. Amos Frazier is right behind me – hear him in there? He's opening it up a bit more. He's gonna crawl through, turn around and open it still more from in here. Then we're gonna—" he paused abruptly, "Where's Eldon?"

"Dad's up there on a slab of slate. He's unconscious," Ben thumbed over his shoulder toward his father.

The men greeted Amos Frazier as he crawled through and immediately turned back to open the tunnel more.

"Ben, was Eldon hurt in the explosion?" asked Smith.

"No, sir. The air got to him."

"Scarbrough, you and Ben go get Eldon. He's the first to go out. Brother Fenton will be on the other side to help with him."

By the time the men got to the wall with Eldon, Amos was backing out after completing the enlarging of the still-tiny tunnel.

"The subway is ready for the first passenger, and Brother Fenton is ready to take your ticket," he said as he straightened up, then swallowed as he saw the men carrying Eldon. "Oh my, Mr. Stoneworth—is he alive?"

"He's unconscious, Amos, but he'll make it, thanks to you fellers," said Ben. "The air's already a little better, over there by the hole."

"Let's go!" yelled a new voice from within the tunnel. A smiling Eli Fenton, lying in the passage, waved to them.

"Amos, you and Fenton get Eldon through that tunnel and over by the air duct. We'll follow."

Smith turned to the rest of the men. "Here's what we're gonna do. After they get Eldon through, we'll follow. Carver first, then Rager, then Scarbrough, then Ben. Listen to me! You take your time, stay together. We're about to crawl into the old abandoned workin's that parallel Right South Entry. It's sealed off at Central South. There's fresh air pumpin' through an air duct into the old entry. Stop at the air duct and fill your lungs with some good air. Eat a bite. Rest. At least rest the best you can standin' in ankle deep water.

"Take this as a warning'," he continued, "don't one of you make a run to get out through the seal. If you do, I'll deck you, sure as I'm standin' here. Central South Entry was full of white damp yesterday, and the fans were broke down. They're prob'ly fixed and blowin' out the gases now, but we can't take a chance of openin' that seal from inside and having white damp flood this place. I'm goin' on forward to check out the seal. While you're waitin', Brother Fenton will fill you in on what happened yesterday. Everybody understand?" He paused. "Then head out. I'll follow."

Getting the dead weight of Eldon Stoneworth through the narrow tunnel was a challenge, but it was accomplished without major incident. As they carried him toward the air duct, he began to stir and struggled with the men to put him down. They told him what had happened and where they were taking him. As the fresh air became stronger, so did Eldon. Soon, with support from a shorter man on either side, Eldon was shuffling along on rubbery legs. By the time they got to the duct the rest had caught up with them, except for Smith. Soon, he came through the darkness carrying the tools. Fenton's eyes followed Eldon as the older miner watched the approach of the man his sister had come to care about. Eldon stuck out an unsteady hand and said simply, "Thanks, Smith, ... thanks."

Smith shook his hand and nodded. "Good to see you on your feet, Eldon." He turned to the others.

"Fellers," said Smith to the miners huddled together sucking in the air coming from the small air duct. "You might say a prayer for me as I head to the barricade that seals this old entry from Central South Entry.

"Stay put. Don't try to follow me unless I ain't back in half an hour, or unless you hear a blast on my whistle." He patted his shirt pocket to make sure his little treasure was still there. "If you hear one blast, send someone to help me, but be careful. If you hear two blasts, all of you come hustlin', but watch out." He turned and plodded through the sludge into the darkness.

Much of the passage to the barricade was littered with breakdown from the ceiling. *The floor's gettin' a little drier. At least that'll make it easier,* he thought. Then he climbed over a sizeable slate fall between crossbeams supporting the roof. Shining his dim light up at the irregular ceiling where the breakdown had occurred, he thought, *Gettin' close to the seal. Blast was felt more here. Air's a little bad, too. Bit of smoke and dust musta crept in. Seal was likely damaged. Hope there's no white damp. Uh Oh!* He was almost at the point where the old passage converged at an angle with Central South Entry. Just ahead, where a portion of the left wall had caved in, a precariously leaning upright timber supported a heavy crossbeam. *Look at that – that's gonna be tricky, but we should be able to make it.* Cautiously, he walked under.

Smith had only gone a few feet further when his heart leaped into his throat. He heard voices and the sound of the incoming crew tearing down the barricade. He scampered over the breakdown as fast as he could and yelled, "Easy, fellers, easy!" The noise suddenly stopped, only to be replaced a second later by the frenzied whoops and cheers of the six jubilant workers opening the seal from the other side.

After a moment of celebration, the workers began calling questions through the seal. Smith quieted them and called back, "Everyone's alive. They're about a quarter mile back. I'll go signal 'em to head this way. The last few hundred feet just inside here are damaged pretty bad. Don't try to come in." Smith paused, took a deep breath, then continued, "Just open up the seal a little more. Stand back and let in as much air as you can. There's a couple of bad pockets back here but we can make it." He turned back into the tunnel. "I'm goin' back for 'em. Wait for us," he called back over his shoulder.

Huddled by the air duct, the men, led by Eli Fenton, gave fervent thanks for having been delivered to that point. They prayed for the safety of Smith, for the men working their way to the seal to save them, and for their families. After the prayer Fenton insisted that the men by the air duct finish off the food that was left. He said they would need their strength for the trip out. Eldon was still coughing and shaky but insisted he was fine.

"They're gettin' restless and anxious," Eli said softly to Amos.

Amos Frazier nodded and said, "Freedom and safety are so close, but still outa reach."

Twin blasts from Smith's whistle sounded down the passage. The sound they had been waiting for.

Fenton led the group to where Smith stood by a slate fall. "It's a little tricky from here. Go easy and watch your step. Some timbers are damaged. Fire-boss Thompson has a crew right on the other side of the seal. Go single file, and take your time. We're almost there."

Amos stepped into the lead when Smith signaled him to do so. Carver, Rager, and Scarbrough followed. Fenton stepped in just ahead of Eldon, to help Ben, who trailed his father, should he need it. Smith brought up the rear.

When Fenton ducked under the damaged crossbeam he warned, "Here's another bit of bad air." Then cheering filled the passage. The first of the men was in view of the team at the opened seal. Scarbrough picked up his pace, then glanced back when Eldon began coughing violently. As Ben reached to steady his father, the big man stumbled to his left and staggered into the unstable, leaning upright.

At that same moment, Smith yelled, "Look out!" He hurled himself at the two Stoneworth men, knocking them out of the way of the falling timber, which collapsed across his legs as he tried to scramble to his feet. Then portions of the fractured slate roof gave way.

Ben scurried to his feet, tugging his father forward. Smith did not follow. He was trapped under the beam. In horror Ben shouted, "Delaney's pinned! Roof's collapsin'!" The horizontal crossbeam fell, then wedged precariously. The slate roof broke away and began to fall. The falling debris buried Smith's body.

Amos Frazier was beyond the seal when he heard Smith's warning cry, and the muffled crash of rock that followed. He whirled and sped back down the passage. He passed three of the freed miners stumbling on toward the cage and freedom. He arrived back at the scene just behind Fenton who had also turned back.

Eldon Stoneworth sat on the stone passage floor looking stunned. Ben stood with his hand on his father's shoulder, tears rolling down his cheeks. "Smith shoved us clean outa the way. The timber got 'im. Pinned 'im to the floor. Then the slate came down," he sobbed.

Amos warily eased forward. "Looks like the worst is over, sir," he said to Fenton. Surveying the ceiling with quick eyes, he continued, "Cain't say for certain, but most likely won't be much more to come down. We gotta risk it. I can see his head and arm under there." He began pulling slate away. Fenton and Ben joined him.

Amos continued. "Looks like the slate mostly hit beside him and slid across 'im, 'stead of hittin' 'im directly. We gotta try to get to 'im. Praise God that crossbeam jammed 'fore it come all the way down. It don't look too stable. If we keep movin' this slate out, it's gonna topple down, too. I'm gonna slide under there and hold it up while y'all try to get to Mr. Delaney." Amos crouched low and slid under the timber, taking its weight on his powerful back and shoulders.

Skeet Davis suddenly appeared from the direction of the seal. He walked past Eldon, tossed aside his reporter's pad, and crawled under the beam to help Ben and Fenton pull the slate away from the fallen man.

"Ben, you go on. Get your dad outta here," said Fenton. "When you get up top, send Doc Wilson down. Have them bring a couple of jacks. We gotta keep that crossbeam from sliding down any further. Amos can't hold it forever. Go on, Son. We'll do what we can here."

As Ben turned to leave, tears twin-tracked through the coal dust on his cheeks. Eben Bivins, one of Thompson's men hurried past him.

"Amos, looks like you could use a little help," the newcomer said.

"Yes, sir. I'm just a mite uncomfortable. Feel free to join my party." He looked past Bivins at Ben and Eldon. The reflection of their lights danced on the dark walls as they slowly moved down the passage toward the seal. The boy looked back and called to them, his voice cracking, "I'll be back. You tell 'im, I'll be back."

"Forrest, how much longer do think it'll be?" asked Rose Ellen, leaning against one of the poles holding up the tarpaulin over the makeshift café. "Surely they'll be comin' out soon! I just don't think I can stand it much longer. Watchin' those women yesterday ... seein' 'em bring up the bodies ... How did Hattie survive it when she lost Jack?" The anxious woman pushed off the pole, then paced as she talked.

Forrest put out his hand to take hers under the weak November sun. "C'mon, Rose Ellen. In your head you're playin' a movin' picture of the awfuls. Let's have us another cup of coffee," he said as he led her over to the table. Annie Radburn poured fresh coffee into the weary woman's cup.

"Yesterday," Forrest continued, "Smith asked Morgan to have a crew open that barricade down there by noon today, but he wasn't guaranteeing he could get Eldon and the rest out by then. We know that. He was just sayin' 'Get it done—have a crew there in case.' Ain't no tellin' what him an' Frazier and Brother Fenton ran into to slow 'em down. We gotta try to be patient. It's just past noon now, so if they're runnin' on schedule ... "

Another forty-five agonizing minutes passed. Then the cage whistle blew the signal to be brought up. The huge pulleys at the top of the tower over the shaft began to whir, and taut cables started moving. People from the "Paradise Café" jumped to their feet and ran toward the shaft. People poured out of buildings. Those dozing in cars threw open the doors and scrambled out. Coaltown's population converged at shaftside.

"Here it comes! Here it comes!" yelled one of the men looking down into the pit from a vantage point high on the structure above the shaft. Fear and hope fought frantic battles in the minds and hearts of the onlookers. Hands went to cheeks, or covered mouths or eyes. Some people held their breath and looked away, unable to face what they might see. Forrest held Rose Ellen. Hattie and Marva hugged. Carrie and Chloe clutched each other.

The cage top came slowly into view. The watching crowd could see men through the open-sided cage. There were Ben, Scarbrough, and the others.

"Ben!" screamed Rose Ellen. "Where's your daddy?" Then she could see him. He was huddled on the floor of the elevator. Aided by two others, he struggled to get to his feet. Rose Ellen shoved past burly grown men and wiry miners, past other women and spectators.

Before the cage came to a slow halt, and the door opened, Ben yelled, "Get Doc Wilson and a stretcher! Get two jacks on here. Hurry, we gotta get back down there." The young man would not leave the cage.

Hattie's eyes swept the faces that crowded the cage: Ben and Eldon, Scarbrough, Carver and Rager. All the trapped men were out, but where was the rescue team? Where were Smith, Fenton and Frazier? Her stomach clenched into a knot and she had to breathe through her nose to keep from passing out. Her hands tightened into balls at her side. Memories of another day, another cage, flooded through her mind. Sickening despair overwhelmed her.

Forrest trotted beside Razz Morgan as he hurried toward the cage. They nodded to the men and spoke to Eldon as he was placed on a stretcher. "You okay, brother?" Forrest asked.

Eldon nodded. "Smith," he swallowed hard, coughed and uttered another name, "Ben." The he was silent. Workers carried him to the field hospital where Doc Wadkins, sleeves rolled up, waited.

Morgan and Forrest approached Ben, who was still standing in the cage, hands on hips, staring into space. "Come off of there, Son. Tell us what happened. Where's the men who came to rescue you?" Morgan asked.

"Uncle Forrest, Mr. Morgan. Beggin' your pardon, but I ain't comin' off. Gotta get back down there. We was almost to the seal – almost out! There was a cave-in. Smith saved Daddy's life, and mine, too, from a fallin' timber. It got him instead. Part of the roof fell in on top of 'im. Amos and one of your men are holdin' the crossbeam off of 'im. Brother Fenton and Skeet Davis are down on their knees draggin' the slate off Smith as fast as they can. He ain't movin'. We gotta get Doc Wilson and get back down there. I promised!" Ben was pleading. Forrest nodded.

Morgan turned and said, "Get a move on," to no one in particular. He quickly turned back to Ben. "Did you say Skeet Davis is down there? How'd he get down there?"

"Don't know, but he's there, workin' away." He beckoned to the workers bringing the jacks. "Hurry y'all! Hurry!"

They loaded the jacks, then right behind them Doc Wilson and an assistant carrying a folded stretcher rushed onto the elevator. The cage whistle tooted its descent signal, and dropped out of sight. Forrest walked to Hattie and took her arm. He gently propelled her toward the field hospital where Rose Ellen hovered over her begrimed husband.

Eldon was trying to talk. "Smith saved us, and then he saved us again. Now, he's lyin' down there ... " his voice trailed off.

213

"Shhhhh, you just rest now, Eldon," said Rose Ellen. "You and Ben are mighty ... " She stopped suddenly. "Where *is* Ben? Didn't he come up with you, Forrest?" Her eyes searched frantically.

Forrest looked at his feet and shook his head.

"He went back down, ma'am," said Billy Scarbrough from a cot nearby. "He went back down fer Smith Delaney."

An hour later, Doc Wadkins stood talking to the group of reporters behind a cable that marked the boundary to DeKoven General, the open-sided shed that had been turned into a field hospital.

"I don't have to tell you gentlemen that Mr. Stoneworth has been through a horrific ordeal. I gave him a shot and he slept a little while. He's awake now, but he refuses to leave for the hospital until the men that are still underground are brought up, and he learns the fate of Smith Delaney." The doctor looked toward the mine shaft, then toward the field hospital. "As you can see, Eldon's family is with him. Forrest Stoneworth, his brother, is going to see if Eldon can recount what happened. I'm going to make a concession to you men and let you in close enough to listen. However, you are not to question Mr. Stoneworth, nor any member of his family. Not one question while under the roof of this building. Do you understand?" The reporters nodded in reluctant agreement.

Doc Wadkins leaned against one of the support pillars, watched, and listened while Eldon talked about what had happened from the time he and the others in Right South Entry felt and heard the blast in Central South Entry. He explained that he was unconscious at times during the ordeal, but others had filled him in on some details. He recounted the horrible closing moments before he was brought to the surface. While Eldon was talking, Hattie stood at the foot of her brother's bed. She looked worn and haggard. Anguish and despair swept over her

214

gaunt features as Eldon told how Smith Delaney had shoved him and Ben out of harms way, only to take the blow of the falling timber himself.

"When me an' Ben left, they was tryin' to get the slate off'n him. There's a saint lying injured down there. I'm just prayin' he's a *livin'* saint," Eldon concluded.

When Eldon paused and tried to collect himself, a reporter from the *Birmingham Bugle* pushed his way between Chloe and Carrie. He thrust his reporter's pad in Eldon's direction and said, "What do you think the odds are ... "

That was as far as he got before the steel grip of Ol' Doc Wadkins clamped his shoulder and propelled him out. The doctor's stern voice announced firmly, "Your time is up, gentlemen. You are dismissed, one and all. Clear out! Now!" They did—though grumbling.

As the area cleared, Hattie placed her hands on her face and walked slowly away across the grounds of Coaltown Mine. When she had placed some distance between herself and everyone else she stood with her back to the turmoil behind her. She gazed unseeing over the vast area that surrounded the mine.

Lord, I'm tryin' so hard to hold onto hope, but I'm scared. I'm so scared, I'm sick. Please don't let him die. I care about him. Look what he did for Eldon and Ben and them others! He didn't have to do any of it, Lord. He coulda just stood there and watched like everyone else. He ain't kin to us. He coulda just waited it out, but he didn't. He risked his life for them. More'n once. Please, Lord, oh please, don't let him die.

Skeet Davis sweated in the cold, dank air as he dragged out slate. Beside him Eli Fenton tried encouraging the trapped man underneath the rock fall. "Hang on Smith. We'll get you out. We're gettin' there, fella, we're gettin' there." Fenton was panting, but while tugging on the flat slabs of slate, he kept a patter of words going in the direction of his trapped friend.

"His hand just moved, Brother Fenton. I know it did, I seen it!" shouted Amos Frazier. Amos was sweat-soaked, as was Bivins, though not from moving slate. Their exhaustion was from the strain of supporting the crossbeam perched precariously just above them. If it slid downward it would not only trap the men underneath, but would permit the collapse of more of the roof.

Five minutes later they were able to clear Delaney's head, shoulders and upper torso. At this point they could see that his lips, where not covered in coal dust, were blue.

"Hey, Smith, you're gonna make it! C'mon, Smith, let's see you breathe," said Eli Fenton.

"Yes, sir, Mr. Delaney. Gonna make it for sure! You promised to tell me about them monkeys in the Philippines. C'mon, Mr. Delaney, c'mon and breath fer us." Tears in the eyes of the black man belied the smile on his face and the hope he forced into his voice.

An insistent "Let me in there!" announced the arrival of Doc Wilson. Skeet and Fenton backed carefully from the tight space.

Fenton pointed to the leaning timber over the narrow crawlway and said, "Doc, that's not stable, you'd better wait."

"I said 'Let me in there!' and I meant it. As long as Atlas and Hercules," he nodded toward Amos and Bivins, "hold steady for a couple of minutes longer, we'll make it. The men with the jacks are right behind me."

Fenton looked away from the doctor who was crawling toward Smith, dragging his bag with him. Sure enough, the workers with the equipment were there. He held up his hand for them to wait and followed the doctor to see if he could help. Skeet crawled in right behind them.

"He's had a lot of weight pressing down on him, probably hardly able to breathe," said the doctor as he prepared to give the unconscious man a shot. "This'll give his heart a boost and maybe get his lungs functioning better." He cut the cloth away from Smith's shoulder and gave him the injection.

216

"That twisted leg doesn't look good, from what I can see of it. Better get the jack under this crossbeam and give these men a break."

Ben Stoneworth reached a hand to help Davis, then Fenton, and then Doc Wilson to their feet as they crawled out of the narrow opening between the floor and the rockfall where Smith lay. The crew from atop ground moved in to put the jacks in place.

The toot of the whistle at shaftside again signaled the ascent of the cage from the deep bowels of Coaltown Mine. The gathering crowd cheered as the top of the cage came slowly into sight. Then it grew somber. There was Doc Simpson, Ben, Fenton, Davis, and two men holding a stretcher with someone—it had to be Smith—on it. The cage stopped, opened, and those on the elevator stepped aside for the stretcher-bearers. A cheer rocked the hillsides and floated down the valley. Smith Delaney, without lifting his head, had raised one arm from the elbow and waved.

As they prepared to load him into the ambulance, Hattie approached and smiled through her tears. He crooked a finger for her to come closer. When she did, he said, in barely more than a whisper, "Hattie, they talk like I'm gonna rest up for a while at the hospital." He reached into his shirt pocket and pulled out the whistle. "Would you keep this for me?"

15

"Ashes to ashes and dust to dust ..." Brother Fenton dropped a handful of dirt onto the pine box. The mourners stood at the graveside. Hattie stood with the rest of the little community gathered around the grave, with the baby on her shoulder and Dulcie by her side. Dulcie's eyes were big and round. She'd never been to a funeral before. The rest of the family was there, too. Zonie was with Smith since his injuries were too severe for him to leave his bed for the service. He'd stayed only a short time at Outwood Veterans Hospital in Dawson Springs and was happily back in the smokehouse.

Quince Bidewell's widow stood across the grave from Hattie, her face white. She clutched his miner's cap between her hands. It was about all she had left of him now – that and the six children lined up beside her, each looking more forlorn than the last. The baby's nose was running, and twelve-year-old Minnie wiped it with her handkerchief. She jogged him on her hip, then put her other arm around the sobbing four-year-old. Patty was a pretty little girl who looked lost in her too-big dress. All of the adults were crying, so she cried, too.

The final prayer was said, and the mourners broke up into small groups to comfort each other. Hattie made her way to Minnie.

"Honey, I'm just down the road. If ... if there's anything I can do, you let me know, hear? You're gonna have to help your mama. She's not gonna feel like doin' much for a while. And you try to be real patient with her. It's not fair, but you're gonna have to carry the load. You gonna be able to do that?"

"Yes, ma'am. Miz Crowe, she don't talk or nothin'. She jes' sits – like she ain't there no more. These babies – they's needin' her awful bad ... "

"I know, Honey. You're gonna have to be their mama for a little while. Think you can?"

"I reckon I'll have to. The boys don't mind me too good, but I'll try." Minnie's eyes filled with tears. "The company man said we was gonna have to move outa the house. He said weren't none of us allowed to stay since Earl ain't old enough to go down the mines yet."

Hattie gritted her teeth in frustration. It wasn't fair. Every mine but Coaltown would have waited until after the burying to inform the family of their eviction. Old man Sawyer was living up to his reputation! "Minnie, listen here. You tell your mama to pack up and come down to my place. We'll clean out the attic and find a place to put y'all, all right?"

"No, ma'am. Thank you, ma'am. Mama's brother's comin' from Hopkinsville. Him and Aunt Polly are takin' us to live with them on Tuesday. I already got most our things ready to go. Weren't much to pack."

Hattie's shoulders slumped. "Honey, I'm real proud of you. It's a mighty big load you're carryin'."

Minnie lowered her eyes. "I didn't do it by myself. Miz Dunford come down and some of the other ladies. Miz Shropshire brought food, and so did Miz Wester and Ma Collier. They been real good to us."

"We'll sure miss you, Minnie. Y'all are good kids. I'm just real proud of you," Hattie repeated.

The mourners moved away from the grave and toward their cars and trucks. A soft rain began to fall. This was the last of the simple funerals for the dead miners—Quince had lingered a few days. It had been a long few days. Hattie was worn out with taking food to bereaved families, and sitting with widows, trying to keep up with her own family, and taking turns sitting with Smith. But Hattie was doing what you always did when tragedy struck—you pulled together and did what you could to bring comfort to those that were hurting.

Carrie hurried to Hattie through the rain. "Sorriest situation I ever saw," she said as they walked to the waiting car.

"I know. I tried to talk to Minnie but that little girl's almost as shocked as her mama. You reckon Purly's gonna snap out of it?"

"I reckon. It'll take awhile," said Carrie. "You know yourself how hard it is."

"Yeah, I do. When Jack died, I just wanted to lay down beside him and go too. It seemed like I couldn't go on, but there was Dulcie and the baby comin'. I guess I just had to, so I did."

"Madge Foley's at Western State Hospital in Hopkinsville. Her sister said she was took so bad when they brought John's body out of the mine they had to have her locked up to keep her from hurtin' herself. Sheriff Westerfield come got her kids yesterday mornin'."

"You don't mean it! I knew she was bad off, but why didn't her sister take the kids, or spread 'em out with the rest of the family? They let the law come get 'em? Why?" Hattie couldn't understand how any family would let that happen.

"Hattie, we'd be hard pressed to take in six younguns. We'd do it, of course, but, lets face it, it would be mighty hard to make ends meet."

"I know, but ... " Hattie thought of her offer to take in the Bidewell family. She *would* have had a hard time feeding them all, it was true, but she would have found a way or died trying.

"Ain't no buts, Honey. That's just the way it is," said Carrie.

Gene joined them at the car. "Y'all ready? I've had about as much of funerals as I can stand." He sounded strained. They quickly loaded into the car, and Gene turned the car toward Hattie's.

"You all right, Gene? You look like you could bite a ten-penny nail in half."

221

"Some of the men were talkin'. They said Obie's gonna call the strike tomorrow mornin', first thing. Said the explosion was bad enough, but the way the mine rough-handled the families was the last straw, and they wasn't gonna take it no more."

"No! They can't just up and strike!" Carrie exclaimed.

"Yes, they can. They're roundin' up the miners now for a big meetin' down in the grove in the bottoms near Coaltown, away from the mine. They're gonna tell 'em what's what and find out who's with 'em and who's agin' 'em. I'm afraid it's ... it's gonna get ugly."

"You ain't goin! You hear me?" Carrie practically shouted. "You ain't gonna be part of that rabble! I ... I won't have it!"

"I got to go. They ain't rabble, Carrie. Some are, but most of 'em are just like us, good men determined to make it better for their families. If'n I don't go, well, I'll be counted against 'em and I ain't sure I am. I ain't for 'em neither, but I got to go."

"Gene, I'm scared. What if ... " Carrie didn't seem to even know which 'what if' she was scared of. "I was thinkin' that you, Forrest and Eldon, and the rest of our boys got to make 'em see sense! Can't you at least try?"

"Eldon'll try. He's been tryin'. Says he can't afford to go without work just to prove a point. He says the mine owners know we need better wages, an' he thinks they're plannin' to pay more. He says strikin's just gonna make 'em hold off an' dig their heels in. He ain't gonna strike. He's put us all in a bad place by bein' so open with his opposition. He'll go down the mine tomorrow mornin' while the rest of us are on the line."

Hattie, in the back seat, with Dulcie looking out the window on one side and Jackie asleep on the other, leaned forward between Carrie and Gene. "But, Eldon's barely back on his feet! How can he even think of goin' back so soon after what happened?"

"Says it ain't gonna get no easier goin' back in the first time. He's gonna do what he thinks needs doin'. He ain't thinkin' about what it's gonna do to the rest of us."

222

"Well, if he's up to workin', ain't that his right? Ain't this America? Don't he have a choice? Why does that put the rest of us in a bad light?" Hattie asked.

"He's got a choice, all right. But if he chooses to scab mine while the rest of us is strikin', it'll make for some mighty bad blood. It weakens the strike to have men goin' to work."

"But, this is a free country. A man's got a right to decide what's best for him and his, don't he?"

"Sure, Hattie. But makin' choices mean you got to take what comes, if you make one that other folks disagree with. Eldon's goin' against' the majority. He's already been chose as a target from what I hear."

"What do you mean 'a target'? They was just pattin' him on the back sayin' how he was about as much responsible for gettin' those men out safe as the rescue crew was. He kept a cool head and made the rest of 'em be still and wait. Now they're turnin' on him?"

"That's not the way they see it," said Gene as he shifted gears to climb from Pond Creek up the hill toward Ebenezer. "In their eyes, he's the one who turned. You ladies are lookin' at the situation like it's all black and white, and it ain't. All the management men ain't bad, and all the miners ain't good. All the miners ain't bad, and all the management ain't good, neither. There's good an' bad on both sides, but the management won't see no reason to make things better if we're still goin' down to work in the mines every day. We got to make 'em see things different, an' I guess this strike is the onliest way we know how to do it."

"What if there's killings, Gene Beckwith? You gonna be able to live with that? You gonna come home some night and tell me they done shot Eldon, but it's all right 'cause they done it for a good reason?" Carrie sobbed.

"Aunt Carrie's mad at Uncle Gene, Mama," whimpered Dulcie, as she crawled into her mother's lap in the back seat of the car. She apparently had been riding along in silence listening to the adults and sensing the tension in the air.

"No, Honey, she's not mad at Uncle Gene," said Hattie. "She's mad 'cause the miners are upset and actin' foolish, and their bosses are actin' foolish, too. We're all mad about that, but it's not Uncle Gene's fault. Aunt Carrie's just worried is all."

"Den I'm worried, too." Dulcie's little face puckered. "Dey gonna shoot Uncle Eldon?"

Carrie's face softened. "Dulcie, Honey, don't pay no attention to me. My mouth's like a runaway train sometimes. Ask your Mama. She'll tell you."

"It's true, Honey," Hattie said. "Your grandma Stoneworth used to say Carrie could talk the white off a sheet. Ain't that somethin'?"

"What color would it be if she did?" Dulcie asked.

"Hmmmm. I don't know. I'll have to think about that. What color do you reckon, Carrie?"

"Well, now, I don't guess I know either."

"I gonna ask Smiff," said Dulcie. "He knows eveweeyfing. He even knows how to catch a monkey, sorta. You want me to tell you how?"

When the adults had nodded in agreement, Dulcie launched into a vivid description of monkey catching. The story took them the rest of the way home.

"Well, I never heard the like. Ain't that something? And Smith seen it with his own eyes?" Carrie helped Dulcie out of the car.

"Yes'm and his buddy's the one knowed how to do it. He showed 'em all. Wasn't that nice? I'm gonna show Jackie when we go to the Philippines."

Dulcie skipped ahead into the house. Gene turned to Hattie and said, "I'm goin' up to talk to Smith. He up to a visit, you think?"

"I 'magine he'd be glad to see anyone 'sides me and Zonie. He must be gettin' tired of us by now."

"Gene, I ain't done with you. We're gonna talk about this here strike business. You hear?" Carrie exclaimed.

"Yeah, Carrie, I figgered you'd have more to say, but I got to get up to that meetin'. I'm just gonna say hello to Smith, then I'm goin'. You want to stay here or have me to take you home?"

"Stay, Carrie. Otherwise, I won't know what happens at the meeting. Y'all can have supper with us when Gene gets back."

Carrie scowled. "All right. I'd just be pacin' the floor if I was home. Might as well stay."

"Don't sound like it's a prison sentence! Is it that hard to spend time with me?"

"Shoot, Hattie, I didn't mean it that way ... "

"I know, I'm teasin'. You're way too serious, Sister. I know this is hard. I'm scared, too, but we got to find a way to get through it. Okay?"

"It's easy for you to say. Ain't your man in the mine ... " Carrie's hand flew up to cover her mouth. Her eyes grew pained as she realized what she'd said. "Oh Hattie! What am I sayin'? You already lost your man. I'm just outa my head. Can you forgive me?"

Hattie put her arms around her big sister. "'Course I forgive you. It's powerful hard to stay mad at you for long. 'Sides, I know what you're goin' through. When Jack was hurt, and then when Smith ... Well, I do know. It's awful hard. But nothin's happened yet. We got to pray it don't, instead of thinkin' the worst. That's what you've always told me."

Carrie pushed her hair back off her forehead. "It ain't the same as Jack and Smith. They was fightin' the mine. Eldon, Gene, and Forrest, they're fightin' other men, and each other. It just ain't right. I know what to do with a disaster, but this is beyond anything I've had to cope with afore."

"That's true, but we got to find the faith to go on. Right?" asked Hattie. "We can't lay down and wait for bad to come. We got to fight, too, even if the onliest weapon we got is prayer. I think there's more we can do, though. We can talk to the other wives. I reckon they're all feelin' 'bout like we are, don't you?"

"I reckon," said Carrie. "It just don't make sense to me. Bringing in gunmen? Why? Who they gonna shoot? What's the matter with Obie Perkins? He's got mush for brains! Which one of his friends and neighbors is he willin' to see die? Does it even matter as long as they scare the livin' daylights outa the rest of 'em?"

"I don't know. I just don't think that way. Neither do most of us, I guess. I know it'll just make Forrest and Gene sick if there's killin'. That ain't why they're in it. You know that. I believe they'll try to cool the hotheads. If enough of 'em stand against killin', surely there won't be any."

"I hope you're right, Hattie. I just hope you're right."

The miners met in a grove of trees in the bottoms between Coaltown and Drakesboro. No one wanted to be seen. It was a secret meeting called by the strike organizers.

"Men, we been treated like dogs for too long. It's gonna stop, and stop, now!" Obie Perkins stood on a tree stump. He looked over the crowd of men gathered there. "We got one chance to make this here strike work and that's to stand together. We can't have no scabs goin' into the mines when we're strikin'. You got to make a choice. You gonna stand with us or agin' us?"

"Yeah!" shouted one of the outsiders. A few of the miners responded in kind.

"That sounds real good, Obie, but I got to feed my younguns," a voice shouted back. "How'm I gonna do that if'n I ain't workin?".

"We're gonna help each other. That's how. We'll all pitch in to make sure everybody's got somethin'. That's what we're gonna do."

226

"Yeah, 'til it runs out. Then what?" asked another man in the crowd.

"It ain't gonna run out. When management sees we mean business, they'll cave in."

"How long's that gonna be?" the first voice called.

"Yeah!" came the second voice.

"Yeah! How long?" another voice added.

Obie's scowl showed his anger. The meeting wasn't going the way he'd planned. "You can cry 'bout your starvin' kids from now 'til Easter, for all I care. But you ain't goin' in that mine if you know what's good for you."

"What you gonna do about it if I do? called out a slender man in his early thirties. You ain't stoppin' me. I'm gonna work like I always done."

Obie gestured with his right hand. Two of his boys stepped into the crowd with baseball bats. They swung the bats at the man who was shouting at Obie. He went down. One grabbed his feet, the other his arms and dragged him to the edge of the clearing where they threw him on the ground. Heavy boots kicked him. He curled into a ball and then went still as a final kick landed on his temple. Blood poured from his head.

"Men! Men! Look here," yelled Obie. "We ain't wantin' no more of that. Right? We want to get this strike goin' and get it over with so we can all feed our children. Right? That's why we're doin this. Right?"

The frightened men looked from Obie to the beaten man and back again. The thugs stood by Obie, slapping their bats against their hands.

"We don't want no more of that, Obie," came Forrest's strong voice. "Most of us agree we got to do somethin', but I ain't for beatin' and killin'. How 'bout you, men?"

Men shuffled their feet and looked at the ground. They adjusted their jackets against the cold, but they said nothing.

Gene, with Mahlon Hennings on his heels, moved to where Forrest was standing. "That's right, Obie. We ain't wantin' killin'. You hear?"

A few men nodded.

"Well, now. I ain't wantin' no bloodshed either," said Obie. "That ain't why we're here. We wanta get a strike goin' and learn them mine operators a thing or to and git it overwith. We're here to organize and find out who's with us and who's agin' us, that's all."

"And if we're agin' you, are we gonna get what Digby got?" Eldon's tired face still showed strength. "Is that what you're sayin'? Most of y'all are church goin'. Some of you, deacons. I see other church leaders among this crowd. You gonna condone what just happened here? You gonna stand by and watch as a workin' man, tryin' to do his best for his family, gets his head beat in? Is that what union means? If it is, I don't want no part of it. Neither does my boy. I can see where folks get real worked up, but that's takin' it too far. Y'all gonna have to answer for what you done."

One of the enforcers moved toward Eldon. Obie raised his hand. The thug stopped and stared. Eldon stared right back. Obie stood silent. Stoneworth was a powerful name. Right now, Eldon was a hero, not one to take lightly. There was time enough to deal with anyone standing with Eldon Stoneworth, but he'd leave him alone for the time being. Obie cleared his throat, and the outsider reluctantly stepped back into place.

Eldon and a handful of men turned and went to where Digby lay. Gently they picked him up and carried him to Eldon's truck. He moaned as they laid him in the bed. It was a sad, lonesome sound that carried to the rest of crowd. The truck slowly pulled out of the grove and headed toward town with Eldon and his small band of supporters.

"Now, men, that was real unfortunate," said Obie. "We ain't wantin' those kinds of things happenin'. We ain't here to hurt nobody. We're here to change the way the mines is run. We're gonna do it. It's gonna happen. I give you my word, we won't be seein' much of what happened here. Is that good enough for you?"

A few men answered in the affirmative. Then a few more. Soon there was a roar of approval from those gathered there. The men were ready. They'd been convinced either prior to the meeting or by what they'd seen at the meeting that the strike was the only way out—the only way to relieve the wretched conditions most of them were enduring.

Hattie bundled Jackie into a quilt and carried him up the rise to the smokehouse door. The baby laughed as she jogged him up and down.

Smith lay on the bed, bandages wrapped around his head, his broken leg propped up on pillows.

"Who's that you got there, Hattie?" Smith chucked the baby under his double chins. A gummy, open-mouthed grin was his reward. He reached for the baby. "C'mere, short stack."

"Are you sure? He's mighty wiggly."

"I got my head bumped and broke my leg, not my arms. I reckon I can hold this mite for a bit."

"Zonie'll be up around midnight. She and Dulcie are sleepin', but this boy thinks the night belongs to him."

"That right, boy? You a night owl?" Smith tickled the chubby baby. Jackie doubled over in baby chuckles, clear from his belly. "You're a sight is what you are. You come clean up here just to play with me?"

Jackie's little face grew serious as he watched Smith. Dimpled hands patted Smith's cheeks. The baby blew a bubble and yawned. Smith laid him on his chest and patted the small back. Baby Jackie nuzzled his shoulder until he found just the right spot, then he settled.

"I declare, I been tryin' to get that boy to sleep for pert near an hour and you have him five minutes, and his eyelids are droopin'!" Hattie exclaimed.

"Reckon I'm just naturally boring, like a long-winded preacher."

Hattie snorted, "You're not like any preacher I ever knew."

"No? Well, maybe you're right."

They sat, comfortably together, in the silence for a few minutes, then Smith asked, "Gene say anything about the union meetin'?"

"Not much. He was mighty worked up about somethin' but wouldn't say what, other than the strike's on for tomorrow."

"Can't say I'm sorry not to be minin' right now."

Hattie shuddered, "I'm downright glad you aren't. It's bad enough havin' the boys up there."

Smith smiled at her use of 'the boys' to describe Eldon and Forrest, one in his forties, the other thirty-seven. "The boys'll be all right, Hattie. They know what's what. How was Carrie when they left? Still carryin' on?"

"I ain't never seen her in such a state. Some of the things she said ... Well, it just weren't like her."

"She's no different than the rest of the wives and mothers— and sisters too, I'm thinkin'. You ain't said a lot about it. How come?"

Hattie didn't answer for a minute, then looking at her hands, she said, "I guess I don't know what *to* say. I see this county comin' apart at the seams, and there's not a lot I can do about it. I'm scared though, Smith. Real scared. Scared for the men, for the boys, and for the family. It ain't a good feelin'."

"Hattie, Darlin', if there's one thing you've taught me, it's to take it to the Lord. I reckon that's what you need to do. Take all that fear and worry, wrap it up, and present it to Him. He'll know what to do with it."

Hattie looked up at Smith. "That's what I'm doin'. That's what I've been doin' and I'll keep on doin'. It's the only thing I know."

16

Christmas time came, and with it a cold, biting wind. Smith took Dulcie and limped up the rise, leaning heavily on a cane. They headed into the woods near the house in search of the perfect Christmas tree.

"Dere's one! Get it! Get it!" Dulcie's face peeped out of the knitted hat her mother had tightly tied over her curls. "See it? It's bootiful!"

"You're right about that, Sugar. It's a real beauty, but don't you think it's a little big for your Mama's house?" His eyes measured the tree, top to bottom. Had to be thirteen feet if it was an inch.

"What about dat one, den? It's littler."

"Weeeeell, I reckon we could get that one, but do you see any reason why we shouldn't? Look real close. Your mama mightn't like it if we took that one."

Dulcie looked at the tree. There in the branches was a small, neat bird's nest.

"Oh. Better not take dat one. It gots birds. Mama wouldn't wike it if we cut da bird's house down."

"That's my girl. Birds don't always come back to the same tree, but they might come back to this one. What do you think of the tree over there on the edge of the clearing?"

"Da one by da fence?"

"Uh huh."

"It's perfect! Let's go get it." She started off at a run, then saw Smith wasn't behind her. She turned and came back for him. "You can't run with dat fing on your leg, can you?"

"Nope, not yet. But ol' Doc says it won't be long now 'til I can take it off. Then I'll be able to move a little better. Maybe limp a little, but I'll be faster than I am now."

"I'll wait for you. Can you carry da twee? Will it hurt you?"

"I think I can handle it. You're gonna help me."

"I am? I never carried a twee before."

"Well, why do you think I brung you?"

"Cause you love me." Dulcie gazed up at Smith with nothing short of adoration and dashed just out of his reach as he lurched after her.

"I do at that, Sugar. C'mon. Let's go get us a tree."

Smith swung the small axe down from his shoulder. "Dulcie, go stand over there where I can see you. I don't want you in the way while I'm swingin' the axe or when the tree falls."

Dulcie scooted out of range and watched as Smith's powerful arms swung the axe. It only took a few blows for the tree to creak and fall.

"There we go. Let's take it home."

"D'you know dat's a cedar tree, Smiff?"

"Uh huh. That's the kind of tree my daddy always brought home for Christmas. It smells good in the house."

"Mama has a box made of cedar. It smells weal good when you open it! She keeps all her special fings in it. Ma Stoneworth's Bible's in there. It's just fallin' apart. Mama said she loved it to pieces."

"That's nice," said Smith.

"Smiff, know somethin'? If I loved one of my books that much, I don't think Mama'd be happy."

"Why not, Little Britches?"

"'Cause I'm not allowed to wite in my books, but Ma Stoneworth wote all over her Bible. Mama says she wote things she wanted to wemember. And she dwew lines under lots of words. That's to help wemember, too."

"Uh huh."

"So, if I wote in my books, Mama would fuss at me. But not at Ma Stoneworth."

Smith limped along dragging the tree behind him. "You reckon your mama would let me see her Ma's Bible sometime? I'd kinda like to look at what she thought was important enough to underline. Might need help with some of the words, though."

"She'd show you if you ask and say, 'Pwease.' She showed me. She's a good weader, too. She says weadin' takes you anywhere you want to go. I want to go to da circus, so I want a book about it. Where you want to go?"

Smith thought of the little house under the hill. That's the only place he really wanted to be. In that house, with that sweet, reading woman and her precious, wonderful children. "Oh, 'bout anywhere, I reckon, long as you go with me."

"'Kay! We'll have us a fun time. Want to?"

"Sure!"

They pulled the tree to the house. When they got to the side porch, Smith asked, "See those two crisscrossed boards over there? Can you bring 'em to me, Honey?"

"Uh huh. You gonna make somethin'?"

"Already did. See, when I saw the tree off level, I'll be able to nail the boards on and then the tree will stand up."

"Oh. Want me to fetch the nail jar? I can weach it."

"Okay. Be careful."

While Smith sawed off the very end of the tree trunk, Dulcie raced to the shelf and stretched as tall as she could to reach the jar. Pudgy fingers wrapped around it and pulled it down. Back she ran. "See, I told you I could weach."

"Yes, you did. You're gettin' bigger everyday! What's Santa Claus gonna bring you?"

"Ummmmm. A penny! And a glass bird for Mama. She told Aunt Zonie about a glass wedbird at the drug store. She said it was the purtiest thing she ever saw. D'you think Santa would bwing that for Mama? She's awful good!"

"Well, maybe. Most of the time though, Santa brings things to boys and girls. Maybe someone else could get the redbird for your Mama. How would that be?"

"That'd be okay, I reckon, if you're sure Santa won't bwing it. You sure? She's just da bestest mama. Santa might bwing it."

"Hmmmm ... you might be right about that. She's a mighty good Mama. Yep, Santa might not like it if someone else got that redbird. We'll just have to leave it to him."

"You all done? Let's see? Yea! Look at da twee! It's standin' up all by itself. Mama! Mama! Come see!"

Dulcie's excited cries brought Hattie and Zonie to the door. "Hurry and bring it in, it's cold out there. Hurry now." Zonie called.

"Oh, look. It's beautiful," said Hattie. "Can we get it to the front room?"

"Sure," said Smith. "Just hold the screen door open and stand back out of the way."

Smith tugged the tree, bottom first, through the kitchen, with Dulcie tagging along behind holding the very top up off the floor.

"Watch out, Smith!" yelled Hattie, "Don't bump into the water bucket."

They turned the corner from the kitchen and into the front room. Smith moved a chair from near the window and set the tree up. "Wow, Smiff! Wow!" shouted Dulcie as she clapped her hands and hopped on one foot, then the other.

"Good job, Little Britches!" he said to the exuberant youngster. "Well, ladies, it that about the right spot for it?"

"No, over to the left just a little," Zonie directed. There— perfect!".

"Why, I believe it's the nicest one we ever had!" exclaimed Hattie.

The excited women gathered up the decorations they'd been making and circled around the tree.

"Look, Dulcie, see all the popcorn we strung. It's gonna go all the way 'round and 'round the tree. Where's the paper chain you made?"

"It's wight here, Mama. Do you like it? I made it just da way you showed me—wed and gween, wed and gween."

"Honey, it's perfect," said Hattie. "Let Smith help you with it. That's the way. Isn't that pretty and notice how good the tree makes the room smell!"

Hattie had a few blown glass ornaments, and they were carefully placed high enough on the tree that excited little hands couldn't knock them off. Thin foil icicles added shimmering sparkles to the tree and soft cotton spread at the base gave a blanket of snow. When all the other decorations were in place Hattie handed Smith a tinfoil star. "Think you can reach up there and put this on? It's the last one."

Smith placed the star on the top of the tree, and they all stood back to admire it. Each declared it the best ever.

Hattie wanted so badly for Christmas to be perfect. Thanksgiving had been a trial. Eldon, Forrest, and Gene had barely spoken to each other. She prayed Christmas at the old homeplace would bring them back together.

Smith swept Jackie up off the floor and high into the air. "What's a matter, big guy; is that tree botherin' you? You wonderin' what it's doin' in the house?" Smith looked at Hattie. "Don't you reckon all this commotion is confusin' to a little'un?"

"I s'pose. Never thought about it before. Bet you're right though. We been hustlin' around here like pigs let outa their pen and into the garden. He's sorta been left out. Haven't you, little feller?"

Smith held the baby at arms length and with mock severity began to lecture him, "Boy, If I was you, I'd be raisin' a ruckus. Don't you let them women ignore you."

Jackie laughed at Smith's fierce face. He was so funny!

Hattie grinned at the two of them and said, "All right then, Mr. Delaney. You just set yourself in that rockin' chair, and you

235

play with him. See if you can keep him happy so I can go make my jam cake."

"Why, sure I'll play with this boy. Hey, don't bite my finger. Wait a minute— Hattie, this boy's got a tooth!"

"He does? Well I swan! I knew one was comin', but it musta popped through durin' his nap. He didn't have it earlier when he nur ... "

Smith laughed at Hattie's red face. "Don't you go gettin' all flummoxed, Hattie. That's the naturalest thing in the world. It don't bother me. It shouldn't bother you, neither."

"Hush! Don't be talkin' like that. It ain't fittin'! We're not ... I mean—well, it just ain't fittin'! I'm goin' to bake my cake." Hattie almost flew through the heavy brocade portieres in her haste to leave the room.

"How come Mama got all wed-faced, Smiff? You tease her? Sometimes she gets wed when Uncle Forrest teases her."

"Maybe I did just a little. Here, Jackie, let's go for a pony ride." Smith put Jackie on his knees facing him. Holding him by the hands he chanted,

"Trot a little horsey
　　up to town.
　Trot a little horsey,
　　　don't fall down!"

When Smith got to 'down', he spread his knees and let Jackie's little bottom slip through to the seat of the rocker. Jackie laughed great, gulping, baby chuckles.

"Do it again, Smiff. He wikes it!"

Smith did it again, and again, and then again. Dulcie had a turn with Jackie seated in front of her.

"Whoa, this old horse has got a lame leg. I can't go as far as I used to. I got to quit."

"Awwwww! It was fun! Just one more time? Pwease?" Dulcie pleaded.

"Just one more time."

236

Smith and the children played while the women got things ready for the big Christmas Eve meal they were having for the family. Hattie made her jam cake. Zonie stuffed the turkey and pressed cloves into the ham. Hattie ran out to the smokehouse and brought in a load of sweet potatoes, which she cooked, measured and stirred until she had a sweet potato pie ready for the oven. Everything that could be done tonight would make tomorrow easier.

By eight o'clock all was prepared that could be. Everything else would have to wait. Smith told them goodnight and slipped out. Zonie climbed the stairs to the room that had been cleared for her use. Dulcie and Jackie were asleep and Hattie was about to drop from exhaustion. She climbed into bed with Dulcie and prayed.

Lord, I'm 'bout nervous as a cat. What happened up at Carrie's on Thanksgiving just wasn't right! It like to tore me up seeing them boys so hard set against each other. Help me give them the kind of celebration that will remind 'em first of You, and next of Mama. I know they'd never act the way they are if she was here to see. Give me the wisdom to know what to say to keep the peace. And thanks for always bein' there when I need You. In Jesus name, Amen.

Christmas Eve dawned bright and clear. Every surface in the house was polished from top to bottom, and the smells coming from the kitchen were incredible. The brothers and sisters arrived one family at a time throughout the afternoon until all were there.

"Cain't nobody else have no more children. We ain't got room in this house!" Forrest said.

Lindy, Carrie's oldest daughter, tugged her sleeve. "Mama, what can I do? Isn't there somethin' for me?"

"Honey, go corral those children into the bedroom and read 'em a story or somethin'. The noise in here is about to deafen

237

me. Grab Junior! Get outa that cake, boy!"

Lindy grabbed Junior around the waist and hauled him into the bedroom. She gave strict orders to Martha to watch him while she went after the rest of the cousins. There was a bunch to corral. Ben was with the men, but he looked like he'd rather be playing with her and the kids. She smiled and waved as she plucked another cousin out of the crowd and headed back to the bedroom. Dulcie tagged along behind.

"Let's play church! I'll be the preacher," Martha said. The children took seats on pillows on the floor. "Bretheren and Sisteren, I'm gonna preach today on the sins of the flesh. Why flesh is just the worst thing. It's the kinda thing that will take you straight to perdition. That's what it'll do. You don't want none of that flesh business. Now listen here, church, you got to straighten up and leave that flesh alone. It will lead you down the wrong road. The wide road. An' the road you're lookin' for is narrow. So just don't be thinkin' about no flesh. Whatever you do, don't be fleshly."

The children "Amened" from their pillow 'pews'. They all came to pray for their fleshly cravings and were forgiven.

Smith stood in the doorway, halfway listening to the men but more interested in "church." *Whew-weeee! If their mamas knew what they were praying deliverance from ...*

"Hallelujah, Thine the glory,
Hallelujah, Amen.
Hallelujah, Thine the glory.
Revive us again."

The children sang. Junior led them, pumping his arm up and down, almost in time to the music. He was Brother Harrison. He led the singing just the way Brother Harrison did. He threw his head back and closed his eyes. He gestured and nodded with exaggerated facial expressions.

No one knew why Brother Harrison did that, but he did it every time. Most of the children who went to Jackson Chapel could do a fair imitation of him by the time they were four or five years old. At six, Junior was a master mimic.

"Now, we're gonna sing number four hundred and sixty-eight."

"No, we ain't Brother Harrison. I ain't done preachin' yet!"

"Well, you got to be, 'cause you ain't supposed to be preachin' nohow. 'Women should keep silent in the church,'" Junior quoted. "That's what the Bible says."

Smith snatched up the new 'Brother Fenton' just as she swung her doll at 'Brother Harrison's head. "Whoa! Hang on a minute, there! We can't be havin' a free-for-all in church. That ain't right."

"I'm sorry, Mr. Delaney, but he just makes me so mad!" Martha stuck her tongue out at her brother and muttered, "Junior, you're a doo doo!"

"Martha Faye Beckwith! What would Mama say?" Lindy was righteous indignation personified. "Shame on you! Do you want me to go tell her right now? You better say you're sorry and mean it."

Chastened, Martha hung her head, "I'm sorry, Junior. Lindy, please don't tell Mama, or—" Her eyes widened in terror at a sudden thought—"She might tell Santa Claus!"

"Course I won't tell, but you got to be good, or else! Now, let's do somethin' else. Somethin' peaceful."

Smith laughed. He thought playing church *should* have been peaceful. Guess not when the preacher's nine, the song leader's six, and they're brother and sister to boot. He stepped back into the front room.

"I don't care. It ain't workin'!" said Eldon. "Y'all been strikin' for weeks, and all it's done is cause trouble. When you gonna see that you're makin' things worse 'stead of better?" Eldon sat on the couch looking fit to be tied.

Forrest jumped to his feet. "We ain't makin' nothin' worse. It's management that's the problem. They won't give an inch. Cain't you see that?"

"Y'all think you got 'em over a barrel, but you don't. There's plenty of men in this here Depression needin' work," said Eldon. "And they'll take it, even if it means crossin' the line. I hear the mine owners are workin' on a plan to raise our pay to as much as twenty- eight to thirty-three cents an hour, but they ain't gonna give in to you hotheads."

Gene rocked forward and leaned on his knees. "That ain't fair, Eldon—callin' us 'hotheads.' Don't paint us with the same brush as them fellers. Me and Forrest are doin' our best to stop the hotheads. We ain't part of them."

"When they beat up Cal Monroe, where was you? Did you stand up for him? Did you tell 'em to back off? No, you didn't."

Forrest shook his finger at Eldon, "Hey, we didn't have nothing' to do with that. We didn't even know they done it 'til it was too late. Both Gene and me's been up to sit with Cal. He's our friend. We ain't likin' what they done to him any more than you are."

"You better watch your backs then. If Obie and them think you're playin' both ends agin' the middle, it ain't gonna go well for you."

Smith leaned on the doorjamb and watched the escalating argument. "Eldon, you ain't had any trouble?" he asked.

"Nah, Smith. Just name callin' and rock throwin' as we walk to the cage every mornin'. Ain't nothin' more than that."

"They're jumpin' the workers pretty regular, ain't they?" asked Smith"

"Yep. Most of 'em's been beat up or threatened, at the least," replied Eldon. So far they're leavin' me alone. Reckon I should count myself lucky, but it kinda makes me nervous, waitin' for it. They hassle Ben some, but not too much. Got him in a circle one afternoon comin' outa the store. Shoved him around some, but that's all. Takes a brave man to bully a youngun who ain't dry behind the ears yet!"

"You know we wouldn't do nothin like that," said Forrest. "You ain't got the right to lump me and Gene in with that bunch.

240

We're just tryin' to make a better life for our kids."

"Yeah, well, you're doin' a fine job of it!" said Eldon, bristling.

"And it ain't helpin' any when you scabs ... "

"Hey y'all," Smith interrupted. "Hold off a minute. Hattie's worked real hard to put this day together. It'll fair break her heart if you go to sluggin' it out. How 'bout we agree not to get too worked up about the strike today. Eldon, you doin' what you think's right, but so are Gene and Forrest. Seems to me y'all got strong convictions. Oughta be proud of takin' a stand, no matter which side you're standin' on. Me, I ain't likin' none of it. I'm thinkin' it's gone on long enough now that somethin' big is gonna have to happen to get management to bend."

"What do you mean, something big? Like what?" Gene sat back in the rocker.

"I don't know, I ain't been in it like y'all have. I'm just thinkin' both sides is trenched in. It's gonna take somethin' major to bust up the stalemate. Sorta like when I was in France in the Big War. We was in our trenches, and the Germans was in theirs. We'd shoot at them, pick a few off. They'd do the same. We did that for days. Weren't gettin' nowhere. Finally the tanks rolled up behind us and shot the liver out of their position. That broke the stalemate. See what I mean? Looks to me like one side or the other's gotta bring in the tanks if you want to see somethin' happen."

"I don't know if I like the sound of that," said Eldon. "It don't sound like that'd be good for any of us. It'd take an awful big 'tank' to shake either side, don't you think?"

"Reckon so, Eldon, but that's the way I see it. Y'all have decided the other side's the enemy. Even family. That don't sound good neither. What do you want? More of the same or a solution?"

"S'pose I want to see an end to the ugliness," replied Eldon. "It's wrong for us to be fightin' amongst ourselves. I guess that's bothered me more'n anything."

241

Forrest looked down and scuffed the toe of his boot against the linoleum floor before he spoke. "You think it ain't bothered us, too? Gene and me ain't exactly been happy sittin' on the other side of the fence from you. We're family. We always will be. And we're Christians. We don't want no more beatin's neither."

Eldon rubbed his hands over his face. "I know that. I just want to work and take care of my own. Never thought I'd live to see the day when a man'd be looked down on for workin' hard."

"Don't reckon none of us did," Gene said.

Forrest walked over to where Eldon sat. "Big brother, I been a first-class polecat for not speakin' to you."

"You ain't the only one. I let my anger get the best of me. I hope you understand," said Eldon.

"Sure, I do. You always was a stubborn mule. Cain't tell you nothin'. Don't figure that's gonna change now." Forrest grinned.

"I'm a stubborn mule? Who was it that decided he should climb down the well to hide from Carrie, then got stuck and wouldn't call for help 'cause he didn't want to get in trouble? You'd still be in there if I hadn't told!" Eldon laughed.

"Yeah, and who got the trip to the woodshed 'cause you told? I almost forgot I ain't forgive you for that yet!"

"Hey, I went too, 'cause Daddy said I shoulda watched you better. I ain't forgive you, neither."

They were still laughing when Hattie called them to eat.

17

As Carrie covered the leftover food with a clean dishtowel, she said, "So, do you have feelin's for Smith, or not? I know you do. You might as well say."

"Carrie! Honest to Pete! All right. I do have feelin's for him. I ... I'm just not sure what they are yet. It ain't the same as with Jack. It's more like comfortable, than anything. I like his company. He's good with the babies. Dulcie loves him. I guess I just never figgered on carin' about no one else after Jack." Hattie stacked the clean plates in the cupboard.

"You've made that decision when you're only twenty-three years old? Child, you *are* foolish. 'Course you're gonna care about another man. You weren't made to be by yourself. You got so much love to give the right man. I just hope he *is* the right man."

"I know. That's kinda how I'm feelin'. He's done so many things that I'd never have dreamed of doin' – good and bad. And the places he's been. It's something to listen to him tell stories about far away places with palm trees and monkeys. And Paris, France! Don't guess I've ever known anyone went all the way to Paris, France."

"It ain't the travelin' in him that worries me; it's the wild streak. He's got a bad reputation, Hattie."

"He does. But you know, I haven't seen him do one thing wrong, 'cept the fight with Mr. Sawyer. He takes me to church every time the doors are open. He's not touched a drop of liquor, that I can tell, since he's been here. He never uses bad language, though he's had to catch himself a time or two. Zonie's

243

just as sweet as she can be. There's got to be good in that family, even if the boys do have a wild streak. 'Sides, after what Eunice's been sayin', my reputation ain't that pure either."

"The difference is, you ain't done nothin' to deserve yours. He's earned every speck of his." Carrie reached around behind her back and untied her apron.

"I know that, but isn't that what God's grace is for? To cover all those poor choices we make? If we believe in Him, don't we have to believe that He can change a heart that's wantin' to change?"

"Yes, but how do you know he's *wantin'* to change?" Carrie folded the apron and hung it on a hook beside the door.

"Well, he reminds me to pray when I'm hurtin' about somethin', like when the strike broke out. I was so scared and he said, 'Take it to the Lord'. I can't see a man who ain't a believer sayin' that.

"The other day, Dulcie fell down. She skinned up her knee somethin' awful. He just grabbed her up and loved her. She was smilin' before the bleedin' stopped. He's just got a way with her. And little Jackie..."

"Has he declared hisself? I mean ... "

"No. We've sorta danced around it. I'm not ready, anyway, but he's made it clear he thinks a lot of me, and I know I'd just be lost if he weren't here. I even miss him when he goes to town. Silly, huh?"

"Hattie, it's not silly. You're in love, you goose! You just ain't lettin' yourself admit it yet."

"You reckon? Well, I swan! I s'pose I am a little bit." Hattie raised her hands to hide her pink cheeks. "My, my! I didn't think I'd ever be in love again."

"Well, Merry Christmas to you!" Carrie chuckled. "You are a caution. Can't believe I have to tell you you're in love before you believe it. How's it feel?"

"I don't know. Scary. Wonderful. A little sad. I sorta feel unfaithful to Jack. I did love him, Carrie. I still do. Guess I always will. You think it's possible to love 'em both?'"

"I 'magine so. If Jack was alive, you wouldn't give Smith a second look, so you don't have nothin' to feel guilty about. It's not cheatin' to care for Smith, if that's what you mean."

"That's exactly what I mean. It feels a little like cheatin'. Jack ain't been gone a year yet. Seems like I oughtn't t'be feelin' anything for any man yet."

"Says who? Eunice? Who cares what she says. Not me, and not too many others, either."

"No, it's not Eunice or anyone else. It's me, what's inside of me. It's like bein' in a tug-a-war. One side of me's so *happy,* but the other side's still sad. The sad side keeps tellin' me I ain't ready to be happy, yet."

"But, Honey, you *are* happy. You walk around singin' all the time and playin' with your kids. I don't never see you without a smile on your face."

Hattie looked thoughtful. "I don't always feel like smilin'. In the beginning, I smiled for Dulcie. Now, it don't seem right to wallow in sorrow, but it don't seem right to be jumpin' up and down for joy, neither."

"Hattie, you're thinkin' way too hard about this. Either you're in love or you're not. Which is it?"

"I ... I am. I reckon I'm just scared is all."

"Prob'ly. You'll be all right. Mama and Daddy raised you good, and me and Gene didn't do too bad by you, neither. You're smart, and I think you know what you want. You just have to decide if you want it bad enough to get over bein' scared about it."

Lalie popped her head around the doorframe from the other room. "Hey, y'all. They're wantin' to sing in there. You gonna come join us?"

"Tell 'em we'll be there in a minute, Lalie," Carrie answered.

"I'll tell 'em, but they ain't gonna like it. They're gonna start without you if you don't hurry. " Lalie turned back to the crowded front room.

Hattie untied her apron and hung it beside the one Carrie had worn. As she moved toward the door, Carrie laid a hand on her arm to stop her.

"Least'un, you did real good with the dinner. I just want you to know I think Mama and Daddy would have been real proud."

"You think so, Carrie? I prayed so hard that things would go well today. I've just been sick to death worryin' about it. I felt so bad about Thanksgivin'!"

"Honey, it's been almost perfect. The boys ... well, they been better today than I seen 'em since the strike. You done good, Honey," said Carrie. "Maybe things'll get better from now on. If our boys can come together, then maybe the rest of them miners can see reason, too."

She didn't tell Hattie that Gene had told her what Smith had said to the arguing brothers, that it would tear Hattie up if they fought about the strike today. Carrie also didn't tell her that it was that act of kindness that had won Smith a place forever in Carrie's heart.

Arm-in-arm the sisters walked into the room where the family was gathered.

The rest of them had made good their threat. They were already singing. A simple melody poured forth in harmony, the likes of which only comes from blended family voices. Together, they sang the gentle song of coming home:

> Turn back time to that place,
> Where I knew love's embrace.
> Simple hearts holdin' fast,
> In that place where love lasts.
>
> Shadows play among the trees,
> And again, my mind sees,
> Sheltered there in that place
> Every lifeworn, loving face.

Young and old gathered 'round,
Generations bloodtie bound.
Yet again I still hear,
Echo whispers of yesteryear.

Turn back time to that place,
Where I knew love's embrace.
Simple hearts holdin' fast,
In that place where love lasts.

I recall once again,
Quilted patchwork, Kentucky kin.
And my mind's memory
Of the hills of Tennessee.

Turn back time to that place,
Where I knew love's embrace.
Simple hearts holdin' fast,
In that place where love lasts.

Sweet harmony drifted out of the little house under the hill, blown on a breeze of love. They sang old songs and then hymns. Finally, they joined in much-beloved Christmas carols. Babies were put to bed, toddlers nodded sleepily, and children yawned. Still the adults sang on. This family, this tradition, this Christmas.

Hattie got up early that Christmas morning, even though the old clock had struck midnight before the last family had gone home to wait for Santa Claus. She fed Jackie and threw together breakfast. Then she dropped two shiny pennies into Dulcie's stocking, followed by an orange, a peppermint stick and a new outfit for her doll. She took a large flat package from her bureau drawer and put it under the tree along with another square box. Finally she added a small box for Zonie and one for Jackie. There was a larger one from her closet for Smith. The tree looked wonderful.

She heard Smith stomping the mud off his boots and ran to pour the coffee. Zonie would be down any minute. Already Hattie could hear her moving around.

"Merry Christmas. Have you been a good little girl?" Smith smiled from behind an armload of presents. "Got some place to put these?"

"Oh, my goodness! Of course. Put them under the tree, but what did you do? You never said ... "

"I don't tell you everything, you know. Merry Christmas, Zonie."

Zonie descended the steep stairs with four small packages. "Same to you, little brother. Mornin', Hattie. Let me take these in to the tree, then what can I help you do?"

"Not a thing! You do enough around here. I feel guilty keepin' you from your family on Christmas day."

"Hattie, you *are* family. You been family since the minute I saw you lyin' in that bed, so sick and all. I just wanted to take you home with me, right then and there."

"Instead, I kept you here," said Hattie.

Zonie walked out of the kitchen, smiling, to add her gifts to the growing pile under the tree.

"Is Dulcie gonna get up this mornin' or sleep 'til this afternoon?" asked Smith.

"What'sa matter, Smith? You ain't excited about the Christmas tree, are you? And you a grown man!" Hattie teased.

"I just want to see Dulcie open her presents."

"I reckon she'll be up any minute. I'm surprised she's still sleepin' with all this ruckus. She was so excited last night, I didn't think she'd ever go to sleep."

Me, too, thought Smith. *I didn't think I was gonna be able to get that stocking up without you seein' it last night. Then I*

248

worried all night long it'd fall and break before you got a chance to open it.

"Smith, you listenin'? I asked if you brought in a bucket of coal." Hattie looked at him hard. "What are you doin? Woolgatherin'?"

"Guess I was, at that. Yep, the coal's on the porch. You need it now?"

"No, it'll wait a little bit ... "

"Mama, did he come? Did Santa come? Let's go see!" Dulcie's little body hurtled through the door into the kitchen on the way to the front room. Smith grabbed her as she ran past.

"Whoa. I think you need to eat a big breakfast 'fore you go in there. Don't you think so, Hattie?"

"Real big. Eggs and bacon and biscuits and gravy. Maybe even some grits. It's cold outside. Gotta have somethin' to stick to your ribs."

"But, Mama, I feel weal stwong dis mornin'. I'm not a bit hungwy. I could wait 'til after ... "

Smith and Hattie laughed at the crestfallen child.

"We're teasin' you, Dumplin'. 'Course we're gonna go open presents first. Then we'll all eat breakfast. You ready?"

"Yes, ma'am!"

Dulcie led the way as they went to the front room. Zonie hurried to get the baby.

"Look, Mama! Just look! Lookit all da pwesents!"

Hattie sat on the couch with Dulcie on the floor at her feet. Zonie and Jackie sat in the rocker, and Smith played Santa, parceling out each gift to its rightful owner.

Dulcie got paperdolls from Zonie and a jointed teddy bear from Smith to go along with the things Hattie had put in her stocking. She had a new jumper and a picture book from her Mama, too.

Zonie loved the hand-embroidered handkerchief from Hattie and the warm gloves from Smith.

Smith opened his big box to find a new shirt Hattie had made. Zonie added socks to his pile, and Dulcie gave him a rubber ball.

"She said you had to have it. I couldn't talk her into anything else," Hattie said.

"'Course not. I needed a new ball real bad." He bounced it a few times. "Don't know what happened to my old one. Lost it years ago." Smith hugged Dulcie tight. "How'd you know I needed a ball?"

"Don't know. It just come to me."

"Well, I sure do thank you. It's just what I wanted."

"Mama, is dat stockin' up dere for Jackie?"

"What stockin'?"

"Da one back dere," Dulcie said pointing.

Tacked to the wall behind the tree was a stocking with a suspicious lump in the toe. Hattie reached in and pulled out a small, brightly wrapped package. She read the tag aloud, "To Hattie, the bestest Mama. With Love, Santa." She tugged gently on the ribbons that bound the small bundle. Peeling back the paper, she lifted the lid from the little box. Nestled in a bed of excelsior, sat the little glass redbird she'd admired. She gasped and hugged it to her breast.

"See Smiff, I told you Santa would bwing it!" Dulcie jumped up and down and clapped her hands. "She *is* da bestest Mama. I told you!"

"Shhhhh! That was our secret, Little Britches. You weren't s'posed to tell that you knew Santa was gonna bring it."

"But, I told you!"

Hattie laughed, "I'll speak to you later, Mr. Delaney. Zonie, I love the slippers. You must have seen my old ones. They're in pretty bad shape. Smith, the locket you gave me is lovely. It's so delicate. Thank you."

Jackie patted the jack-in-the-box from Smith, then cried when the clown popped out.

250

"Guess it's too big a surprise for such a little guy, said Smith."

"He'll get used to it. By tomorrow he'll be laughin' when he sees it. It just startled him, that's all," Hattie said.

They sat in contented fellowship, enjoying each other and the delights of the day.

In the middle of the afternoon on Christmas day, Hattie and Smith went to house after house in Drakesboro dropping off small gifts of food to families they knew. A loaf a homemade bread here, a plate of cookies there. Each was received in the same spirit it was given. When there was only one plate left on the seat between them, Smith headed to the far side of the small town and down the old highway toward Browder.

"I still don't see why we need to go to Eunice's. I thought she was out of the picture," said Smith.

"Smith, she's always going to be my babies' grandmother, whether I like it or not. I'm not invitin' her to the house. I'm just taking her a cake. It's a small enough thing, but maybe it'll bring peace."

"You're dreamin' if you think a cake is gonna fix what's broke with that woman!"

"I don't want to argue with you. This has been such a good day. Love reaches even the unlovable. I'm gonna take the cake in and leave. That's all. Just let me do this without any guff from you. It's Christmas, for goodness sake! It won't hurt me any, and she don't have no one else but Ferd."

"It's not just a cake. There's presents in that bag you're totin', too. What did you do?"

"It's nothin' really, socks for Ferd and a hanky like I made Zonie. That's all. Shame on you for begrudgin' an old lady a little bit of Christmas!"

"She's gonna throw 'em back in your face. Then where you gonna be? Right back where you started."

251

"Fine! If she does, I'll at least know I tried. Don't you understand? It doesn't matter what Eunice does. What matters is what *I* do. I got to live with my conscience, not hers."

"So you don't care if she slams the door in your face? It won't bother you?"

Hattie fiddled with the buttons on her coat and looked out the truck window and the countryside whizzing by. "Course it would bother me. It would hurt real bad, but it's the right thing to do. I ain't sayin' I'm gonna welcome her back with open arms ... "

"You better not. That woman's a menace!"

"You stop tellin' me what to do! It's not up to you. You got no right."

Smith slammed the palm of his hand down on the steering wheel. "Don't you think I know I got no right? Don't you think I'm fully aware of that? I know I got no place to tell you, but I'd like to have the right, if you'd let down that wall you throwed up between us!" Smith shouted.

Hattie blinked. "I'm sorry. I know you'd like things to be different between us. I didn't mean to say you got no right. That wasn't fair. You're my friend. I reckon friends have a right to say how they feel."

Friend! I'm a friend! Smith took a deep breath to calm his frustration. He didn't want to be a friend. He wanted to be a husband, a lover, a father. Well, friend was better than nothing. He'd be there to pick up the pieces when Eunice tossed her out on her ear, and maybe if he was a good enough friend, ... perhaps someday ...."

"I meant to tell you how much I love the redbird. That was real sweet of you. I reckon Dulcie planted that idea in your head?" Hattie deliberately changed the subject.

"It weren't nothin'. I did it for her. She was sure Santa would bring it, and I couldn't see lettin' her down," he answered.

"Smith ... "

"Hattie, don't say nothin'. I think we said enough for to-day."

"But ... "

"No, I mean it. I ain't feelin' much like talkin' right now."

Fine! If he don't wanna talk, we won't talk. He ain't the only one got feelin's. Thinks I've thrown up a wall! Hattie turned her face to the window and blinked hard to keep the welled-up tears in her eyes from running down her cheeks.

They rode in tense silence the rest of the way to Eunice's house. When they parked Hattie waited for Smith to walk around the truck and open her door. When he didn't, she got out, snatched up her small bundles and slammed the door. Smith leaned back on the seat and closed his eyes as though a nap would be just the thing this fine day. She glared at him and turned on her heel. Picking her way through the cluttered yard, she went to the door of the old house.

Ferd answered her knock. "Hattie, ain't you a sight for sore eyes!"

"Merry Christmas, Ferd. I brought y'all a jam cake. I know how you like 'em. And there's a little something for Christmas, too. Can I come in?"

"Well, I don't know. She's in a mood today." Ferd lowered his voice to a whisper. "It ain't a good day for her, Hattie."

"What do *you* want? Come to beg my forgiveness? Well, I ain'ta forgivin' you! You can just get back in your man's truck and get outa here." Eunice stood in the dark interior of the house. She wore an old housedress and looked as though she hadn't bathed in weeks. Her stringy hair hung in greasy strands around her twisted face.

"Mother Crowe, are you all right? You look like you been having a hard time. Is there somethin' I can do to help you?" Hattie's sweet heart felt only compassion for the sick woman. All the past was wiped away by what she saw in Eunice's lined face.

"You cain't do nothin' for me. Get out. I ain't wantin' you here. You're a shame to all that's holy, that's what you are."

Hattie stepped through the door. "Let me make you somethin' to eat. I can whip up somethin' real quick. You like my biscuits and gravy. Let me fix you somethin'. You look like you ain't been eatin' right. You got to take care of yourself, Mother Crowe. Jack wouldn't like to see you this way."

"Don't you even speak his name! You gave up the right to even *think* his name when you moved that man in with you!" Eunice hurled the words at Hattie like bullets, striking her in the heart.

"Ferd, help her to that chair. Now, listen, Mother Crowe." Hattie knelt at Eunice's knee and took the old woman's cold hands between her little ones. "I loved Jack with my whole heart. He give me the most precious treasures of my whole life. Dulcie and Jackie are his legacy. Ain't nothin' can take that from his memory. No matter what I do, they're still his. And they're still yours, too. But I can't let you hurt 'em. Understand?"

"I ... I wouldn't hurt 'em. You just don't want me around. That's all. You don't want me seein' what you're up to." Eunice snatched one hand from Hattie's and slapped her hard across the face. "Get out. I don't need your help! I don't need no one!"

Hattie's hand flew to her burning cheek. Backing away, she turned toward the door. Ferd reached for her. "I'm sorry, Hattie. I was thinkin' maybe she'd see reason, but she's gettin' worse. I called the doctor in, but she wouldn't let him past the door. I don't know what to do anymore. I'm just real sorry. You're a good girl to try like you done ... "

"Ferd, see if you can get someone up here to help you. I got a little money laid by, if you need help to pay for it." Hattie looked back at Eunice kicking the rocker into a mad ride, ranting about Jack and Big Jack and the book of Revelation, all in a jumble of nonsense. "She needs help. Maybe Ma Richards could give you somethin' to help calm her some."

254

"I'll do that, Hattie. Thanks for comin'. I just want you to know, I'm real sorry. She ain't been right since she was a little girl. It's just gettin' worse." Ferd rubbed tired hands over his weary face.

Heartsick, Hattie stepped through the door and breathed in the fresh winter air. The door flew open behind her, and Eunice flung the cake at her. The plate shattered on the frozen ground at Hattie's feet. Ferd wrapped one arm around his sister's waist and hung on for dear life. He tried to protect himself from her flailing arms with his other hand while she screamed obscenities, spittle flying from her mouth. Hattie stood rooted to the ground, shocked beyond belief.

"Go on, Hattie, she'll be all right. She'll calm down once you're gone. Sister, let's go back inside. You ain't got your shoes on. See? You're gonna catch your death of cold out here." Ferd turned his sister back to the door. She still struggled, but less now.

Smith stepped out of the truck and silently gazed at Hattie's reddened cheek. He'd known this was a mistake. He wrapped her in his arms as she sobbed against his coat.

"Come on, Honey, let's go home."

18

"Dulcie, don't get too close to the road."

"Yes, ma'am."

Hattie clipped another sheet to the clothesline with wooden clothespins. She'd spent most of the morning on the side porch washing clothes. Washday called for bone-wearying work. Hauling bucket after bucket of water from the well to the big black kettle in the yard to be heated over a fire. Carefully carrying the hot water to the first of two galvanized washtubs sitting side by side on low benches on the porch. Filling the second tub with cold water for rinsing. Bending over, rubbing in the lye soap and scrubbing the clothes by hand on the old washboard that bruised the palms and skinned the knuckles. Poking and stirring the soaking clothes with the old wooden axe handle. Lifting each water-laden item into the rinse water, then running the clean clothes, one piece at a time, through the hand-turned wringer. Pinning them, at last, to the clothesline where the sun and breeze would dry them and leave them with the cleanest, freshest smell imaginable.

After while, Hattie thought, *when I gather these clothes all off the line, and lay my cheek against 'em and feel and smell how good and fresh they are, I'll know it was all worthwhile, even if I'm a bit tuckered out.*

It sure helped having Zonie around to keep an eye on Jackie so she didn't have to keep running in and out! If only Smith hadn't gone off by himself today, he would have helped her. Carrying the heavy buckets didn't seem to bother him at all. But he'd driven off around ten o'clock, and she hadn't seen him since. She called down to where Dulcie played with her doll, "When I'm finished hangin' this washin', you're gonna have to come back up to the house."

"'Kay, Mama," Dulcie answered Hattie, then turned back to her world of make-believe. "Now, be a good boy and put your cap on. It's still cold out here. Don't want you gettin' da cwoup. Dat's better." Dulcie placed Smith's old cap on her doll. It drooped down over the little button eyes. "Now you'll be warm enough. When we get home, we'll have us a snack. What you want to eat? Jelly biscuits? Dat's my favowite, too."

Slowly, carefully, Dulcie pushed her doll back and forth on the swing. She carried on a steady stream of conversation with her baby. "When you gwow up, you gonna be a fine man just wike Smiff and my daddy. I'll make you clothes so you can go to work. You be weal handsome, huh? 'Course you got to wear shoes. Everybody gots to wear shoes when dey go some place special."

Dulcie was so engrossed in her little pretend world, that she didn't hear the car approach.

The large black car came slowly down the hill and eased to a stop in front of the house. It was full of strange men. The door opened, and one started to get out. Startled, Dulcie grabbed her doll and ran up the drive to her mother. The cap slipped from the doll's head and lay at the edge of the yard.

Jeb Sawyer gazed after the fleeing child until he spotted Hattie. "Scuse me, ma'am. Could you help me out? We're lookin' for Snead Piper's place. Thought it was down this road, but we musta made a wrong turn somewhere." Jeb Sawyer acted as though he knew he'd met her somewhere but couldn't place the dark-haired beauty. "Hey, ain't you ... ?"

"Hattie Crowe, Mr. Sawyer. We've met, briefly." Hattie drew herself up to her full height and slowly walked toward the car. "Who'd you say you're lookin' for?"

258

Sawyer, on hearing her voice, immediately recognized her as the little spitfire who'd witnessed the humiliating beating Delaney had given him at Coaltown! She'd even told him to "Git" and that she'd hold Smith off of him! Red-faced, he puffed out his chest and blustered, "I said I was lookin' for Snead Piper's place."

"You and your friends came out the wrong road. If you go back to Drakesboro and turn right on the highway, go up to the last road on your right before leavin' town. Turn there, and Piper's will be about a mile out on the left-hand side on the edge of Jacksontown. It's got a white mailbox with Mr. Piper's name on it. You can't miss it."

"Me and Mr. Farnsworth got bizness to take care of. He's an important man, you know. Him and Mr. Baxter and me, we're making the rounds today, talkin' to management about the strike. We got a lotta things to do."

Hattie didn't know whether to be irritated or amused by Sawyer's obvious attempt to impress her. "Well, you'd best get to it then." She didn't want to be unfriendly, but she wasn't particularly warm either. "If that's all you're needin' ... " She turned her back as Mr. Farnsworth rolled down his window.

"Quit flappin' your jaw, Sawyer. Get in the car! We ain't got all day."

Hattie was already on her way back up the drive and didn't turn around to see the look on Sawyer's face. Nor did she see him kick at the cap on the ground, or hesitate, then stoop to pick it up. Dulcie saw though. She was scared of that big man with the red face. It wasn't a nice face at all. And he took Smith's cap!

"Mama, did you see what he ... "

"Hush, Dulcie. Go in the house now. I'll be in in a minute, and we'll have lunch."

"But Mama, he ... "

"Dulcie, I said go in the house. They're turnin' around, there's nothin' to see."

Dulcie, dragging her feet, went into the house. It wasn't fair. That man took Smith's cap—her cap! And Mama just let him have it. Why'd she do that?

Smith leaned back against a tree trunk. Around him the woods were thick and quiet. Next to him on the ground lay his rifle and a small pack. He'd tramped through the woods for hours 'til the ache in his weak leg forced him to find a place to rest. He wasn't hunting, he'd just needed to get away for awhile. He'd done nothing but wander around trying to figure out what to do about his relationship with Hattie. He'd even shot at a rotten tree stump in an attempt to distract himself from the jumble of emotions that threatened to overwhelm him. It hadn't worked.

Things had been different since Christmas day. He and Hattie were closer, but still she held him at arm's length. It was driving him to distraction. He couldn't seem to get her out of his head. He evened dreamed about her. And what dreams they were! Wonderful images of Hattie floated through his mind: Hattie standing at the back of the yard gazing out at the sunset, the colors reflected in the pools of her eyes; Hattie kissing roly-poly Jackie; Hattie, eyes closed in prayer; Hattie with Dulcie making thimble biscuits; Hattie sleeping in his arms, burning with fever. Hattie in his arms, Hattie in his arms, Hattie in his arms. ...

Smith dropped his forehead onto his drawn up knees.

What's it gonna take, Lord? I love her with all my heart, and I know she feels somethin' for me. I know I ain't never gonna be worthy of her but ... I never much cared what folks thought of me before, but now I do. I wish I could turn back time and do my life over, ... better, ... more like one of them Stoneworth boys. But I can't. I can't change who I was or what I done. He raised his arms up and covered his head. The wind whispered through the trees. *I been tryin' to show her, to give her time. I*

260

know she's still heart-tied to Jack Crowe. It don't matter to me, Lord. I just want to be part of her life. Even if it's just a little part. But, I'd rather be her husband and father to her children. I know they can get along without me, but I sure do want to be there for 'em. I just don't know what to do about it, Lord.

The wind rustled through the winter-dried leaves and seemed to whisper, "Have you asked her? Have you asked her?"

No, I ain't asked her. I just figgered she'd tell me, I reckon.

"Better ask her," the wind whispered back.

Smith's head jerked upright. A sudden grin lit his face. "I reckon I'll do just that!" He spoke aloud to the wind, and his Father in Heaven. Then he snatched up his rifle and pack. The long walk back to the truck didn't seem as burdensome as the walk in had been. His step seemed lighter than it had been since his cast had come off. The limp didn't seem so awkward. Smith moved like a man possessed, He was heading home to ask Hattie to be his wife.

Two men held their horses at a standstill at the edge of the rise. They saw Smith from a distance and exchanged a silent glance as he strode on. They knew who he was but didn't speak or raise a hand to greet him.

The car with Farnsworth, Sawyer, and Baxter had driven all over the county. They'd even picked up an escort car of armed men early in the afternoon. Now, they were heading from Drakesboro to Greenville for one more stop. They were close to having a deal to end the strike. It would be touch and go, but they had the makings of a settlement.

Earlier, at the meeting with Mr. Piper, it was obvious that Sawyer was disgusted. He didn't see any point in dealing with the miners. He grumbled that management was caving in. By his expression it was clear that it rubbed him the wrong way to even consider some of the concessions Farnsworth was willing to make. Sawyer had argued long and hard that they needed to stick to their position, but Farnsworth, the manager of Little Creek Mine, was authorized to talk to the other mine managers and owners to win consensus. "Enough was enough," Farnsworth said. He wouldn't listen to Sawyer's whining complaints.

"Don't see why we have to settle," Sawyer griped. "There's plenty willin' to work without us havin' to do nothin fer them ingrates that's strikin'."

Farnworth scowled. "Sawyer, shut your mouth. You aren't helping. If you don't have anything worthwhile to say—just be quiet. You're like a dog with a bone. We're gonna settle this strike whether you like it or not." Under his breath he muttered, "Razz Morgan owes me one for sending this idiot along."

As they came over the brow of Ebenezer hill, the escort car wasn't in sight. Sawyer plucked at the gray cap he'd picked up down at Hattie Crowe's. Turning it over he saw 'S D' written on the sweatband. *Smith Delaney.* An angry flush rose from Sawyer's florid neck and rose 'til it covered his jowly face.

Turning to Farnsworth he said, "Know who this cap belongs to? Smith Delaney. Now there's a man who needs to be taken down a peg or two. Too full of hisself by far. Typical miner! Always wanting more. Always acting like he deserves better than he's gettin'. Like the rest of them miners, he's a graspin', snatchin', whinin' slug."

Without warning, a hail of bullets smashed through the windshield, killing Farnsworth instantly. Brains, flesh, and fragments of bone splattered across Sawyer's face and the interior of the car. Terrified, he clawed at his face to clear his vision and braced himself as the car, its driver dead, careened to the left, into an embankment and toppled onto its side. Baxter was thrown from the car. He dragged his injured body in a bellycrawl toward a culvert. A slug through the stomach stopped him. Sawyer flung himself to the bottom of the car, hauling Farnsworth's body on top of him in desperation, using it as a shield. One shot blew off the rear view mirror. Holes appeared in the floorboards. A door handle pinged and swung on its axis. Death whizzed past his head. He jerked from one side to the other trying to dodge an unseen enemy. Warmth spread down his legs as his bladder let go. Heart pounding, he hid, waiting for death to come.

As quickly as the horror began, silence descended. Dead, deathly quiet, then the squeal of tires. Again, nothing. Just the stillness of death and the acrid scent of new blood. The snipers were gone. Suddenly, he recoiled from the feel of Farnsworth body on his, the blood oozing down, covering him in stickiness. Shoving the body aside, Sawyer crawled through the window. Baxter lay on the ground, arms flung out. Dead, too.

Sawyer shook. He couldn't stop. He bent over and sucked in gulps of air. A tree creaked. He threw himself into the ditch, expecting a bullet that never came. Nothing. Just the wind.

Lying in the ditch, he realized that in his hand he clutched the cap. He stared at it like it was a foreign object until recognition hit. Shock, fear, and hatred for Smith Delaney and the miners rose up in his throat. He retched and retched again. Then, without stopping to think about it, he jumped to his feet. Screaming a curse against all miners, he sailed the cap deep into the underbrush where the snipers had hidden.

"You did it, Smith Delaney! You did it, you no count, puffed-up banty rooster of a miner. You did it!" He shouted.

The escort car found him there, rocking by the side of the road, his hands over his face. He was silent. The evidence would show who did the killing.

"Zonie, why hasn't Smith ever married?"

"He prob'ly coulda if he'd wanted to. I reckon no one ever struck his fancy. 'Course, he ain't always made it easy to love him, either."

It's easier than fallin' off a log, Hattie thought. "He's a hard worker, and I know he'd be a good husband to the right woman. Just seems strange to me is all."

"There was a few women we thought he might get serious about, but he never seemed to get past the courtin' stage. I reckon some of 'em just didn't suit him, and then I s'pose one or two might have been afraid of his temper. He does get his back up. Musta scared 'em off."

"But he'd never hurt a woman! He ain't that kind!" Hattie jumped to his defense.

"'Course not, but he's set himself up for folks to wonder about him. Know what I mean? All that foolishness. He just didn't seem to care at the time, though now I think he's beginnin' to regret it."

"Why do you say that?"

"Well, I know he thinks an awful lot of you, Hattie. I reckon it ain't my place to say, but I think he's real fond of you."

"I'm fond of him, too. He sure can make me mad, though. Only one other man ever could get under my skin like Smith and that was Jack!" Hattie laughed at herself. "Your brother was so dead-set against me goin' to see Eunice on Christmas Day. Turned out he was right, too, but the funny thing is, he never said 'I told you so'. He just brought me home. He coulda read me out like a madman, but he didn't. That don't sound like a man whose temper gets the best of him."

"You see his knuckles the next day? He had 'em wrapped. He punched a board outta the wall of the outhouse. Had to put a new board in. He was so angry at Eunice for slappin' you."

"I saw the board, but I never realized. And I knew his hand was hurt, but he didn't say. You mean he punched that board clear out of the wall? Oh, my!"

"Someone had just hurt the woman he lo ... cares about. What'd you expect him to do? It hurt him somethin' awful to know she'd hit you like that."

"Oh, Zonie. I was awful to him on the way up there. I told him he had no right to tell me what to do. Even when I said it, I knew I was hurtin' him. I'm so ashamed of myself."

"He told me. I gave him what for. He *don't* have the right to tell you what to do. He ain't your man." Zonie paused and smiled gently. "But if someday he should be, and I ain't sayin' he will, I just want you to know I couldn't ask for a sweeter sister than you."

Hattie swiped at the tears on her cheeks. "Thank you, Zonie. I feel the same about you. I can't believe he told you, though. It's embarrassin'."

"Well now, listen. Don't you talk to Carrie? I'm his big sister just like she's yours. We may not be as open about how we feel, but we love each other just like y'all do. Don't you know that?"

"'Course I do. I know how much you care about each other. It's that carin' that's showed me as much as anything how lovin' he is."

"And Colt is that way, too. We're kinda quiet when it comes to soft words, but we feel 'em just the same. Anyway, Smith's a good man. He's done some dumbfool things, but under all that bluster and struttin' there's a good heart beatin'. And I ain't just sayin' that 'cause I'm his sister, though that don't hurt none either."

"Do you really think folks dump him in the same barrel with Deke Dunford—I mean, with a man that'd beat his wife?"

"Hattie, I think most folks don't know what to make of Smith. And, up to now, he's kinda liked it that way. Keeps 'em on their toes and they don't mess with him. There's not too many willin' to take him on in a fair fight. He's proved himself over and over with his fists."

"Why? I mean, why'd he get in all those fights? I don't understand that at all."

"I don't know. I always figgered it was 'cause he ain't real big. I mean he's powerful, but he's close to a head shorter than any of your Stoneworth men. Maybe he's got a bit of a chip on his shoulder. I think he musta felt like he had to strike first, strike furious, and do it up right, or he'd have to keep provin' himself. That's what he done, anyway. Him and Colt are about the same size, and you ain't never seen nothin' like the two of them when they got their backs together fighten' their way out of a bad situation!"

"I saw enough when he whipped Mr. Sawyer. It scared the liver out of me. But the minute I told him to quit, he stopped. That don't sound like a dangerous man to me."

Zonie snorted, "Ha! If it'd been me tellin' him to quit he'd still be there. He hears you better'n he does anyone else. That's why I'm sayin' he cares about you. It's 'Hattie said this,' 'Hattie said that,' and 'Did you see Hattie when ...' It's a good thing I'm fond of you or I'd be mighty sick of hearin' about you by now."

The porch-swing squeaked when Hattie sat down with her book. A few minutes of peace would be nice. She'd just enjoy the quiet and lose herself for a little bit before she went in to make supper.

Hattie laid the book aside when she realized she'd read the same page three times, and still didn't know what she'd read. She just couldn't seem to get Smith out of her thoughts long enough to concentrate. Where was he anyway? He'd been gone all day.

Watch out for him, Lord. He's real important to me. I know I prob'ly shouldn't care so much, but I do. Hattie saw herself in Smith's arms. She groaned. *What am I gonna do, Lord? He's just so special. He's caring and gentle and warm. He's also cocky and way too proud, but I love him, Lord. I think I'll just die if he up and leaves. I know he gets the wanderlust and takes himself off from time to time. I can live with that, but if he was to pull up stakes and go forever—You can make the blind to see*

266

*and the lame to walk. Can't you make him want to stay? I reckon
You can, if You want to, but don't do it if he won't be happy
here. He's got to want to stay. It's gotta be his choice. Please.
Please let it be his choice.*

"Smith, quit pacin'! You're makin' me nervous," Zonie
snapped.

"Huh? What?"

"Light somewhere, boy. I can't stand you traipsin' back and
forth anymore. What's wrong with you?"

"Nothin'. Ain't nothin' wrong, I'm just a little edgy's all. I
got somethin' needs doin', and I'm tryin' to work out the best
way to do it."

"Well go outside and bother the chickens. You're drivin' me
up the wall!"

"How much longer you think Hattie's gonna be?" Smith
asked.

"I don't know. How long does it usually take her to put Dulcie
to bed and feed the baby?"

"A while I reckon," he muttered.

"What is so all fired important? You needin' to 'fess up about
somethin'? You done somethin' you wantin' to talk about?"

"No, I ain't done nothin'. Not yet anyway. But I'm gonna."

"You're gonna what? Quit talkin' in riddles, and just tell
me." Zonie was getting a little concerned.

"I can't. I got to talk to Hattie about it first."

"Well, all right, but hurry up and talk to her. You're 'bout to
worry me to death."

"Will you watch the babies?"

"When?"

"Now."

Zonie blew out a breath. "I reckon. You sure you're not in
trouble?"

"No, I ain't in trouble, not yet anyway. I reckon that'll depend on Hattie."

Zonie's frustration had turned to concern and now was full-blown worry. She'd never seen Smith this flustered. She was just about to question Smith further when Hattie came into the room.

"Hattie, will you go for a drive with me?" Smith blurted.

"When, now? It's dark out there!"

"I know, but I got somethin' I want to talk to you about, and Zonie said she'd stay with the younguns." His eyes pleaded with hers.

"Where we gonna go at this hour?"

"Just drivin'. No place special. I just want to go for a drive."

"I guess it'd be all right. Let me get my coat."

She didn't see the relief that washed over his face.

Smith drove to Black Diamond Lake. His mouth was so dry he hadn't been able to speak since they'd left the house. Sure could use a drink. But those days were past and gone.

They sat in silence looking out at the moon reflected on the water. He couldn't think of one word to say. What words do you use when you ask a woman to marry you?

Swallowing hard he looked straight ahead out of the windshield. "I been thinkin' a lot about us, and I know you ain't prob'ly feelin' like I do, but I got real strong feelin's for you." He risked a quick glance at Hattie's face. She was listening.

"You and Dulcie and Jackie are 'bout the best things that ever happened to me. If you think you could forgive my past and maybe think about the future, I ... I'd ... well, um ... I'd like you ... I mean ... I want to m ... marry you. If you'd have me, that is ... "

Oh my goodness! Tears welled up in Hattie's eyes. This tough-talkin', hard-as-nails, precious man could hardly speak he was so choked up.

268

"Do you love me?"

"Well, yeah! Ain't that what I just said? I mean, you don't think I'd ask if I didn't, do you?" *I'm messin' this up. She's gonna laugh in my face,* thought Smith. "I know I ain't much to look at, and I ain't got a lot to offer, and I ain't got the kind of book learnin' you do, but I went up to Old Hebron this evenin' and fetched this. I'd be proud if you'd wear it. Will you, Hattie?"

The ring was gold filigree with a six-point setting. "It was my mother's. She give it to me when she died. Colt got her wedding band and give it to Virginia. I got her engagement ring. It ain't a real diamond, but if you'd have it … it's yours if you want it."

"It's lovely! Oh, Smith. Of course I'll marry you. I love … "

Smith had her in his arms by then. The moon shone down on the truck as he gently, carefully lowered his lips to hers. The kiss was warm and sweet and full of promise. He set her away from him and jumped out of the truck. "She said 'yes'! Did you hear that, Lord? She said 'yes'!" He ran around the side of the truck, yanked open the door and grabbed Hattie's hands to pull her into a hug under the stars. Laughing, he awkwardly danced her around the truck. "She said 'yes'!"

"Hush, Smith, you're gonna wake up all of Ditney Hill, Drakesboro and the rest of Muhlenberg County and get us hauled off, you nut!" Hattie laughed as hard as he did.

"Wait. I still got the ring! I forgot to put it on your finger. Here, let me do it. There. It's perfect." His hands came up to cradle her face. "You did mean it, didn't you? You'll really marry me?"

"Yes! I really will marry you, Smith," she said with simple conviction" "I love you, too."

He kissed her again. "Honey from the hive ain't as sweet as you!" He turned his face toward the stars and exclaimed, "She said, 'Yes,' Lord! You said to ask her and I did! She said, 'Yes.' Ain't that somethin'?"

Hattie marveled that he was ignoring her to talk to God again. What a man he was!

"What do we do now?" he asked as they walked arm in arm toward the edge of the lake.

"I don't know. What do you want to do?"

"I reckon we could just stay here a while."

"Or we could go tell Carrie. She'll be so happy for us!"

"Awwwwww! I ain't wantin' to share you with anyone right now—just look at that moon reflectin' on the water. Can't we just stay here and kiss a little more?"

"One more kiss, then we're gettin' in that truck and goin'. D'you hear me?"

"Yes, ma'am!" He dropped his hands to her waist and pulled her close. Once again he lowered his head and found her sweet lips with his own.

"Mmmmmm ... maybe you're right," Hattie said with a shiver. "Maybe we ought to kiss a little more. That's awful nice!"

"Uh, no. You were right. We best be goin'. I'm thinkin' this kissin' business could be a little dangerous 'til we get the vows said."

"Smith! The things you say ... " Hattie blushed as he led her to the truck.

"Have you set a date? How 'bout Valentine's Day? That's just a couple of weeks off. You said you didn't see no reason to wait. Where you gonna get married? At Jackson Chapel? Is Brother Fenton gonna do the service? Oh, I'm so excited!" Carrie bubbled like a stewpot.

"Wait, wait, wait! I can't think as fast as you can ask questions," said Hattie. "No, we haven't set the date. Valentine's Day is awful soon."

"Hogwash. We can put together a humdinger of a weddin' by then. Now, we'll get Willa to bake the cake, and ... "

"Carrie, this ain't your weddin'!" Gene smiled as he interrupted his excited wife. "Hush and listen for a minute." He shook his head in amusement.

"Oh Hattie, I'm sorry. I guess I just let myself get carried away. Well, what *are* your plans?"

Hattie and Smith looked at each other, grinned and shrugged. "We don't have any yet," said Hattie. "He just asked me a few minutes ago. We came here to tell you before going back home. So far we haven't had time to make plans."

"The girls are gonna be so thrilled!" Then Carrie's brow furrowed—"What about Eunice, though? You think she'll give you any trouble? I don't want that woman messin' things up for you, Hattie."

"I don't think Eunice can hurt me anymore. She's just the most pitiful thing, Carrie. You'd know what I mean if you'd been up there at her place on Christmas Day. It was sad seein' her like she is now."

Carrie shook her head slowly, "I don't know, Honey, I wouldn't be feelin' too sorry for her just yet. She's still got venom in her fangs."

"Let's don't talk about Eunice. I'm gettin' married!" Hattie turned to Smith, "Dulcie's gonna be so excited. She loves you already, Smith."

"I love her and Jackie, too. I'll be proud to raise 'em up. I don't expect you'll want to change their names to Delaney. Their daddy was a good man."

"No. I think they need to know who they are, but that won't change their love for you."

"Sure won't change my feelin's about them, neither."

"Y'all are so sweet, I could cry! Now, quit that mushin', and let's get to makin' plans. Do you want Willa to make the cake or not?" Carrie blew her nose hard.

"I reckon. She's the best baker in the family. Might as well, if she's willin'. I'll start savin' sugar."

"We all will. Now, what are you gonna wear?"

"Goodness. I don't know. My church dress?"

"Nonsense! You're gonna have a new dress. I'm gonna help you make it. What color? That blue that's so purty on you? Or a soft green. You look good in either one."

"Well, since I'm a Jezebel, how 'bout red?" Hattie laughed. "That'd make the biddies stand up and take notice."

"Quit that. You're not wearing red! Hattie Delaney ... Oh, I like the sound of that!"

Smith and Gene grinned at each other and let the women bubble on. They had all kinds of ideas, and each was more outrageous than the last. They laughed until they had to wipe the tears that ran down their cheeks. Such joy!

The knock on the door barely registered to Carrie and Hattie. They were caught up in their own world.

Gene brought Sheriff Westerfield into the small living room. He cleared his throat. "Uh, Smith. The sheriff, here, wants to see you."

"Hey, Sheriff, been climbin' any ladders lately?" Smith stuck his hand out. Sheriff Westerfield shook it slowly.

"I was just on my way down to your place, Miz Hattie, when I saw Smith's truck. Saved me the trip. Sorry to interrupt."

"Smith and Hattie are gettin' married. Ain't that wonderful? We were just plannin' the weddin'. You and Mrs. Westerfield will have to come ... " Carrie's voice faded as she saw the grim expression on the sheriff's face. Something was wrong. Something serious. "What's happened? Is it Eldon? Did he ... "

"No, Miz Carrie. It ain't Eldon. It's ... There was an ambush at Ebenezer today. One of the Coaltown foremen and Mr. Farnsworth were in a car that was hit by a sniper, maybe more than one. Farnsworth and Baxter are dead."

"Oh my gracious! How could that be? They were down to the house askin' directions this afternoon."

"Miz Hattie, that might be important to my investigation, but in the meantime, I got to take Smith in."

"What? Why? He didn't have nothin' to do with a killin'. He was ... " *Where had he been all afternoon?* "You don't have a reason to take him in. He wouldn't have any part in somethin' like that!"

"No, ma'am. I never thought he would, neither, but so far the only evidence I got points to him. The only livin' witness says he seen Smith runnin' through the woods away from the scene. I got to take him in, or folks'll be callin' for my badge."

Hattie ran to Smith and threw her arms around him. "Tell him you didn't do it, Smith. Tell him. I know you didn't. Tell him!"

Smith gently disengaged her arms from around his waist and took her face in his hands. "I didn't do it, Hattie. I promise you that. Don't never, *ever* doubt it. We'll figger this out, and then I'll be home. Okay?" With his thumbs, he brushed the tears from her eyes. "Don't you cry. You're strong. Remember? Our babies need you to be strong. I need you to be strong."

Hattie's eyes pleaded with his. "I ain't strong, Smith," she whispered brokenly. "I ain't. I'm breakin' apart inside. Please don't let 'im take you. I just found you ... "

"I was there all along. God just opened your eyes. He'll find us a way, Hattie. I know that now. He give you to me, and he'll find us a way. You hang on, Honey. I'll be home soon."

Westerfield stepped forward and handcuffed Smith's hands behind his back. With his head he motioned toward the door and tugged on Smith's arm.

"Noooooooooooooo!" Gene held Hattie as she struggled to get to Smith. "Don't you take him! He didn't do it! He didn't!"

"Hush, Hattie!" Smith spoke sharply. "Go home to our babies. They need you now."

Hattie's cries changed to sobs as Smith was led away. Carrie rocked Hattie in her arms as they both cried. They cried for broken dreams and broken hopes and broken hearts.

19

Forrest slammed his hand down hard on the oak table. "You got to listen to reason, Hattie. I just don't want you getting' hurt any worse. Facts is facts. Smith's the only suspect they got. He was missin' that whole day. Sawyer seen 'im runnin' through the woods with his own eyes."

Hattie's eyes flashed with anger, "I don't care. You can say it from now 'til doomsday but that doesn't make it true. You never put any faith in Sawyer's word before. *Why now?*" Hattie rubbed the back of her neck. Her shoulders sagged and she dropped her hands into her lap. She and Forrest had been arguing for an hour. "Why are you believin' him now?" she repeated, her tone weary.

"Because they don't arrest a man and charge him with murder without evidence. They say they got evidence, and that's gotta mean somethin'."

Hattie turned her coffee cup in her hands. "It don't mean a thing if it's Sawyer's word against Smith's. Weren't you the one who said you'd never known Smith to lie? Didn't you sit right here at this table last summer and tell me that?"

Forrest threw his hands in the air and turned away from Hattie. They'd been over this ground before.

"I give up!" He wheeled back to face her. "Just tell me how can you be so sure? How can you be so dad-blamed sure?"

"Don't you cuss in my house!" Hattie set her cup down so hard it was a wonder the handle didn't break off.

"I'm sorry!" he shouted. "I just don't get it. You standin' by a man who's about to be convicted of murder! Hattie, there's a side of Smith you ain't seen. You better face the fact that he may well be the one who done the shootin'."

Hattie shook her head. "No, Forrest! You didn't see his face. He looked me in the eye and said he didn't do it. He said 'don't never, ever doubt it.' I believe him, and nothin' you or anybody else says is gonna change that." Hattie lifted her chin and glared at her brother.

"You been readin' the papers?" asked Forrest. They're draggin' up every fool thing he ever did. They're sayin' it was just a matter of time before he come unhinged altogether. They're sayin' ... "

"They're sayin' whatever will sell the most papers. That same paper called him the 'Saint of Coaltown' when he squeezed down that airshaft to lead Eldon and those other men out. They nominated him for a citizenship award, remember? Then that awful Tennessee paper turned it all around and put out that head-line 'Saint of Coaltown – Satan of Ebenezer?' They'll say any-thing to sell a paper! What do you think the newspapers are gonna do? Muhlenberg's got itself a couple of murders—they got 'em a story. Their turnin' their backs on Smith don't mean he did those killin's."

Forrest wagged his head back and forth as though he couldn't believe what he was hearing, "Hattie, this just ain't like you."

Carrie shook a finger at Forrest. "It's exactly like her, and you quit badgerin' her. I've heard about all I'm gonna listen to. And if you think for one minute that Eldon believes that Smith did it, you got another think a comin."

"Oh come on, Carrie! You ain't fallin' for this, too?"

"You're forgettin' somethin', little brother. I saw his face when he told Hattie he didn't do it. I believe him. So does Gene. The man that rescued our brother and our nephew ain't a mur-derer."

Forrest slumped into a chair at the dining room table. He threw himself forward on his elbows. "All right, all right. I'll stand with you, but I still say, where there's smoke there's fire."

276

Hattie jumped to her feet, so angry she was shaking. "Don't you say you'll stand by me and then tell me you don't mean it. If'n you don't believe in Smith then just go on home. You just go on home to Vida and Clifford and keep readin' the paper and believin' lies. But you're not gonna stay down here and keep throwin' your doubts at me! I won't stand for it."

"Hattie, you don't mean that…" Forrest stared at Hattie, his dark eyes reflecting the pain in his voice.

"Yes, I do. You either be here 'cause you know I'm tellin' you true, or just go on home."

Forrest turned to Carrie, looking for support. She folded her arms across her chest. The set of her jaw told him he'd get no help from her. Gene stood beside Hattie with one arm around her shoulders. He wasn't going to listen to either. With a look Zonie dared Forrest to speak one word in her direction.

Forrest sighed. "I just don't want y'all to get hurt any worse. I don't know what to think about Smith, but I do know my family. If you truly believe Smith is innocent, he must be. I had to hear with my own ears how convinced you are. I'll stand behind you. He must not have done it."

Hattie's eyes, bright with unshed tears, stared at Forrest. "You mean it?"

"Yes, Little'un. I believe you. If you say he didn't do it, then he didn't do it."

Hattie flew to him and wrapped her arms around him. "Thank you, Forrest. You don't know how much that means to me." She whispered against his neck, "It'll mean a lot to Smith, too."

"Colt's here." Zonie spoke from where she stood at the window. "Virginia's with him. I'm goin' out to meet 'em."

The last week had aged Zonie. The gentle lines around her mouth had deepened into crevices. No one had taken the news of Smith's arrest and subsequent murder charge harder than she had.

"Bring 'em in Zonie. We're all family now," Hattie said gently.

Hattie's heart fluttered when she saw Colt Delaney for the first time. He had Smith's auburn hair, same blue eyes, same build. Only the amount of gray at his temples betrayed Colt was the older brother. Virginia was a plump little wren. Her reddened eyes betrayed earlier tears.

Hattie crossed to the door. "Please come in. I'm Hattie. I'm so sorry we have to meet this way," she said. She swallowed hard, then remembered her manners. "This is my sister, Carrie, and her husband, Gene Beckwith. That's my brother, Forrest Stoneworth."

Colt nodded at the women and shook hands with the men. Virginia gave Hattie a quick hug then held her at arms length to look her over. "Why, you're purtier than a picture, ain't she, Colt?"

Colt smiled a slow smile so reminiscent of Smith's that Hattie had to stop herself from gasping out loud.

"She's mighty purty, Virginia, he said."

Colt's speech was slow and country. "I been to the jail. They let me see Smith for a few minutes. He said to tell you he's thinkin' of you and the younguns. Said y'all was gettin' married. He told me to be good to you."

"Is he all right? Will they let me see him?" Hattie's hands flew to her mouth, prayerfully.

"I don't think so. The sheriff said it's family only."

"But we're ... "

"Yeah, but y'ain't yet," Colt interrupted. "Sheriff Westerfield said he'd do what he can for Smith, but it ain't lookin' good for him. Folks are pushin' for a speedy trial. Looks like Smith's gonna go before Judge Curtis in the Circuit Court by the end of next month if nothin' else turns up."

"Did he say what his evidence is? I mean 'side's Sawyer's talk?" Gene asked.

"Nope, he's bein' real closed-mouthed about it. I reckon y'all should know that I called Fletch Sommerall. He said he'd represent Smith if we want him to."

278

"Fletch's a good man. He ever try a murder before?" asked Forrest leaning against the wall.

"Nope. Not too many have around here. This ain't Louisville or Nashville. But he said he'd do his best. Don't reckon we can ask for more than that." Colt reached over to pat Virginia's hand where it rested on the table.

"Trotter, the D.A., is playin' it up real big in the papers. He's chompin' at the bit to take Smith to trial." Hattie fluttered a hand in the air as if to dismiss the importance of her statement.

"Well, it is an election year." Forrest's sarcasm hung in the air like December icicles from the eaves of a house.

"Virginia, can I get you anything?" Hattie asked.

"No, I'm fine. Just worried sick is all."

"Yeah, I reckon we all are," Hattie responded softly.

Exactly one month later, the circuit court held jury selections for the trial. Because the nature of the crime was murder, one in which the defendant, if found guilty, could receive the death penalty, the district attorney himself would be the prosecutor for the State. Tom Trotter was an outlander. He wasn't from Kentucky. In fact, he wasn't even a southerner. He'd been raised in the state of Indiana. After his Harvard law education, he had moved to his wife's hometown of Greenville. He was considered a pompous man who seemed to think himself a little above the good people of his adopted state. By contrast, Fletcher Sommerall was Kentucky all the way. Born and raised in Graham, the son of a coal miner, he was a hometown success story. His quick mind won him a full scholarship to the University of Kentucky. He studied law and then came back home to serve the people he knew best.

About thirty Muhlenberg County residents were called for jury duty, receiving their notices from the sheriff about four weeks after the murders. As is done in jury trials, the defense attorney and the prosecutor were allowed to question the prospective jurors about several matters: their knowledge of the crime; their kinship to the defendant, prosecutor and sheriff; and their feelings about the death penalty.

By three o'clock on the day of the jury selection both sides were satisfied with the final choices. Judge Curtis dismissed the chosen jury and alternates for the day, advising them the trial would begin promptly at nine o'clock the next morning.

The honorable Judge Craig Curtis had presided over the circuit court for twenty-three years. His circuit consisted of the counties of Logan, Todd, McLean and Muhlenberg. He was known for his sense of humor outside the courtroom, but didn't tolerate any nonsense in his court.

On the morning of the trial Tom Trotter, dressed in a gray, pinstriped suit, looked confident as he rose to present his opening argument to the jury.

"Gentlemen of the jury, it's a sad day in Muhlenberg County when we have one of our own on trial for murder. I'd rather be doing anything in the world than prosecuting a neighbor for the heinous crime that Smith Delaney's been charged with. It's painful to think that there is someone, *right here in our community*, with so little regard for human life. The facts are, that's exactly what we have. We have a man—sitting right over there—who's been a powder keg just waiting for the fuse to be lit. The next few days will be some of the longest of his life. We're going to look at this man's past. We're going to look at who he is and where he came from. We're going to see from his past just exactly what kind of man he is. When you hear the kind of life he's led you'll have to agree that he is, beyond a reasonable doubt, the sort of man it takes to commit the kind of crime that's been committed here.

"Now, some of you are going say that you can't convict a man of murder just because he's sown a few wild oats. And that just because he's taken a few drinks, been in a fight or two, he isn't necessarily a murderer. That's true. I can't fault that logic one bit. But what we have *here* is an angry man—a man with a bent toward using violence when it serves his purpose. A hard-drinking man. A man who can't hold a job in the mines of this county. We've got a hostile man who's carrying a grudge—and has been for a long time." Tom Trotter paused dramatically to adjust his tie.

"We have his rifle that, by his own admission, he fired on the very day of the murders." He walked over to the evidence table and picked up Smith's rifle, turned it over in his hands and sighted down the barrel.

"This same man hasn't got an explanation for his whereabouts on the afternoon the crimes were committed—no alibi."

Tom Trotter carefully laid the rifle back on the table and turned back toward the jury. "He's guilty based on the evidence sitting right here on this table—and there's more. He's as guilty as they come, and we're going to prove that beyond a reasonable doubt."

Mr. Trotter walked back to his table and sat down, satisfied with his opening statement and with the reaction of the jury.

Fletcher Sommerall nodded as he passed Trotter on his way to the podium.

"Well, now. That was real convincin'. Only problem is, it isn't true. Oh, parts of it are. But the whole package just isn't wrapped up tight. It's got little curled up edges where the bindin's a little loose. Has Smith Delaney done violence in his past? Yep. Has he had a nip or two of the old corn whiskey?" He winked at an older man in the jury box. "Yep. Probl'y made some, too. Has he been fired from the mines? Uh huh. That's true.

"What my distinguished colleague didn't bother to mention, is that none of that proves the defendant has committed murder. Something else Mr. Trotter didn't bother to mention is that the defendant has been hired back by every mine that ever fired him. '*Why is that?*' you ask. Well, sir, I'll tell you. It's because he's a good man to have around. He's a hard worker. He pulls his weight. He's also got strong ideas about right and wrong."

Fletch walked over to rest a hand on Smith's shoulder. "When Smith Delaney thinks somethin's wrong, he does somethin' about it. That gets him in trouble once in a while. He's what I call a 'man of principles'. He doesn't take injustice lyin' down. He doesn't take bein' cheated without recourse. He won't see a friend bein' walked on without takin' to task the person doin' the walkin'. That's the kind of man he is. Mr. Trotter over there is gonna tell you he's a smoulderin', angry man. Someone lookin' for a fight. That isn't so. He's been in fights. Not too many of us country boys can say different. Does that make us murderers? No sir! It does not."

Fletch walked over and picked up Smith's rifle and held it out for the jury to see.

"Did Smith Delaney have his rifle in his possession on the afternoon of the murders? Indeed he did. Did he offer that information to Sheriff Westerfield? Indeed he did. Did he try to hide that rifle? He did not. Did he lie about its whereabouts? Again, he did not. No, sir. He told the sheriff right off where the gun was and where he'd fired it. Does that sound like a man with somethin' to hide? I don't think it does. Do you?

"Now, let's move on to the eyewitness. Jeb Sawyer's an important man up at Coaltown Mine. Most of y'all know him, if not by sight, certainly by reputation." Sommerall paused to let that thought sink in. Then he continued. We're gonna prove that Mr. Sawyer has a grudge against Smith Delaney. He doesn't like him. Not one little bit. And that's his right." Fletch narrowed his eyes and stared hard at the jury. "But that don't make Smith Delaney a murderer, either.

"Mr. Trotter's a good prosecutor. He knows all those big words. He knows how to tie a fancy tie. He can prob'ly talk rings around me, but that doesn't mean he's right in the matter under consideration. I'm gonna prove he's wrong. Just watch and see if I don't."

282

The honorable Judge Curtis swiveled back and forth in his chair. "Thank you, gentlemen. Mr.Trotter, call your first witness."

"Your Honor, the Commonwealth of Kentucky calls Jebidiah Sawyer."

The witnesses, including Hattie and Forrest, were not allowed into the courtroom until after they had testified. This was to keep them from hearing what others said in the trial. It was too easy for a person to change his story to fit what another witness said, or to refute that person's testimony.

The bailiff stepped to the door of the witness room and called Sawyer's name. Sawyer swaggered to the bench in the shiny suit and tie he reserved for weddings and funerals. He was sworn in.

Mr. Trotter asked Sawyer to identify himself to the jury and then got down to the business at hand. "Now, Mr. Sawyer, you were in the car with Mr. Farnsworth and Mr. Baxter on the day of the murders. Is that true?"

"Yes, sir."

"Where exactly in the car were you?"

"Lessee. Me'n Mr. Farnsworth, we was in the front seat, and Mr. Baxter, he was in the back. Mr. Farnsworth was drivin'."

"Did you have any warning before the shots were fired at the car?"

"No, sir. We was ridin' along, and I had just turned around to look out the back window when the first bullet come through the windshield. Killed Mr. Farnsworth right off the bat."

"How was it that you came to survive this act of violence?"

Sawyer sanctimoniously intoned, "I reckon it was the hand of God."

Mr. Trotter nodded sympathetically. "Now, you stated in your deposition that as you were crawling from the car, you saw a man running from the edge of the clearing into the woods carrying a rifle. Is that right?"

"Yes, sir, it is."

283

"And you recognized that man?"

"I sure did." Sawyer's eyes shifted to the right.

"It was a man that you knew personally. Is that right?"

"Yes, it was."

"How was it that you knew him?"

"I was his boss at Coaltown Mine for a time."

Trotter cocked his head sideways and rubbed his chin thoughtfully. "Did this man have any distinguishing features that made him stand out from the crowd?"

"Well, he ain't nothin' much to look at, if that's what you mean."

Someone in the crowd tittered. The judge banged his gavel.

Mr. Trotter smiled. "No, I mean, was there something special about him that caused you to recognize him right away?"

"Well, there's that auburn hair of his. Ain't too many folks around here got hair that color."

"So that's how you knew who he was?"

"That and the fact that I saw him with my own eyes." Sawyer leaned forward, eyes wide.

"Is that man in this courtroom?"

"Yeah. I mean, Yes, sir."

"And would you point him out for the jury."

Sawyer looked confused. "Well, Mr. Trotter, he's right there. Next to Mr. Sommerall." He pointed directly at Smith.

"Let the record show that Mr. Sawyer pointed out the defendant, Smith Delaney."

"So ordered," Judge Curtis responded.

"No further questions."

The judge turned to the defense table. "Mr. Sommerall?"

"I have no questions for Mr. Sawyer right now, Your Honor, but I reserve the right to recall this witness at a later time."

"So ordered. Mr. Trotter, call your next witness."

Sawyer lumbered down from the stand and left the courtroom.

The prosecutor called Sheriff Westerfield.

284

Sheriff Westerfield stepped forward. He was quite a presence in the county. Everyone knew him. When he'd been sworn in, Trotter glanced at his notes.

"Sir, on the night you arrested Mr. Delaney, he had in his possession a rifle. Is that right?"

"Objection! Leading the witness, Your Honor." Mr. Sommerall unfolded his lincolnesque frame from the chair at the defense table and rose to face the judge.

"Sustained."

Mr. Trotter glanced quickly at the judge and then stated, "I'll rephrase." He turned back to the witness. "Sheriff, on the night Delaney was arrested, did he tell you that he had a rifle?"

"Yes."

"And that rifle had recently been fired, is that correct?"

"Objection!"

"Sustained."

Trotter stopped and took a deep breath, then started again. "Sheriff, were you able to tell if the rifle had been fired recently?"

"Yes, it had."

"And Mr. Delaney, in his statement to you that evening, said he'd fired that rifle himself that day. Correct?"

"Yes, that's right."

"Where did he say he'd fired the rifle?"

"Said he'd had a lot of thinkin' to do and needed to get away from everyone for awhile. He told me he'd driven up to Mud River and spent most of the afternoon traipsin' around. Said he fired the rifle at a tree stump." The sheriff leaned back in the chair, relaxed.

"Did you find any evidence to back that story up? That he was firing at tree stumps?"

The sheriff shook his head, "Mr. Trotter, there's an awful lot of tree stumps in the woods at Mud River."

Once again, a twitter or two rippled through the courtroom. The judge glared from the bench until quiet was restored.

"Now Sheriff, you've had dealings with Mr. Delaney off and on for years, haven't you?"

"Off and on, yes."

"He's been in a lot of trouble, hasn't he?"

"Objection! Leading the witness," said Mr. Sommerall.

"Sustained."

The sheriff watched the by-play between the lawyers and the judge then answered. "I reckon you could say he's been questioned about a lot of trouble."

"How many times have you arrested him?"

"Just this once — for the murders." The sheriff pushed himself a little more upright.

Fletch Sommerall was on his feet. "Objection, Your Honor. No one has found that Mr. Delaney murdered anyone."

"Sustained. The jury will disregard."

Tom Trotter smiled. It was obvious he was happy that murder and Smith Delaney had been connected by the sheriff's words. The jury wouldn't forget that in spite of the judge's instruction. "All right, how many times have you questioned him on other matters?"

"Well now, let's see. I ain't exactly sure. A fair number. We've had a go 'round a time or two. Had to bring him in several times for questioning."

"What's he been 'brought in' for?"

"Him and Colt, that's his brother, they were cut ups when they was boys. I guess I had to talk to 'em several times."

"You had to talk to them? What about specifically?"

"Oh, the usual boyhood pranks. Tippin' outhouses, stealin' small stuff from the mines, fights, not goin' to school."

Again, Trotter checked his notes. "Let's talk about the fights. They were numerous, I believe?"

"Objection! Mr. Trotter is testifyin'," Sommerall called out.

"Sustained. Please confine your remarks to questions, Mr. Trotter," the judge responded.

The prosecutor inclined his head in the judge's direction and asked with exaggerated patience, "Sheriff, would you please give me some idea of how many times you questioned the defendant about fights?"

"Oh, several, I'd say. I don't rightly recollect how many exactly, if you're lookin' for a number." Westerfield shifted his not inconsiderable weight on the chair.

"He's quite the fighter, I hear."

The sheriff nodded, "Don't too many tangle with him anymore. He's proved hisself."

"I see. So he's a good fighter?"

"Pound for pound 'bout the best I ever seen in these parts."

"I'm sure his mama's proud of him." Trotter's sarcasm dripped like molasses from a jar.

"Objection!" Sommerall leapt to his feet again.

"Sustained."

"Withdrawn." Trotter, paused, then started again, "Now, as Delaney got older, the trouble got worse didn't it?"

"Well, he was gone for a time. Bein' in the war and all. Things were pretty quiet then."

"Objection! Mr. Trotter's calling for a conclusion."

Trotter exploded, "Your Honor! Mr. Sommerall's constant interference with these groundless objections is only slowing down testimony. Surely we can proceed ..."

The judge glared at the prosecutor, "Mr. Trotter, I have sustained Mr. Sommerall's objections because he is correct under the law. Stop stepping over the line, and I'm sure he will stop objecting."

His face flushed with anger, Trotter turned back to his witness. "When Smith Delaney returned from the war, was he involved in an incident at the pool hall at Beech Creek?"

"Sure was."

"And, I believe firearms were involved in that incident. Is that right?"

The sheriff hesitated, "Well, yes, that's true. Smith said he'd been cheated at cards and wanted his money back. Shot the place up purty good."

"Didn't he shoot at you?"

"When?"

"Sheriff, did the defendant shoot at you, or not?"

"Not at the pool hall."

The prosecutor took a deep breath, "All right. Then, in still *another* incident he shot you."

"Nah. Shot around me when I was lookin' in his barn through a high window. I was up on a ladder outside and he was inside on the ground level."

"So he did shoot at you."

"Sorta, I reckon."

Trotter was getting aggravated. "Sheriff, he either shot at you or he didn't. Which is it?"

"He fired a six shooter, and I fell off the ladder. He didn't hit me."

"Fine. Now do I understand correctly that he deliberately fired a weapon in your direction?"

"I guess that's right."

"What exactly were you doing at the time — why were you looking in his barn?"

Sheriff Westerfield sighed and then recounted, "I'd heard tell he had moonshine in the loft. Him and Colt were s'posed to have a still back in their old mine and it was said they were storin' the whiskey up there in the barn. Leastwise that's what I heard."

"So you went to investigate?"

"Yes."

"And in an effort to keep you from seeing what was in the loft he shot you off the ladder?"

Fletch Sommerall once again called from the defense table, "Objection! The sheriff has already testified that he *fell* off the ladder."

288

Judge Curtis' mouth twitched at the corners. "Sustained, the jury will disregard that testimony."

"Now, Sheriff," Trotter asked, "would you say Smith Delaney has a bad temper?"

"Objection! Drawing a conclusion," said Sommerall.

"Your Honor..." said Trotter.

"Sustained!"

Trotter slapped his hand down on the rail that separated him from the sheriff. "Sir, in your opinion, the man who ambushed the mine managers would have been someone with an axe to grind. Is that right?"

The sheriff looked first to the defense attorney, then at the judge as if waiting for another objection. When none came he answered, "Yeah, he, or *they,* woulda had to feel real strong about the strike, I 'magine, to have gone so far as to do what they did."

"Thank you, Sheriff. No further questions."

Fletcher didn't even get up from his chair. "No questions at this time."

20

"**W**hat kind of defense is he runnin'?" asked Forrest, as he and Hattie paced the hall outside the courtroom. The court was in recess. Everyone was waiting to be called back inside.

"You mean he ain't askin' questions? How does sayin' 'no questions at this time' help Smith?" Hattie asked.

Forrest stretched his back as he leaned against the wall. "I don't know, Hattie. All I can think about right now is that they're gonna be callin' me next."

Carrie and Gene had been in the courtroom and had explained the proceedings to Hattie and Forrest when they came out for the recess. By order of the judge they couldn't discuss the actual testimony they'd heard, but they could tell how they thought Sommerall and Trotter were doing. They'd told about Sommerall's apparent refusal to question the witnesses and that he'd done a lot of objecting, but they couldn't explain his conduct.

Hattie wandered to the end of the hall and then back again. "Did you see Smith? Does he look like he's been eatin' right? You think he's okay?"

Carrie stood next to the courtroom door watching for the signal that they were to go back in. "Honey, he looks tired, but I'm sure he's fine. This is hard on us, but think how much harder it must be on him. It's got to be awful wearin' on him."

"I know that. It's wrong! Here we are in a murder trial on the word of that Sawyer. Surely the jury will see through him. I mean, how can they think Smith did it? It doesn't even make sense."

"Hattie, when I go up there I'll try to say that. Somehow we got to make 'em see it wasn't him," said Forrest.

"I know you will, Forrest. I'm just worried is all."

Carrie moved away from the courtroom door, "The bailiff's comin'. I think they're ready."

She and Gene returned to their seats in the oak-lined courtroom as Hattie and Forrest went back to the witness room to wait. Smith was brought back into the courtroom in shackles from the holding cell where he'd been waiting. The judge came in from his chambers, and they were all seated.

Trotter called Forrest to the stand.

"Now, Mr. Stoneworth, you told Mahlon Hennings about a conversation you and your brothers had on Christmas Eve with Mr. Delaney. Would you tell us about that conversation?"

Forrest looked at his feet. "We talked about a lot of stuff that day. It was a family gatherin'."

"The part I'm interested in was Mr. Delaney's theory about what it would take to end the strike. He told you what he thought. What exactly did he say about it?"

"He said it was a bad situation that didn't look like there was an end in sight."

"And ... ?"

Forrest's face flushed a deep red, "He said ... he said it was gonna take somethin' big to end the strike," he mumbled.

"Excuse me, Mr. Stoneworth, I don't think I heard you clearly. Please repeat what you just said."

"He said it was gonna take somethin' big to end the strike," Forrest repeated while staring at the tips of his shoes.

"Something big? Like what did he have in mind?"

Forrest looked up at the prosecutor. "He didn't really say. He just said both sides was dug in and didn't look to budge. That somethin' big was gonna have to happen to break the stalemate."

"He didn't offer any suggestions?"

292

"No sir, he was just tryin' to get us to quit arguin' about it."

"No further questions."

"But he ... "

"No further questions, Mr. Stoneworth."

"But ... "

"That's all Mr. Stoneworth." Judge Curtis spoke from the bench. "Counselor, do you wish to question this witness?"

"Not at this time, Your Honor."

"I call Hattie Stoneworth Crowe."

Hattie, looking frightened and pale, came through the door of the witness room and walked to the bench. Her eyes gazed tenderly at Smith. She had not been allowed to see him in the six weeks since his arrest.

Mr. Trotter stepped between Hattie and Smith so that he blocked Smith from her sight. "Mrs. Crowe, I know this must be hard on you. You've been through a lot in the last year. I believe you were widowed last spring. Is that right?"

"Yes, sir, in April."

"You have my sincere condolences. Seems you found comfort in the arms of another man. Is that right?"

"Objection! Irrelevant. Where is the relevance?" Sommerall looked furious.

Judge Curtis leaned forward on the bench, his chin cupped in one hand, a finger held to his lips. He didn't answer for a moment, then turned to the prosecutor, "Go ahead, Mr. Trotter, but this testimony better be relevant, or it will be stricken."

Trotter looked expectantly at Hattie. She blushed and stammered, "No! I mean, yes, sir, I am engaged to be married, but ... "

"But what? Are you saying you didn't find comfort with your *new* relationship?"

"Of course I find comfort, but not like you make it sound."

"How long were you a widow before Mr. Delaney came to live at your place?"

"About three months. I hired him in late July, I think."

"You hired him. How long had you known him when you hired him?"

"I'd just met him that day."

"Are you telling this court that you hired a man that you knew nothing about on the very day you met him?" Trotter looked incredulous.

"Well, yes, I guess I did."

"You didn't know anything about him, did you?"

Hattie shook her head, "I didn't know much about him. But my brother, Forrest, vouched for him as a hard worker. One of my sisters went to school with him and said she'd always liked him, and he's related to a friend of ours, Annie Radburn, so I thought it would be all right."

"Sounds like you made an error in judgement, doesn't it?" Trotter shook his head.

"No, I don't think so."

"Apparently, Mrs. Crowe, you don't think much at all."

"Objection. Mr. Trotter is badgering the witness!"

"Sustained."

"I'll rephrase. Mrs. Crowe, how much thought did you put into your decision to hire Mr. Delaney?"

Hattie hesitated for a moment, "Not a lot, I reckon. I needed the help, and he seemed like a good man."

"Not a lot. In fact Mrs. Crowe, I believe you went against older and wiser counsel not to hire Mr. Delaney. Isn't that right?"

"Not that I recall."

"Your mother-in-law, Mrs. Eunice Crowe, gave a deposition to this court that says she urged you, in fact begged you, not to hire Mr. Delaney. Isn't that true?"

"Well yes, but ... "

Trotter waved a sheaf of papers. "She states and I quote, 'I begged Hattie to reconsider her decision. She expelled me from

294

her home in a fit of temper and has not allowed me to see my grandchildren since the night of our confrontation.'"

What in the world? Eunice doesn't talk like that! thought Hattie before she said "Mr.Trotter, that's not exactly what happened. Yes, she objected to my hiring Smith, but ... "

"Didn't you eject her from your home under threat of death?"

Hattie was mortified. She'd never wanted anyone to hear about that night. "I did ask her to leave, but ... "

Again, Trotter interrupted, "Now you have two little children, is that right?"

"Yes, sir. Dulcie and Jackie."

"And you haven't let Mrs. Crowe see her grandchildren, your two little children, since that night. Isn't that right? We can call Mrs. Crowe if we need to."

"I haven't allowed her to see the children because ... "

"All right. Now ... "

"Wait, you're not lettin' me finish. The reason ... "

"You answered the question, Mrs. Crowe. Now, on the afternoon of the ambush, where was Mr. Delaney?"

"He was at Mud River." Hattie twisted her handkerchief in her damp hands.

"How do you know that?"

"Because he told me."

"That's what he told you. And you *believed* him?"

"Yes, I did."

"Tell me, Mrs. Crowe, didn't the thought ever cross your mind that you didn't know this man very well and that just 'cause he *said* he was at Mud River doesn't mean he wasn't somewhere else at the time?"

"No sir! He said he was at Mud River, and that's where he was."

"Mrs. Crowe, we've established that this has been an emotional year for you. Is that right?"

Trotter's fast-paced switches of direction had Hattie's head spinning. "I s'pose it has."

"You've been through an awful lot. We talked about that right?"

"Yes."

"Would you say that in the emotional state you've been in your judgement has always been good?"

Hattie thought of her anger at Eunice and the threat to shoot her with the shotgun. She thought of her impulsive invitation to the Bidewell family and wading into Smith's fight with Sawyer.

"I ... I reckon my emotions have gotten out of hand a few times, but ... "

"So your judgement has been rather questionable hasn't it?"

"I wouldn't say questionable, but ... "

"You come from a highly respected family. Isn't that right?"

"I'd like to think so."

"They were probably concerned about your deepening romantic relationship with someone like Mr. Delaney. Would you say that?"

Carrie's words on Christmas Eve floated through Hattie's memory. "Well, they were a little concerned."

"Yet, in your emotional state, you flouted their concerns, the concerns of your older brothers and sisters, and promised yourself to Mr. Delaney."

"Well, yes, but ... "

"You regret that now, don't you?" He took a step away from Hattie. He no longer obstructed her view of Smith Delaney.

Hattie looked at Smith's sweet face. It was furrowed with heartbreak for the ordeal she was going through. All she saw was pain.

"No, I don't." Tears slid down her cheeks.

"Then why are your crying?"

"I ... I'm ... "

"I would submit, Mrs. Crowe, that you are crying because you realize you have made a monumental error in judgement — one that you regret with all your heart at this moment."

"No! You're wrong! I ... "

"No further questions, Your Honor. This witness is obviously in an emotional state that makes it impossible to make sense of her answers."

"No questions at this time," said Sommerall.

"You may step down, Mrs. Crowe," Judge Curtis said.

"I'm sorry, Smith. It's not true." Hattie reached one hand out toward him as Mr. Trotter escorted her back to the gate that led to the gallery. She sobbed into her handkerchief as she slid into the seat next to Carrie.

"The Commonwealth of Kentucky calls Smith Delaney."

Smith rose from his chair and stood to be sworn in.

"Now, Mr. Delaney, you've been a citizen of Muhlenberg County your whole life. Is that right?"

"Yes, sir."

"You know these folks and this county pretty well, don't you?"

"I reckon I do."

"So, if you were planning an ambush you'd have a pretty good idea of where the best place to accomplish it would be. Right?"

"If I thought about it, I reckon so."

"You would have looked around and seen a place where you could hide and take your aim without being seen. You'd choose one with a good way to get out when you were done. Right?"

"Yeah."

"Uh huh. And that's exactly what you did isn't it."

"No, sir. It ain't."

"Objection, Your Honor. It ain't been established that Smith's the shooter. Mr. Trotter's trying to introduce facts that ain't in evidence." Sommerall stood at the defense table.

"Sustained."

"I withdraw the question." Trotter paced back and forth in front of Smith. "Where were you on the afternoon of the ambush?"

"I was out in the woods at Mud River." Smith leaned forward with his hands on the rail in front of him.

"Anybody see you or talk to you that can corroborate that?"

"Does that mean that could say they saw me?"

"Yes."

"No, sir. I was by myself."

"You didn't run into anyone the whole afternoon?"

"No, sir. But about five o'clock I ran up to Old Hebron. I saw my grandmother and waved at my nephew on my way by."

"So the only people who saw you were members of your family. You think they might lie for you?"

"Objection! He can't testify to what someone else might or might not do!"

"Sustained. Mr. Trotter, you know better than that."

"I apologize, Your Honor." Trotter didn't look a bit sorry as he turned back to Smith. "You said you were up at Old Hebron around five o'clock. Now the ambush took place around 3:30 in the afternoon. You could have committed the murders and had plenty of time to get up there, right?"

"*If* I was the sniper, which I ain't, I could have made it up to Old Hebron by 5:00. But ... "

"All right. Now you said your family saw you. I'm sure you know we can call them to testify to your whereabouts. Right?"

"Reckon you can if you want to, but they wouldn't lie for me, if that's what you was implyin' earlier."

"I wasn't trying to imply anything. I'm just trying to establish your whereabouts on the afternoon in question. But since you brought it up, how do you feel about lying?"

"I think it's wrong. I don't believe it's necessary to lie. The truth makes more sense."

"So you don't lie?"

"No, sir!"

"Now, Mr. Delaney, how old were you when you joined the army?"

"Objection. What possible relevance does that have to this case?" Fletcher Sommerall, red faced, was on his feet again. He was angry with the way Trotter had decimated Hattie and the way he was trying to do the same to Smith.

"Your Honor, Mr. Delaney has just testified to his strong belief in honesty. I'm trying to establish he hasn't always held himself to that standard."

Judge Curtis appeared to think about that a moment and then stated, "Overruled, you may answer the question."

"I was sixteen, but ... "

"Sixteen? I thought you had to be eighteen to go into the military. How was it you were able to get in at sixteen?"

"I lied about my age," Smith muttered.

"I beg your pardon? You what?"

"I lied about my age. It was ... "

"You lied. I see. All right then. So you haven't always been as careful about telling the truth as you claim to be now. Is that right?"

"They needed men in the army. I wanted to serve my country."

"You don't think the military people in Washington D.C. have good reasons for their age requirements?"

"Yes, I'm sure they do."

"But you know more than they do so you figured you'd lie to circumvent their rules."

"No, sir!"

"You didn't lie?"

"Yes I did, but ... "

"All right, so we've established that you *are* a liar."

"Now wait just a minute, I ain't a liar." Smith's was breathing fast. The muscles in his jaw flexed as he moved it to the right, then to the left. There was fire in his eyes.

Hattie held her breath. *Don't lose your temper, Honey. That's what he wants!*

"What's the matter, Mr. Delaney? You getting angry?"

"Yeah, you got my dander up a bit. You ain't got no right to stand there callin' me a liar!"

"Well, now." Trotter smirked and looked at the jury. "The way I see it, you called yourself a liar. You admitted you lied about your age to get into the army."

"You're makin' it sound like I make it a practice to lie. That ain't true."

"I guess we'll never know, will we?"

"Now just a minute!"

"Mr. Delaney, that well-known temper of yours is showing. Is that what happened the day of the ambush? You got to thinking about the strike, and the more you thought about it the angrier you got. The time had come for 'something big' to happen. You took your rifle and went for a drive, looking for a good place to set up for the killings. Isn't that right?"

"No, it ain't. I never killed no one. It wasn't like that. You ain't listenin'."

"Oh, my! That's another lie isn't it?" Mr. Trotter made tsking noises with his tongue, as though deeply regretting what he was hearing.

"Wha...? *What* was another lie?"

"You were in the Big War, weren't you?"

"Yes, sir. I served in France."

"Uh huh. And in the course of your time in France you *did* kill people didn't you?"

"Maybe. I don't know. Probably did. But that's not what I was talkin' about. You're twistin' my words!"

"Your words. That's exactly right, your words. You said you don't lie. But you do. You lied to get into the military. You said 'I never killed no one' but you did. We know that for a fact."

"You ain't listenin' to the whole ..."

"Well, why would I listen to anything you say? You are a self-confessed liar. Nothing you say would have much veracity, now would it?"

"What's that mean?"

"It means, Mr. Delaney," Trotter continued, "that you have established for this court, and this jury of your peers, that you cannot be trusted to answer any question truthfully."

Smith slumped back in the chair.

Trotter walked over to the evidence table and reached into a paper bag. He pulled out Smith's gray cap. Smith looked startled and straightened up.

"Mr. Delaney, I want you to see something that was found at the scene of the ambush. I would remind you, sir, you are still under oath. Have you ever seen this cap before?"

Hattie gasped. *Where had it come from? It's Dulcie's, the one Smith traded her for the whistle.*

"Yes, sir. It's an old cap of mine."

"That's right. It is. It has your initials on the sweatband. Did you write them there?"

"I did."

"I would like for you to think carefully and tell me how *your* cap got to the woods at Ebenezer on the very day the mine managers were brutally shot and killed in cold blood, if it wasn't on your head, and *if you were at Mud River,* as you claim."

"I ... I don't know." Smith wearily rubbed his hands over his face.

"No further questions."

Hattie cried quietly in her seat. Mr. Trotter was destroying them.

Mr. Sommerall rose. "No questions at this time, Your Honor."

21

"Hattie, Honey, please stop cryin'. You ain't helpin' Smith bein' so upset," said Carrie. The family sat at a corner table at Cotton's Corner trying to eat lunch before going back for the afternoon session. Everything tasted like sawdust, and no one was eating, but they had to try. Carrie continued, "Chloe's gonna be here any minute with Dulcie. You don't want her to see you like this. You got to stop, Honey." Carrie had her arm around Hattie's shoulders.

"I c ... can't. I'm tryin'. It's just so ... they're gonna send him to the 'lectric chair!" Hattie covered her face with her hands. Sob after sob racked her body. Carrie had never seen her so upset. It shook her to the core.

"Honey, they are not gonna send him to the 'lectric chair. Where's your faith? You think God's gonna walk away from you? He ain't never yet! Why would He today?"

"Oh, Carrie, don't you understand? This ain't about God! It's about that lyin' snake, Sawyer, and Tom Trotter standin' up there makin' us all out to be ignorant half-wits. I ... I can't stand it. I just can't! How'd they get Smith's cap? It just doesn't make a lick of sense."

Carrie lifted Hattie's face and spoke quietly, "I don't know. But Smith didn't do it, and we've got to prove it, somehow. Think Hattie. When was the last time you saw that cap?"

"I don't know!" Hattie wailed, "Dulcie was always wearin' it around or puttin' it on the baby or her doll. I can't remember."

Forrest was desperate to help. He knew Smith was in big trouble. "Hattie, Carrie's right. Chloe's gonna be here with

Dulcie anytime now. You don't want her to see you carryin' on, right? This is supposed to be a special treat for her, getting' to come to a restaurant. You got to calm down. Now, think about that cap. Did Dulcie have it at Christmas?"

Hattie sniffed, took a handkerchief from her purse, and blew her nose. "I think so. Yes. I'm sure she did. I remember her puttin' it on and paradin' around the day we went up to Eunice's."

"Okay. That was Christmas Day, right?"

"Yes."

"Well, what about since then?"

"Um ... let me think. She had it ... I can't remember. What's the matter with me? I don't guess I've seen it since the day of the ambush."

Forrest leaned toward her. "Did you see it that day? If you did, then they could have planted it sometime after the ambush!"

"I don't think so, Forrest," Gene answered. "They said they found it at the scene *on the day* of the ambush."

"Well, somebody put it there! There's a missin' piece of the puzzle, I just know there is. But what — and where is it?"

Hattie was calmer now. "Let's think! Where, who, and why? Why would anyone want to frame Smith?" Again she struggled to remember the last time she saw Smith's cap.

"I reckon those are the questions we got to answer, some-how," said Carrie.

Gene took a drink of his coffee. "I asked Sommerall what he thinks he's doin' not questionin' any of the witnesses. All he'd say was 'all in good time.' I reckon we can appeal a conviction if he don't question 'em. Don't you, Forrest?"

"I don't know. I reckon." The big man shook his head.

"Colt lit out of the courtroom like a scalded cat when they sent us out for the lunch recess. I was gonna ask him to come eat with us, but he was in a state."

Hattie raised her head. "Do you blame him, Gene? That's his brother they're makin' out to be a murderer." Tears filled her eyes again. "It's so unfair."

"Hattie, I know you don't want to hear this ... "

"Then don't say it, Forrest. If you're gonna say maybe he done it, you just keep your mouth shut!"

"Hattie ... "

"Forrest, that's enough." Gene clamped one hand down hard on Forrest's shoulder. "We agreed to stand by Smith as a family and that's what were gonna do. You understand?"

"Yeah, Gene, I understand." Forrest kicked at a paper straw on the floor of the restaurant.

"Now here comes Dulcie. Y'all smile. Remember, she thinks we're all just having us a treat at Cotton's Corner." Carrie turned her brightest smile toward the happy little girl.

Dulcie skipped across the bare hardwood floor. "Hi Mama! Whatcha been doin? I been playin' wif Aunt Chloe. She's fun! We maked paperdolls."

"You did! That's wonderful!" Hattie's pasted-on smile might have fooled some, but not the family.

"Can I have ice cream?"

"I guess so. What kind do you want?"

"The brown kind."

"Okay."

The grown ups all tried to be happy for the little girl's sake. They'd kept Dulcie completely ignorant of Smith's situation. She didn't know that he was literally fighting for his life in the big courthouse across the street.

It was almost time for the noon recess to be over when Sawyer sauntered in. He looked like he was feeling pretty good about himself; as though the trial had gone just the way he'd planned. There wouldn't be any more ignorant miners messing with him.

Chloe was helping Dulcie into her jacket when Dulcie spotted Sawyer. "Mama!"

"Just a minute Dulcie, I'm speakin' to Aunt Carrie."

"But Mama ... "

"Dulcie, you're interruptin'! Wait please."

"B ... but Mama ... "

"Chloe, take her out to the car!" Hattie frowned at her little girl. "Dulcie, we'll talk about this tonight."

"But it's him!" She cried, tears rolling down her little face. "It's that mean man."

Hattie looked to where Dulcie pointed. It was Sawyer, shoveling chicken-fried steak into his mouth, seemingly oblivious to being watched.

"What did you say? Why did you say he's a mean man, Honey?" Dulcie had Hattie's attention now.

"Don't you 'member? He's da mean man dat took my cap!" Dulcie was sobbing now. She didn't know if she was in trouble or not, but Mama's face looked fierce.

Hattie snatched Dulcie out of Chloe's arms and sat down with her back to Sawyer. "Dulcie, tell Mama about that. When did he take Smith's, I mean, your cap?"

"Didn't you see him?"

"No. When was it, Honey?"

They all leaned forward in their chairs to listen as Dulcie recounted what had happened the morning of the ambush.

"Member? He come in da big car. I was swingin' my baby, and da car came?"

"Yes, I remember."

"You talked to him. Den he kicked da cap. My dolly dwopped it when I wunned up da dwive. And dat mean man tooked it. Didn't you see him?"

"No, I didn't."

"You didn't?" she asked again.

"No, Honey, I would never have let him take your cap."

"Weally? I'm glad. I was afwaid Smiff would be mad at me for losin' it. Can I go tell dat man to give it back?"

306

"No, Honey. You're gonna have to tell someone else about it, though. Think you can do that?"

"Uh huh. But how come I can't tell him. He did da takin'."

"I know that now, but we need to tell a man called a judge."

"Hattie, you can't put her on the stand! She's just a baby." Forrest's face registered shock.

"I have to. Don't you see? She's all that's standin' between Smith and ..." Hattie stopped. She wouldn't say it in front of Dulcie.

Forrest nodded slowly, then responded, "Let's get over there and see if we can find Sommerall."

Sommerall grinned like a Cheshire cat. "Well now, that is an interestin' turn. I figgered somebody had to have taken it, but looks like it was the Commonwealth's star witness. Should make this afternoon all the more excitin'."

He instructed Chloe to wait in the hall with Dulcie while the rest of the family went into the courtroom.

Mr. Trotter had rested his case before lunch. It was Sommerall's turn.

"The defense calls Dulcie Crowe."

Dulcie skipped down the aisle to the delight of the watchers.

Tom Trotter rose from his seat. "Your Honor, I object to this witness on the grounds that she was not on the witness list!" The prosecutor was clearly furious.

Judge Curtis called both lawyers to the bench for a whispered conference.

"Your Honor," Sommerall said, "I realize that the little gal wasn't on the list, but evidence came to light over the lunch recess that makes it necessary to call her."

"What possible evidence can a child of minimal age give to a trial of this magnitude?" Trotter said with a sneer. "I request that this witness be disallowed."

Sommerall interjected, "Your Honor, this witness may be the key to Smith Delaney's defense. You can't disallow her. She has some very important evidence to offer. You understand children's testimony, Your Honor. I believe you'll find Dulcie qualified."

Judge Curtis looked doubtful but after a moment he said, "Mr. Sommerall, I'll allow the witness, but I will not have my courtroom turned into a playroom. There had better be just cause for her presence."

"Yes, Your Honor. There is. Thank you, sir."

Fletch Sommerall took the four-year-old by the hand and walked her to the witness stand. He lifted her up on the chair. "Dulcie, do you know the difference between the truth and a lie?"

"Uh huh."

"Can you tell me what the difference is?"

"A wie didn't weally happen. It's wike pwetend. But it's on purpose. The trufe is what did happen." Dulcie's eyes got big. "Jesus don't wike a wie!"

"That's right, He sure don't. That's very good. Now, I'm going to ask you some questions and you are gonna tell me the truth, right?"

"'Kay."

The lawyer stepped back and nodded to the court clerk. The clerk swore Dulcie in and Fletch Sommerall began asking simple questions.

"How old are you, Dulcie?"

"I'm dis many," she held up four dimpled fingers.

"Let the record show that Miss Crowe is four years old. Who lives at your house, Dulcie?"

"Mama and Jackie and Aunt Zonie. Smiff lives in da smokehouse, but he comes down to play wif me."

"He does?"

"Uh huh." Dulcie swung her little legs and rolled up the hem of her skirt.

"Has Smith ever given you any presents?"

"Yup. He gived me pwesents for Chwistmas."

"He did?"

"Uh huh."

"Didn't he give you a cap?"

"Noooooo!"

"B... but I thought you told me a little while ago he gave you his cap."

"Noooooo! We swapped." Dulcie giggled at Sommerall.

Sommerall smiled, relief obvious on his face. "Oh, I see. What did you swap for it?"

"A whisthle."

"Why do you think Smith wanted that whistle?"

"He said I was a doll in dat cap." Dulcie blinked up at the judge. "So he swapped me for it."

"Where is that cap now?"

"It's gone ..." Her little lip trembled. "It was tooked by da vewy bad man with da wed face."

"Which bad man, Honey?"

"Da one dat asted d'rections from Mama."

"Tell me about that."

"'Kay. He was in a big black car. Mama said dey tooked a turn and dey have to go back."

"They took a wrong turn and needed to turn around and go back?"

"Uh huh. He said he was 'portent and had bizness to do with dem other mens. Mama said he better go do it den. His face got all wed and he kicked my cap. Den he tooked it!" She added breathlessly.

"Did your Mama see him take the cap?"

"Thought so. But she didn't. I'm glad. I din't tink it was nice for her to let him take my cap. It was mine. Smiff swapped me for it." In the age-old way of small children, Dulcie repeated herself.

"Your Honor," Trotter looked and sounded bored by the entire proceeding. "This is an obvious attempt on the part of the defense to bring in a witness to explain that cap away, but really, she's four years old! How much can we be expected to believe?"

Judge Curtis spoke from the bench, "Mr. Trotter. I have found my four-year-old granddaughter to be quite believable. I see no reason to disbelieve this one. Overruled."

Trotter sat back down, a look of disgust covering his face.

"Dulcie, do you see that man with the red face in this room right now?"

Dulcie looked around. She craned her neck to see over the crowd and then stood on her chair and looked. There in the back trying to make himself invisible sat red-faced Jeb Sawyer.

"He's right over dere. See him?" Dulcie pointed.

"Indeed I do, Dulcie. Indeed I do. No further questions."

"Do you have questions for this witness, Mr. Trotter?" asked the judge.

Trotter hesitated. He couldn't make mincemeat of a little girl without creating hostility in the jury. He'd have to prove she wasn't a reliable witness during his closing argument.

"No, Your Honor. I have no questions." He answered as though Dulcie were totally unimportant.

"You may step down."

Dulcie slid to the edge of her chair and hopped down. She grinned as she skipped past Smith and curled one little hand into a shy wave as she passed.

"The defense recalls Jebidiah Sawyer."

Sawyer came forward slowly. He didn't seem as enthusiastic about testifying as he had been earlier when he'd been testifying for the prosecution.

"Mr. Sawyer, we ain't met before. I'm Fletcher Sommerall. I need to ask you a few questions. I b'lieve you're a mine foreman and wear the title of Assistant Manager at Coaltown Mine. Is that right?"

310

"Yes, sir." Sawyer's arms were crossed defensively across his chest.

"Man! That must be a tough job. I 'spect things have been mighty hard up there lately with the strike and all. You, being boss, prob'ly had it harder'n most. Havin' to deal with all those decisions about whether to settle or whether to keep on fightin' the strike."

"If it'd been up to me, wouldn't have been no settlin'," Sawyer stated belligerently.

"Course not. That'd be givin' in, wouldn't it."

"To my way of thinkin'."

"Now, you said you were boss of Smith Delaney. Was he one of them strikers?"

"No, he weren't minin' when they called the strike."

"He wasn't? He wasn't one of them walkin' the line and callin for better conditions and higher wages?"

"Well, no. Not when they called the strike he weren't. He was doin' somethin' else then."

"Huh!" Sommerall appeared to be confused. "So then why do you think he wanted to kill those two men and put your life in danger?"

"Objection! Mr. Sawyer's in no position to discuss Delaney's state of mind."

"Sustained. Mr. Sommerall, you cannot ask him what Mr. Delaney's thinking was."

"Yes, sir, Your Honor. I withdraw the question." Fletch rubbed his chin. "Mr. Sawyer, Smith Delaney hadn't been workin' at the mine for how long?"

"Lemme think. 'Bout six months, I reckon."

"So, he hadn't been around there?"

"Oh, he was up there all right. I seen him sneakin' around one night at Coaltown. He was gettin' in his truck. No tellin' what he was up to."

"You saw him at Coaltown?"

"Sure did."

"Y'all speak, or did you see him from a distance?"

"We spoke. He attacked me. Didn't have no good reason for it. Just jumped me. Jumped me from behind."

"Wait a minute. Didn't you just say you saw him sneakin' around?"

Sawyer realized his mistake and tried to cover it. "Well, yeah, but that was earlier. He jumped me later, when I was walkin' back down the road."

"That's when he jumped you from behind?"

"That's right."

"Uh huh. Now, how much do you weigh? Approximately."

"Around two hundred and sixty pounds, I reckon."

"Two hundred and sixty pounds. Okay, and how much do you reckon Smith Delaney weighs?"

"Not much!" Sawyer sneered. "He ain't much of a man if you ask me."

"Well, now, I heard he was enough of a man to whip your rear end into the ground that night. I understand you got yourself a pretty good beatin'."

Sawyer flushed a deeper crimson than he already was. "He ... he cheated. He had brass knucks!"

"He did not! That's a lie!" Hattie cried from her seat in the gallery.

The courtroom erupted.

"Order! Order in the court. There'll be no more outbursts in this courtroom or I'll clear y'all outa here!" Judge Curtis slammed his gavel down.

Sommerall paced in front of the witness stand. "Mr. Sawyer, there seems to be some question about what happened that night. Maybe we'll come back to that later. Now you've testified that you saw Mr. Delaney running from the clearing at the edge of the woods back into those woods. Is that right?"

"Yeah."

Fletch Sommerall walked away from Sawyer and glanced down at the pad of paper on the defense table. He paused a moment, then looked back at the witness. "So you're sayin' that the shooter shot up the car, came out of the woods, looked around and then run back into the woods. Is that right?"

"No, I ain't sayin' that."

"Did you see him standin' there shootin' at you?"

"No."

"Where was he when the shootin' happened?"

"In ... in the trees, I reckon."

"And then?"

"And then ... I don't know. It all happened real fast. I can't remember every detail." Sweat beaded Sawyer's forehead and darkened the armpits of his suit. He yanked at his collar.

"But you remember it was Smith Delaney."

"I do remember that." Sawyer nodded vigorously.

"Mr. Sawyer, you've testified that Mr. Delaney ran from the scene. Those were your words right?"

"That's right."

"Sir, I would propose that if you saw anyone running from the scene, and that's questionable, it couldn't have been Smith Delaney."

"Was too. I'm tellin' you I seen him." Sawyer leaned forward and shook his fat finger at the defense attorney. "Seen 'im with my own two eyes!"

"No, sir! You did not. You are aware, aren't you, that Smith Delaney's leg was crushed when he threw himself in the way of a falling timber in Coaltown Mine to save the lives of Eldon and Ben Stoneworth and those other men after the explosion?"

"Well, yeah, I guess so." Sawyer squirmed on his chair, shifting his eyes away from the lawyer.

"He cannot run. Hear me! *He cannot run.* ... He will *never* be able to run again. He walks with a pronounced limp. Yet you sit there and tell us you saw him run, saw him with your own two eyes! Would you now like to clarify your statement about the man you saw running into the woods at the ambush?"

"Wha… No… I just forgot to say it. He… He looked like he was running. I was too scared …um, …uh, bothered, to think right. Yeah, that's right, he was limpin'," Sawyer stammered.

"Sir, you were asked by the prosecutor if the man you saw had any distinguishing characteristics. You mentioned auburn hair. You did not mention a limp. Now, you conveniently re-member one?"

"Well, yeah. It all happened real fast. I just forgot," he re-peated.

"I see. All right. Let's move on to the subject of the cap. Did you stop at Hattie Crowe's house for directions on the morning of the ambush?"

"I don't recollect." Sawyer shifted his position on the hard wooden witness chair and looked at his feet.

"You don't? Well, that's interesting. So when I call Hattie Crowe back to the stand and she remembers … "

"Oh yeah, that's right, I guess we did stop down there."

"Do you recall the little girl?"

"Not really."

"Is that a yes or a no?"

"There was a kid playin' by the road. I reckon it coulda been her," Sawyer answered in a mumble.

"And what was she doin'?"

"I don't know. What does any kid do? She was by a swing. When we pulled up she ran across the yard to her mama."

Sommerall smiled at the jury and raised his eyebrows. "Your memory seems to be getting better, Mr. Sawyer. What was the gist of the conversation you had with Miz Crowe?"

"We was lookin' for someone's house. It didn't seem to be where we thought it was so we asked her for directions."

"Whose house was that?"

"What? Oh, um … Snead Piper's place."

"And why were you lookin' for him?"

"Farnsworth and Baxter were all fired up to settle the strike. They figgered they needed Piper's approval of what they was doin'."

"You sound kinda disgusted about that."

"Well, I thought they should hold on a little longer. Let the men get a little hungrier. They'd've come crawlin' back afore long."

"So you were in a pretty foul mood when you got to Miz Crowe's. Is that right?"

"I wasn't real happy, I reckon." Sweat glistened on Sawyer's forehead and ran down his neck. He mopped at it with a not-too-clean handkerchief he yanked from the back pocket of his trousers.

"So you saw the cap on the ground, and out of frustration, you kicked it. Then you took it."

"No, I didn't! I mighta kicked it, but I didn't take it. That's a lie."

Sommerall's lanky frame bent down over the rail until he pinned Sawyer's eyes with his own. "No sir, I don't think that's a lie. I think *you're* the liar and when this trial is over and Smith Delaney's been set free, I'm gonna press for perjury charges against you."

"Objection! The defense is intimidating the witness!" Trotter was furious!

"Sustained! Mr. Sommerall you know better than that! Confine your remarks to questions." Judge Curtis glared at Fletcher Sommerall.

"No further questions, Your Honor. At this time I'd like to recall Sheriff Westerfield back to the stand."

Once again the sheriff was seated in the witness chair.

"Sheriff, I ain't gonna waste much time here. Let's get right down to brass tacks. Do *you* think Smith Delaney was the ambusher?"

"No sir, I don't believe he was."

"Why not?"

"If Smith done it, I b'lieve he'd a done it in three shots, and there wouldn't have been no witnesses left to testify."

"Why do you think that?"

"He's a crack shot. Mr. Trotter made a big deal outa him shootin' me off'n that ladder. Let me tell what happened. That barn, where I was lookin' in the window, is still standin'. If you go out there you'll see that he practically outlined my body with them six bullets in that revolver. If he'd been aimin' to kill me, there'd a been six bullets right under that window pane and I wouldn't be here today. I didn't have no papers, no right to be there, and he knowed it. I got stung by a few splinters and bruised when I hit the ground, but I'm here to tell about it. If it'd been Smith at that ambush, Jeb Sawyer wouldn't be a testifyin' today. If Smith had tried to hit someone, he'd adone it."

"No further questions. I call Snead Piper."

Judge Curtis instructed the bailiff to bring Mr. Piper from the witness room. Snead was a highly-trusted supervisor from Black Diamond Mine at Drakesboro. He was known as a tough, but honest man.

"Mr. Piper, on the afternoon of the ambush you had a visit from Mr. Farnsworth, Mr. Baxter, and Jeb Sawyer. Is that right?"

"Yes, sir, I did."

"Y'all talked about settlin' the strike?"

"We did."

"Mr. Sawyer wasn't happy about it, was he?"

"Objection. He can't testify to Sawyer's state of mind," called Mr. Trotter.

"Sustained."

"Mr. Piper, did Mr. Sawyer seem to agree with the decisions that were made that afternoon?"

"No, sir. He didn't."

"What did he want to do?"

316

"Jeb wanted to drag the strike on, starve 'em, 'til the miner's gave in. Then he wanted to refuse them their jobs back. Said we ort to hire all new miners from those out lookin' for work."

"But you disagreed?"

"We all did. It's hard to find and train a good, reliable, miner. I'm not willin' to give up good men if I don't have to. Farnsworth and Baxter agreed."

"What happened?"

"Sawyer bellyached about the miner's tryin' to drain us all dry and finally Farnsworth told him if he didn't shut up he'd put in a call to Mr. Morgan and Sawyer might find himself back down swingin' a pick."

"My! Strong words."

"Yes, sir. We was tired and tense. We'd all heard about as much from Jeb as we were willin' to listen to at that point."

"Now, at any time during that meeting did you see Mr. Sawyer with a cap?"

"Besides the one he was wearin', you mean?"

"That's right."

"Yeah. He was twistin' one around in his hands the whole time we were talkin'. Even shook it at Baxter at one point. Baxter told him to get the fool thing out of his face."

"Was that cap similar to this one?" Fletch Sommerall handed him Smith's cap.

"No, sir. It *was* this one."

Hattie gasped and clasped her hands in a thankful prayer.

"You sure about that?"

"Yes, sir. See this?" He pointed at the bill of the cap, then continued, "Sawyer kept shaking that cap at Baxter even after he told him to quit. Baxter got fed up and knocked it out of his hands. I picked it up. I seen the tear on the bill right there."

"Thank you, Mr. Piper. No further questions. I'd like to call John Blaine to the stand."

John Blaine, in old overalls, entered from the side door when called.

"Mr. Blaine, you were in the woods at Mud River on the day of the ambush, is that right?"

"Not 'xactly. Me and my brother Orville was ridin' up on the rise looking down on the woods about three-thirty that afternoon."

"What were y'all doin'?"

"Just out for the afternoon. We didn't have nothin' better to do."

"Did you see anyone?"

"Yeah."

"Who was it you saw, Mr. Blaine?"

"Seen Smith over there coming out of the woods."

"Was he alone?"

"Yup. All by hisself."

"How'd you know it was him?"

"We're distant kin. I'd a know'd him anywhere. Hadn't seen him since the mine explosion though. Said to Orville that it sure was a shame he come out with that limp."

"Thank you, Mr. Blaine. No further questions."

"Mr. Blaine, I got a question or two." Tom Trotter rose and walked toward the witness. "You say you and Smith are distant relations. Is that right?"

"That's right."

"You might have a vested interest in his being exonerated then, right?"

"Huh?"

Trotter rolled his eyes. "I mean, it might be important to you that none of your kin go to the electric chair."

"Well, I reckon that would be real sad, but not worth tellin' a lie about. I ain't holdin' to no lies, and neither does my brother."

"No further questions."

Sommerall called Orville Blaine. He testified that he, too, had seen Smith at Mud River that day.

The defense rested.

318

22

The crowd that filled the courtroom on the next morning to hear the closing arguments was restless from the waiting. People jostled each other for seats and pushed their way into already crowded rows of chairs. The press stood at the back, their press passes sticking out of their hats like plumes.

Hattie and the family with Colt, Virginia, and Zonie were in the first two rows behind the defense table. All the Stoneworths were there—even Eldon. He wasn't about to let Smith go to the electric chair without his showing the world he believed in him.

They had all gathered at Hattie's that morning to pray. Each had lifted their hearts and hands to heaven for strength for themselves, but mostly for Smith. They'd prayed God's wisdom on the jury and the judge and a special blessing for Fletcher Sommerall as he presented his closing argument. Now it was in God's hands.

The bailiff called, "All rise for the Honorable Judge Craig Curtis."

The judge, in his black robe, took the bench and they were seated.

"Mr. Trotter, is the Commonwealth ready for closing arguments?"

"We are, Your Honor."

"You may proceed."

Tom Trotter walked around the table and moved toward the jury. He paused, leaned slightly forward, took a deep breath and boomed out in a clear voice. "Guilty!" He stopped, said nothing for a moment and let the word ring. "Now that is a word with heavy meaning. It means that the defendant, Mr. Smith Delaney planned, devised, participated in, in fact conducted the murders of Mr. Farnsworth and Mr. Baxter on an afternoon in January in this year of 1934."

Trotter stopped, raised himself to his full height, slowly turned toward Smith and stared at him. Then he continued. "It means that he took it upon himself to do 'something big' to break the strike, just as he told his friends would have to happen. It means that he got in his truck that day, drove around until he found just the right place, and then he lay in waiting for the moment to come. He saw that car come over the rise and sighted it through his rifle. Then he proceeded to murder those two mine managers in cold blood. He tried to make it three." Trotter held up three fingers, paused, shook his head slowly as he looked at the floor. Then, brightening, he looked at the jury and proceeded. "By the grace of God and good fortune, he missed one. All I can figure is that he didn't see Mr. Sawyer, or he got scared and ran before he finished the job. We'll never know for sure, but we do know that Mr. Sawyer saw Smith Delaney leaving the scene. We also know that Delaney's cap was found in the woods where he came to survey the carnage he had created by his own hand.

"What does he say in his own defense? Nothing! 'I didn't do it. It weren't me.'

"We have motive. He's a recalcitrant miner who's been fired from every single mine in Muhlenberg County. He's got a grudge against management. Why? Because they don't put up with troublemakers. He can't hold a job. Why isn't he working in the mines now? I'll tell you why. They won't have him. He hasn't even tried to get a mining job for at least six months because he *knows* they don't want him. He's a problem, a hothead who solves his problems with his fists and his guns. We've heard direct testimony from the sheriff of this county regarding two separate incidents of violence involving his use of firearms. That fits his M.O., the modus operandi. That means the pattern of the way he conducts himself. The way he has consistently dealt with things before. We can't just pretend he hasn't acted with hair-trigger rashness when riled in the past."

Trotter turned his back on the jury, walked away and let these thoughts penetrate. Then, wheeling about to face them again, he continued, "Jebediah Sawyer was there in that car. He *saw* what happened. He survived to testify against Smith Delaney. Would he do that if it weren't true? Why would he? That would be perjury. He'd be setting himself up for felony charges. That is not something an intelligent man would do. Obviously, he's intelligent or he wouldn't be a foreman and assistant manager at Coaltown Mine. Were some of the details of his testimony a little off the mark? Perhaps, though that certainly wasn't proved to my satisfaction. Would you be able to remember every detail of an attack in which bullets were whizzing by your head? Where two friends died before your very eyes? Could you recall every detail with perfect clarity? I submit you could not!

"We have Delaney's cap at the scene of the crime. Members of the jury, I ask you, how did it get there if it was not on the head of Smith Delaney? Are we to believe the testimony of a four-year-old girl? Are we to let a murderer walk free in this county to terrorize our families on the word of a little girl, barely able to talk? We don't know for sure where she got her story, but let's look at this situation logically. That cute little girl, and I grant you she is cute, is the daughter of Delaney's intended bride." The prosecutor stepped closer to the jury, sofened his voice, and proceeded with a tone of sympathy. "Mrs. Crowe's a nice woman in a horrible situation. She's lost her husband. She's been manipulated by this man to cut off contact with her husband's family. She has no where else to turn, so she talks to her little girl. She says, 'Dulcie, remember that day? Remember, Honey, how that man took Smith's cap? Think real hard. Remember?' This woman is desperate to salvage whatever is left of her life. Did Delaney really give that little girl his cap? Why would he? Did Sawyer pick it up? Again, why would he? What are we supposed to believe? That in the moment of the greatest trauma of his life, after seeing the brutal slaying of his friends, Mr. Farnsworth and Mr. Baxter, Sawyer ran over and *planted* that cap in the woods just to implicate Mr. Delaney? I find that highly unbelievable."

The attorney picked up the cap, looked at it, and laid it back down. "Mr. Piper said that Mr. Sawyer had the cap with him when the managers came to see him that fateful afternoon. Now, I know that Snead Piper's a fine man. I believe him to be an honest man, *but* I also believe him to be wrong. There are a thousand caps, just like Smith Delaney's in this town and the surrounding communities. It could have been any cap that Sawyer held. But the cap that was found at the scene has Smith Delaney's initials written on the sweatband, by his own hand. Piper says that he recognized it. But, let's face it folks, they were in the middle of intense negotiations. I doubt that he was truly concentrating on the cap in Sawyer's hand. I believe *he believes* it was Smith Delaney's cap he saw, but I also believe he's mistaken in that assumption."

Tom Trotter let his gaze wander across the faces of the jury, deliberately meeting each one eye to eye. "Let's move on to the witnesses who *supposedly* corroborate Delaney's testimony as to his whereabouts on the afternoon of the murders. John and Orville Blaine waltzed in here at the last minute and gave him an alibi. Who are they? They're his cousins. Distant kin is how they put it. Who did Delaney say could vouch for his whereabouts? His old granny up at Old Hebron, the nephew he waved at as he drove by, and now these two cousins. That's a stretch. It's a long stretch. He has no credible witnesses to his whereabouts that day. None!

"As to Smith Delaney himself,"—Trotter paused, shifted his eyes to the left and upward at the ceiling, then looked

322

thoughtfully at the jury for a moment, then turned quickly and stared at the defendant—"Smith Delaney is a liar. He proved himself to be a liar on the stand. Not just once, but twice. In the first case he admitted to a lie after stating that he doesn't abide lying. Then, we caught him in one. Flat out caught him! He said he'd never killed anyone, but he fought in France and did kill. He admitted that."

Trotter steepled his fingers under his bottom lip and appeared to be thinking long and hard about what he was about to say. He took a deep breath and shook his head with what appeared to be deep regret. "Here's the bottom line. Smith Delaney is a murderer. He murdered those two men in cold blood. We have motive; we have his rifle; we have his cap at the scene of the crime. We have a witness that saw him there. We have the murderer. There is simply no plausible explanation to the contrary. I ask that you return the only logical verdict—a verdict of guilty."

Mr. Trotter turned and walked back to his table. He sat down. Looking satisfied and disinterested in anything else, he began to pack his things away as though the jury's verdict had already been decided.

Fletch Sommerall just sat in silence. He didn't move for a moment. Then, slowly he rose and walked toward the jury.

"My goodness! Once again, my learned colleague has outdone hisself. He just makes things out so clear and plain you can't help but understand what he's sayin', can you? Whew! He *is* a communicator. Too bad it's all tripe.

"What was it he said about Smith Delaney? Don't let him loose to terrorize our community? Somethin' like that, I think. Well now, we've heard from the sheriff that he doesn't believe Smith's the murderer. Why not? He wouldn't have done it the way the Ebenezer ambusher or ambushers did. He's a crack shot. He'd have taken those three men out with three simple shots. He wouldn't have wasted the time and the ammunition to shoot up that car like was done."

Sommerall walked toward the jury, stopped, and said, "Why is that important? I'll tell you why. Smith Delaney's a crippled man. He can't run. So, *if* he did the murders it would have been important to get the killin' done and get outa there *quick*. He wouldn't have been traipsin' through the woods to see how well he'd done it. He'd woulda stayed as close to his truck as he could get and still be able to aim clear. Could he do that from way back in the trees? Nope. He'd have to been in the edge of the trees to get a clear shot at that car. Then he'd have had to hustle back to his truck and put the pedal to the floor to get outa there. In his condition he wouldn't a had time to do the shootin', come runnin' across the clearin' to the edge of the road, look over the situation then run back to his truck.

"Sawyer *says* he saw Smith Delaney at the scene. Says he saw him *running* from the edge of the clearing. Says he recognized him by his hair and by his face 'cause he knew him. Gentlemen, Mr. Delaney's cap was found in the trees—not in the clearing. Did he drop it, leave it lying there to incriminate himself, go out to check the damage, see Sawyer, turn from that helpless, unarmed potential witness and run back into the woods?" Sommerall looked at the jury and shook his head.

"Now that's ridiculous! If he'd dropped it before the shooting, he'd have just picked it up and put it back on again. If we believe that version, then I would propose it happened something like this: the man Sawyer saw came out of the woods, looked around, saw Sawyer standing there, ran back into the woods and in his haste the cap came off. He left it and kept runnin'.

"Now if that's what happened, how did Sawyer see his auburn hair since he didn't drop his cap till he got to the woods? Like so many of us, Smith's hair is gray around the temples. So, if it was him, when he limped, let me repeat, when he limped, not ran, out of the woods, the cap would have covered the auburn hair on top and in the back. It seems mighty strange to me that a feller who can see *soooooo* well that from a distance he

324

could spot auburn hair stickin out from under a cap, yet didn't notice the awkward gait of a badly-crippled man tryin' to run. Mighty strange! Which would be easiest to see, a bit of auburn hair mixed with gray stickin' from under the cap of a runnin' man, or a badly crippled man strugglin' to run? Couldn't have happened the way Sawyer tells it. It doesn't make sense."

"Let's talk about Dulcie Crowe. Wasn't she a doll! That little girl sat there and told about the 'mean red-faced man'. Y'all saw Sawyer when I called him to the stand? Looked pretty mean to me. Was his face red? Like a tomato! Did she describe him to a tee? She sure did. Y'all saw her little lip tremble when she told about him takin' that cap. Unless she's the next Clara Bow, nobody could have coached her to do that. Not even to please her mama—who must be mighty proud of her." He looked at Hattie, and smiled.

"Y'all ever try to get a youngun like that to say somethin' she don't wanna say? Mine's like a mule. Won't say a word. Sings like a bird at home, won't sing for anybody else, though. Makes me look like a fool every time I try to get him to talk. I'll be braggin' on him and ask him to tell the coal man 'howdy,' and he sticks his finger in his mouth. Mute as a stump around strangers. Never fails." Sommerall shook his head.

"Mr. Trotter'd have you believe that little girl was told what to say. Y'all saw her. Did she seem natural to you? Did she give a little memorized speech? No sir! I asked questions, she gave answers, as clear as you please. She said, 'Jesus don't like a lie'. Yes, sirree, she did! That little girl's been taught the difference between what's right and what's wrong. I ain't gonna believe for a minute she sat up there and lied."

Fletcher Sommerall paused to catch his breath and then started again, "Jeb Sawyer. Now there's a man with a problem. He don't like miners. He don't like troublemakers. He don't like Smith Delaney, in particular. Why not? Ol' Jeb's a little man in a big body. You heard what Snead Piper said about him. Sawyer didn't want to settle the strike. He wanted the miners to get hungrier. Let their wives and children starve a little more. Ain't that nice? He'd been showed up by Smith Delaney. Smith busted him in the jaw up at Coaltown. Whipped him pretty good, from all accounts—and more than once. Sawyer wasn't gonna take that lyin' down. He was gonna get his revenge. What better way than to frame Smith for the murders? That'd take care of him once and for all."

Fletch walked away from the jury and gazed at Sawyer in the back row. "Now, I don't believe for a minute that Sawyer saw that cap on the ground at Hattie Crowe's house and thought about how it would be useful if there was ever a murder in Muhlenberg County. Up to that point nobody knew there was gonna be a killin'." He turned back to face the listening jurors. "But, he saw it lyin' there, and in his hatred for Smith Delaney, snatched it up. Dulcie told you she saw him do it! Later, when the opportunity presented itself, I think Sawyer, in his rage, in the heat of the moment, in sheer frustration and panic, threw that cap, or ran into the woods after whoever it was he says he saw runnin', and he dropped it. Once he'd done that, he couldn't take it back. It was done. One way or the other, the last person *we know for a fact* had that cap in his possession was Jebidiah Sawyer. That's what I think happened. It's the only way it could have happened.

"Why would he have done it, you ask? Sawyer's bitter. He's bitter about his lot in life. He's the brother-in-law of Coaltown Mine's owner, Mr. Morgan. That's got to stick in his craw. He ain't the one in charge. He's got a title but he can't call the shots. Don't too many folks listen to him 'cause he's ornery and thinks he's better'n most. But, the truth is, he ain't. He's just a bitter, twisted soul who's tryin' to be important. And mistreatin' miners is one way he goes about it.

"But Smith Delaney put him in his place. More'n once. That's gotta dig at him. I believe he sees Smith as all that's bad about miners. But Smith's got a good mind. He hasn't got a lotta book learnin', but he's smart. Don't you be fooled into thinkin'

326

otherwise. He organized that rescue after the explosion right down to what tools they needed and what needed to be done on the outside while he was workin' his way down inside. Sawyer can't think like that. He can do one thing at a time, and generally I don't think he does that very well. I believe that's why he hates Smith like he does. Besides that, Smith — a *miner* — is a hero! That must burn in Sawyer's gut." Sommerall paused and paced back and forth as though uncertain as to where to go next. Then he said, "Now let's switch gears."

Leaning down on the railing that separated him from the jury, he lowered his voice. "Any of you men ever took off for the woods on a nice day with your rifle? Maybe you just needed to get away from the little woman for a while? Sure you have. I can see by the looks on your faces you know what I'm talkin' about. Now, does that mean that y'all would commit murder? 'Course not. And the fact that Smith Delaney took off for a day doesn't prove he was up to mischief. And we have witnesses who told us where he was that fateful day." Sommerall straightened to his full height, walked toward the judge, then looked at the two witnesses from Mud River.

"Who are Orville and John Blaine? Two men some of y'all know. They're fine men. A little rough around the edges, I grant you, but good men. Ever known 'em to lie? Me neither. Are they related to Smith? Yes, they are. Does that mean their testimony about seein' Smith the day of the ambush isn't the truth? No, it does not."

Sommerall clasped his hands behind his back and looked out over the courtroom. "I have one last thing to say 'fore I'm done. Mr. Trotter talked about motive. He said Smith was a— what was that word?—recalcitrant miner. That's it. He said Smith was angry about bein' fired from so many jobs. Well now, that would make me angry, too, but not mad enough to kill anyone. Smith Delaney had not worked in the mines for six months when the strike started. Why, then, would he be the one to do 'somethin' big'? Why would he stick his neck out for the

327

strikers? He wasn't workin' with 'em. He wasn't part of 'em. He was workin' for the woman he loves. He was tryin' to establish a family. Why would he risk it all now? He wouldn't!" As he made the last statement, Sommerall firmly punched his right fist into his open left hand.

The attorney faced the jury and, said slowly as he swept his hands outward, palms up, "That's it folks. That's all there is to say. Mr. Delaney is an innocent man. We've proved it! Now it's up to you to come back—with a verdict— of *not* guilty. We'll wait for you."

Sommerall strolled back over to the defense table and folded his considerable length down onto the chair next to Smith, resting one hand on Smith's shoulder.

The judge instructed the jury on several points of law and then dismissed them. They filed out of the courtroom to the small side room where they would deliberate.

The bailiff led Smith away to wait in solitude in the holding cell.

Hattie and the family milled around, fear and worry pinning them together like patches on a quilt. It was all over. No more testimony. No more witnesses. No more time. Now just the waiting.

They stood quietly together in one corner of the hall. They each wondered what they could have done or said differently, that might have made a difference. So many 'what ifs'. They stood, as countless others have done, waiting to hear the verdict: guilty or not guilty, life or death.

23

Smith sat alone on the bench in his cell. He leaned forward, head in hands. He was cold—so very cold. He'd never felt this kind of fear before. He'd faced death in France. He'd fought like a madman when he'd seen fit to. But he'd never had to leave his fate in the hands of others before. The family had tried, Orville and John Blaine had been a welcome surprise. Snead Piper had defended him. Even Sheriff Westerfield, but Smith knew in his heart it probably wasn't enough. Even little Dulcie. Tears sprang to his eyes. How he loved that child!

Slowly, Smith sat up and reached for the paper and pencil he'd asked for on his way back to his cell. Carefully he wrote the words that syllable by syllable chipped at his heart.

> Dear Hattie,
>
> Please forgive me. No matter how this trial turns out, I can't marry you. You've overlooked my past, and I thank you for that, but I can't overlook it myself. The day after we met, I promised you I wouldn't bring you shame. But look what I've done. You deserve a man that you can be proud of—that your children can look up to and admire. I want you to be able to look at your man with all the pride in the world. And have him deserve it. I'm not that man. The love you offered me gave me hope that life could be different, but ...

The letter went on to explain how, in the weeks he'd been incarcerated, he'd come to the hardest decision of his life.

Shame, boiling, searing, shame poured through him. He'd never meant for any of this to happen. Hattie didn't deserve this. She deserved so much better—better than he could ever give her.

Even if he was found not guilty, he'd always know he'd caused her pain. He couldn't live with that. It was *his* past they'd paraded before the world. All those boyhood stunts. The fights, the shootouts, the 'shine. She deserved better. And he was going to give it to her. He didn't know what he'd been thinking when he'd asked her to be his wife. How could he have ever dreamed there could be a chance for them to make a life together?

He loved her. Loved her with all his heart. Loved her enough, in fact, to let her go. Let her find a man who wouldn't bring shame to stain her. If the jury, by some miracle, found him not guilty, let him go, he'd leave. He'd struggled so long and so hard with the decision. He wanted to stay. He wanted to marry Hattie. He wanted to be Dulcie's and Jackie's daddy, but, his daddy had always told him, 'Son, it ain't what you want. It's what you ort.' He'd do what he 'ort'. He knew it would be torture, doing what he ought to do, instead of following his heart's desire. But he'd do it. Find a new life somewhere else, where no one would know him. He'd start again and let Hattie start again, too. Without him.

The jury deliberated through the afternoon and on into the night. The bailiff sent them all home at eight o'clock.

The next morning Hattie left Dulcie with Mrs. Sumner and returned with Gene and Carrie to meet the rest of the family at the courthouse to wait again. Around eleven-thirty the signal came. The verdict was in.

330

Hattie clutched her handkerchief with one damp hand and Carrie's hand with the other. Eldon sat on the other side with his arm around her shoulder.

They brought in the jury. When they had taken their seats, Judge Curtis turned to them.

"Has the jury reached a verdict?"

"We have, Your Honor."

A small slip of paper was handed to the judge. After reading it, his face a mask, he sent it back to the foreman.

"Mr. Delaney, please rise for the reading of the verdict."

Smith slowly got to his feet. He held his head high. He wouldn't go down looking like a criminal.

"Mr. Foreman, how do you find the defendant, Smith Delaney?"

Hattie, bit her lower lip and uttered a silent prayer.

"Your Honor, we find the defendant, Smith Delaney, not guilty on all counts."

The courtroom broke into bedlam. Hattie, slid down in her seat, lightheaded with relief and thanksgiving. The girls cried, and the brothers slapped each other on the back.

Trotter looked disgusted. He slammed his briefcase on the table, stuffed his notebooks inside the case, picked it up and stalked down the aisle. Sommerall looked tickled to death and a little stunned.

Smith stood still as though he hadn't heard what the foreman had said.

Judge Curtis slammed his gavel down and called for order. He thanked the jury and dismissed them. Then it was over.

Hattie quickly moved to his side. "C'mon, Honey," she said, "let's go home. Let's go home now." She threw her arms around him. He looked into her face, that sweet open face that he loved, and slowly allowed himself to wrap his arms around her and hold her close. He knew he shouldn't, but it might be the last time. He just wanted one last time ... So sweet. So precious. So much better than he deserved. How would he ever tell her he was leaving? How could he?

It took awhile to gather up all of their things and accept congratulations from their friends and neighbors who'd come to show their support. Annie and Harwell were there. Miz Shropshire, Clarence Hunt, Brother Fenton and most of the Jackson Chapel congregation, and a big part of the people of Mondray. Finally, they were out the door into the sunshine.

Gene drove them home. Carrie and Hattie chattered nonstop about the closing arguments and how awful Sawyer was. Gene said he thought Sawyer should be tried for perjury. Most of the conversation washed over Smith without a ripple. He didn't even hear Gene tell that Sheriff Westerfield had run up to him on the courthouse steps with surprising news. Three neighborhood boys from near Ebenezer had just come to him saying that on the day of the ambush they'd seen three men with rifles running through the woods. None had a limp. Smith was oblivious to the buzz of excitement this stirred. He couldn't even believe he was free. There was just too much going on in his mind to join the conversation. His brain raced through what needed to be done. Get home. Get packed. Talk to Hattie. Leave. He knew it would bring her more pain for a time, but it was the right thing to do, and he was going to do it. Right now, though, she held his hand as though she'd never let go. It felt so good just to touch her, to be with her. The words of the old song they'd sung on Christmas Eve whispered through his memory:

"Turn back time to that place,
Where I knew love's embrace.
Simple Hearts, holdin' fast,
In that place where love lasts."

That was it. Once again, as he had so often in the last few weeks, he wished he could turn back time. Start over again. Come to Hattie without his past, worthy of her.

They picked up bubbly little Dulcie at Mrs. Sumner's, then slipped down the big hill and pulled up the drive by the old house. Carrie and Gene didn't stay long. They'd planned a big family get-together for the weekend, but for now they had to get back to their homes. There was a lot to catch them up on.

Smith headed to the smokehouse. He unlatched the door and went inside. There, neatly folded on the bed, was his clean laundry—all done by Hattie's hands. He hesitated, then reached under the bed and pulled out the old cardboard suitcase he'd brought with him months ago and laid it on the bed beside his clean clothes. Stiffly, he reached out and picked up each item, one at a time, and placed them inside. He added the ball Dulcie had given him for Christmas and the Bible Hattie had sent him in jail. Then he emptied the small bureau. That was it. It was all packed. Ready to go. He took the folded letter with Hattie's name written on the outside from his front shirt pocket and laid it on the pillow. His left hand withdrew the whistle from his pants pocket—he'd even kept it with him in the courtroom. He reached toward the pillow to drop the toy beside the letter, hesitated, then curled his fist tight around the whistle and stuffed it back in his pocket. He couldn't leave it.

Smith sat on the edge of the bed. All feeling seemed to have left his body. He was numb, except for the constant dull ache in his bad leg. It was his reminder of a different time, a different day when he'd brought Hattie joy and pride instead of pain and shame.

Hattie knocked on the door and then opened it. Her eyes flashed from Smith's face to the open suitcase, the letter, and back again to Smith and the look on his face.

"What are you doin'?" she asked quietly. "You goin' somewhere?"

"Hattie, I'm leavin'," he said, looking at the toes of his boots. "I wrote you a letter, but ... "

"Where are you goin'? When are you comin' back?"

"I ain't comin' back, Hattie. I just think it's for the best if I move on."

Hattie reeled with shock. "Did I do somethin'? Was it what I said at the trial? I told the truth. I know it didn't sound good, but I thought ... " Hattie was desperate. She needed to understand.

"No, it ain't you or nothin' you did. I just realized while I sat in jail that I ain't the man for you, Hattie. I thought I was, but I just ain't."

"Isn't that for me to decide?"

"No. In this case, I reckon it's up to me. I know you'd still have me, even after everything I put you through, but I'm not willin' to let you do it."

"Because you don't love me?" Hattie's eyes searched his face.

"No! Because I *do* love you!" Smith finally looked up at her, begging her to understand, "Don't you see, Hattie, I ain't never been no good. You heard what all they said durin' the trial. I ain't never done nothin' right in my life. I'm just not good enough for you. I'll just bring you more shame if I stay."

"No, Smith! I think you'll give me more joy than I've ever known!"

"Well then, you're wrong! I'm nothin'. Nobody! Just a hothead who don't know when to walk away from a fight. Only this time, this time I *am* walkin'. I ain't gonna put you through any more pain. I can't."

Hattie drew herself up to her full height. "You wait just a minute. Don't you go callin' yourself 'nothin'.' God made you. You *are* something. You're the man I love!" Hattie placed her hand on his shoulder.

Smith violently shook her off. "God? Yeah, He made me all right. He made me and then He turned me loose and let me hurt all the people who cared about me. He ... "

Hattie cut him off. "Uh uh! Any hurtin' you did, you did all by your own choosin', Smith Delaney! When you were cuttin' up with Colt, you did that 'cause you wanted to. When you shot up the pool hall, you did it 'cause you wanted to. When you

334

shot the sheriff off the ladder, you did it 'cause you wanted to! Don't you dare blame God!"

Hattie's hands were fisted on her hips. She was fighting for her life, just as Smith had fought for his in the courtroom. Her eyes were bright as she fought back angry tears. "Listen here. If you want to walk out on me and Dulcie and Jackie, then you go ahead and go, but it ain't 'cause of you bein' a no-account human bein'. It's 'cause for the first time in your life, you're scared. Scared you can't live up to some kind of standard you think I've set for you. Well, let me tell you something, Smith Delaney, the only standard I have for you is that you try from this day forward to be the man God intends you to be. As far as I'm concerned, what you did before we met is wiped clean. Do you hear me? *I don't care!* It doesn't make one whit of difference to me. It's what you've done since we've been together that matters to me. It's the man I've seen here, on this land, in that house, with me and my younguns that I care about."

Smith sat with his head down.

Hattie paced back and forth, thinking. She had to fix this. He couldn't leave her! She wouldn't let him.

"Smith, I know you were raised in a God-fearing home. I know that you know right from wrong. I know that at one time you made a commitment to God. I can tell. How did you feel when you gave your life to the Lord?"

"Hattie, a man don't talk about ... "

"A *real* man does!"

Smith didn't know where this was going, but if it made her happy, he'd tell her. He looked up. "All right. The summer I came back from France, Brother Phy come to Mt. Moriah for a revival. I didn't want to go, but it seemed awful important to my Ma. She was so excited about those meetin's. So, I went with her and dragged Clarence along. We figured hellfire and brimstone preaching was worth a couple of laughs."

Smith's gaze seemed to lose focus, as though he was seeing it happen all over again. "I'll never forget it. Brother Phy didn't pound the pulpit or threaten eternal damnation. He talked about God's grace and how it don't matter what you've done—that grace is a gift from God that's ours for the takin' if we want it. It covers all our wrongs like a blanket. I never expected what happened next. I was hurtin' bad. The things I'd seen in the war …" Smith pushed his hair back off of his forehead. "Shoot, Hattie, the things I'd done in the war … I was just so low down. Brother Phy started tellin' how it only takes acceptin' grace to get it. It was so simple. No preacher I ever heard talked like that. I mean, they all talked about grace some, but mostly they talked about livin' right or goin' to hell, and tithin'. When he asked 'Won't you accept this free gift?', and called us to come, I almost ran down that aisle. I figured Clarence was laughin' his head off, but he was right behind me! We were even baptized the 'same hour of the night' just like in the Bible. Never felt so wonderful before in my whole life."

Hattie sat down on the edge of the bed beside Smith and took one of his hands between both of hers. "So if God covered your sins with His grace, you ain't supposed to be draggin' 'em back out and throwin' 'em back up in His face sayin' He didn't do a good enough job coverin' 'em, right?"

"I reckon, but … "

"So, that's not an issue then. Sounds to me like this leavin' business is just your pride talkin' foolish."

Smith looked her in the eye. "Hattie, it ain't pride. It's shame. I don't want you to be ashamed of me."

Hattie smiled softly. "Smith, I could never be ashamed of you! I'm proud of you! You start rememberin' who you are—one of God's forgiven sons. Stand up and be the man He wants you to be. You can't leave, Smith. You belong here with me." Hattie rose and pulled him to his feet. She pointed to the closed suitcase. "Now, you just unpack that suitcase right now!"

"Hattie … "

"Don't you even 'Hattie' me. I've heard enough of this foolishness. You just start unpackin'. We got a weddin' to plan!"

336

Hattie's love shone from her eyes.

"But ... "

"Ain't no buts, neither. Don't you understand?" Hattie brushed the tears from her cheeks and reached up to put her arms around his neck. "God loves you. I love you. The younguns love you. Shoot, there's so much love around here it's sickenin'."

Smith gazed down at the sweet face he adored. He looked deep into the shining eyes that promised him the world. His heart pounded. Slowly he smiled his lopsided smile. *How could I have wished to turn back time when the future is looking so amazing?* He pulled her closer and lowered his head and kissed his woman, his bride.

Glossary

There are three types of words in this novel which may prove a challenge: mining terminology, slang in vogue during the 30s, and terms adapted from the mother tongues of the settlers of Muhlenberg County. Someone commented fifty years ago that if William Shakespeare should arise from the dead, he'd likely feel more at home, language-wise, in the mountains of Appalachia than any-where else on the earth. Muhlenberg County is not in Appalachia, but many of its settlers came from the Caro-linas and Virginia. This glossary will help you understand this story's people of the 1930s as you associate with them.

Black damp A Combination of carbon dioxide and nitro-gen, or air depleted of oxygen. Can be deadly, but kills more slowly than some gasses.

Bank mule A small, tough, and powerful breed of mules used to pull coal cars out of mines.

Cage An elevator-like hoist, often partially open-sided, used in mine shafts to lift and lower personnel, equip-ment, and materials, including coal.

Carbide A crystalline solid which releases flammable acetylene gas when water is added to it. In lump form it is used in carbide lights or lamps.

Carbide light (or lamp) A small two-chambered lamp worn by miners on their hats or helmets. The lower cham-ber holds carbide, while the upper holds water. Water, dripping on the carbide through a valve, releases gas through a nozzle in the center of a reflector attached to the lamp. A spark from a flint wheel on the reflector is used to ignite the gas.

Dander Temper, anger, or level of irritation. "That stubborn old mule sure got my dander up."

Entry The area where coal is being extracted. It is usually a horizontal or nearly horizontal passage or section of the workings.

Face The vertical plane of coal where miners extract the coal.

Fetch Go, get, and bring back. "Fetch me that bucket of nails."

Fiddlesticks An expression of surprise, disbelief, or mild displeasure. "You sent him? Oh, fiddlesticks! By the time he gets to the store, he'll have forgotten what he went for"

Fire Damp Methane. Forms in coal and decaying matter. Highly explosive. Danger is minimized when there is ample ventilation in a mine.

Fittin' Appropriate or fitting. Also, used at times for "fighting." "They were fittin' over some gal."

I'll be jiggered An expression of wonder. "I'll be jiggered, Jenny, it's snowed on your birthday the last three years!"

Ort Ought or should. Combines in interesting ways: Orta = Ought to; Ortn't = Ought not.

Peaked (Pron. Peek'-ed) Thin, emaciated, unhealthy.

Peart Healthy, Well. "Since I got this cough, I just ain't been feelin' peart at all."

Pert "Pretty" was often pronounced, "purty." But it was shortened to "Pert" when combined with "near" to mean "almost," or "nearly." Example: "Honest, Tilly, when Edith found out that Ed was marryin' her sister, she pert near died."

Reckon Consider, estimate, judge, assume. "Is Jim gonna join the union?" "I'm not sure—I reckon so."

Scab A worker who continues to work in spite of a strike being underway, or a worker who hires on to work in the place of a person on strike.

Shaft A vertical mine opening, at times hundreds of feet deep, by which personnel, materials, and equipment descend and ascend to and from the mine's underground workings.

Slack Very small pieces and particles of coal of limited marketability in the 1930s. Often used to surface road-beds and streets.

Slacker One who avoids work or responsibility—especially in the military.

Slate A dense, fine-grained rock of compressed shale. Frequently it is the first layer of overburden directly above the coal. Easily breaks into horizontally fractured sheets or chunks.

Smidgen A small amount, a dab, a little bit.

Swan Combines with "I'll" as an exclamation. "You don't mean it! Well, I'll swan!" Probably derived from Victorian times when a shocked lady might say, "You don't mean it! Why, I'll swoon!—I'll just swoon!"

Thrush (Thresh) A disease of the mouth and throat, usually in infants, characterized by white patches.

Tipple Originally the superstructure where a loaded car of coal would be tipped and its load emptied. Eventually came to be used in reference to the whole surface structure adjacent to the mine opening.

Vein A layer, channel, or bed of coal

White Damp Carbon monoxide, in coal mines often the result of a methane (fire damp) explosion. Very deadly. Just one one-thousandth of a percent in the blood can result in death.

Workings The entire system of openings created in the extraction of coal.

Sequel to *Turn Back Time*

Becky Dunford's face was that of an old woman, not that of a ten-year-old girl. She looked out at the world with eyes that seemed to have seen the worst of what life has to offer and didn't expect any different. "M ... Miz Delaney? Is Mama gonna be all right?"

Hattie didn't look at the child. She wrung out the cloth she had dipped in cold water from the wash basin by the bed and placed it against Mamie Dunford's bruised cheek. "Becky, where did you say your brothers and sisters are?"

"I ... I took 'em over to the old cabin. They'll wait for me to come get 'em. They won't come out 'til I tell 'em to." Becky's bare toe rubbed a pattern against the bare wood floor. She looked nervously toward the door. "If you think Mama'll be all right, maybe ... you should be ... goin' now."

Hattie glanced away from the badly beaten face of Becky's mother to the little girl. "I'm not leavin' yet. I want to see her open her eyes first. How long did you say she'd been like this 'fore you came to get me?"

"Um, well... she *fell* last night and I couldn't wake her up this mornin'."

"Becky, where was your daddy when she fell?"

"D ... Daddy? He weren't here. She just tripped and fell. You know how clumsy she is, Miz Delaney. Always fallin' down...." Becky's voice cracked and

343

faded.

Hattie gritted her teeth. *Tripped and fell, my foot! Deke Dunford beat her again.* "Honey, I'm thinkin' maybe you better run for Ma Richards. This time, it looks like your Mama's hurt purty bad. Ma'll know what to do better'n me."

"Oh, no ma'am! I cain't do that!" Becky's face radiated pure terror. There was panic in her voice. "Daddy don't hold none with that ol' midwife. Says she's always meddlin' in other folk's business. I reckon Mama'll be all right. You … you can prob'ly go on home now. I shouldn't'a come after you, but—It's just, I was a little skeered when she wouldn't wake up. An' Mama said one time, if anything was to happen, you'd be the best one to help out." Becky hardly spoke above a whisper.

Hattie reached for the child. When Becky cringed and ducked her head, Hattie let her hand fall back in her lap. "Becky, listen to me. However your mama hurt her head, it's bad hurt. I don't know what to do. See how black her eyes are gettin'? They wasn't that black two hours ago. She's bruisin' up on the inside of her head an' I don't know how to stop it. I need help, Honey."

"Miz Delaney. I cain't go get Miz Richards. Daddy'd … I just cain't. Ain't there no one else?"

Hattie closed her eyes for a minute as a wave of nausea washed over her. She hadn't been sick this late in her pregnancies with Dulcie and Jackie, but this time, it seemed like she was sick all the time.

"Miz Delaney, you alright?"

"I'm fine, Honey. Just a little dizzy. That happens sometimes." Hattie swallowed hard. "Could you just bring me a glass of water? That'll help." Hattie pressed the cold cloth to the back of her own neck for a moment. She glanced around the little room. Everything was neat as a pin. The Dunfords might be poor, but they were clean. She'd grant them that. Mamie Dunford's floors were clean enough to eat off of. There were none of the little frills that Hattie had in her own house. No music box. No pretty little embroidered Bible verses adorned the walls. The only adornment here was the beautiful quilt that lay folded across the bottom of the bed where Mamie Dunford lay, made by her own hand, no doubt. Sunshine and Shadow was the pattern. It was one of Hattie's favorites, but oh, the stitching. It was tiny and flawless. *I'm a purty good quilter, but, my land! I could never make such a purty runnin' stitch! She musta put hours and hours in that coverlet!*

"I fetched it cold from the well, Miz Delaney. Is it all right?" Becky handed Hattie a tin glass. Already, the heat of the room had caused condensation to bead up on the outside. Hattie took a careful sip.

"Oh! That's just what I needed. Now, listen Becky. I want you to run up to Ma Richards house and fetch her. If anybody can help your Mama, she can. I'll tell your daddy it was my idea. I'll make sure he understands it was my doin' and not yours."

"Miz Delaney, please don't make me. I'm purty sure Mama's gonna be all right. I just can't go after Miz Richards. Daddy, why he'd..." Becky gulped hard.

"He'd what, Becky?"

"He … He just wouldn't like it none and he might get mad at M…Mama 'cause she went an' got herse'f hurt agin'. 'Sides,I can't leave, I got to go get the young'uns an' I got to get supper goin'. If'n it ain't ready when he gets home …"

You'll be in for it, too. Hattie looked at the misery on the little face before her. "Tell you what I'll do. I'll walk on over to Ma's house and tell her about your Mama and see if she can tell me what to do. Then I'll come back and check on her and help you get supper on."

Relief poured off the child like a vapor. "I'm much obliged, Miz Delaney."

"He pert near beat her to death sounds like to me." Ma Richards glared out the window and across her yard as she talked to Hattie. "He's gonna kill her one o' these days and ain't nobody gonna own up to what's been goin' on here 'til she's dead and gone."

"I just don't know what to do, Ma. Her face is so swollen and her arms are just black where he must of jerked her around and hit her. There's a soft spot of swellin' on the back of her head. It's almost mushy. Her eyes are gettin' blacker by the minute."

"Mercy. She may not live through the night, if'n you're right about that swellin' on her head. I better go down there."

"Ma, I don't know why, but Becky Dunford's in mortal fear of you bein' there. She said her Daddy wouldn't stand for it. Cain't you just tell me what to do? I'll do exactly like you say."

Ma snorted. "If you had done like I said, you'd be at home with your feet up, not runnin' all over the county tryin' to save the world. You ain't in no condition to be seein' to other folks. You got your own garden to tend to without a worryin' 'bout other people's crops! 'Side's, seein' somethin' like that in your condition could mark the baby. Ain't you got no sense?"

"No ma'am, not when a young'un comes to my door tellin' me her Mama won't wake up, I don't. Especially when it's Mamie. You know it's just a matter of time, afore he—" Hattie's eyes filled with tears. "How could he do it to her? How could he beat her like that? I … just don't understand.…"

"'Course you don't, Honey. I don't neither. In that big old family of yourn there's not a man who'd lay a hand on a woman, except in love. This makes me so mad I could spit!" Ma paced back and forth the length of her kitchen. "Tell you what let's do. You reckon your man'd let you bring Mamie and them young'uns down to your place? We could go get 'em and then I could see her down there and Deke Dunford wouldn't have no say."

"I think so. Smith's mighty understandin'. We could put her 'n the children upstairs and …"

"Hattie, you ain't climbin' no stairs to wait on her. I'm tellin' you right now, you ain't! You got that room up in the smokehouse where Smith stayed when he worked for you. We'll put her in there. The young'uns we can put on pallets on the floor. It's clean. I remember it."

"I reckon that would be all right."

"Reckon Carrie'd go get 'em in her Ford?"

"I'm sure she would."

"Let's call her."

Later that afternoon Hattie stood at the stove in her kitchen and stirred the pot of stew she'd made to feed the crowd that had landed on her doorstep. She jumped when two strong arms wrapped around her and then relaxed against the familiar body pressed against her back. She tipped her head back to look at her husband's face.

Smith's eyes twinkled. "Honey, there's a buncha long-faced youngun's out there on the smoke house porch that don't look like they belong to us."

'Course not!" Hattie smiled. "They're the Dunford kids. Mamie's up in the smokehouse."

Smith's smile softened. "Guess that explains why none of 'em called me 'daddy.' You savin' the world again, Hattie?" Smith asked as he sat down on the four-legged kitchen stool.

"Just my little corner." Hattie explained how Becky Dunford had come to the door that morning begging for help and how she'd gone to the house and found Mamie. By the time she finished Smith's face was grim.

"I couldn't just leave her there, Smith. I had to bring 'em down here where we could try to help." Hattie added, "Ma Richards is with her now."

"You did the right thing, Hattie. Only thing is, sooner or later Deke's gonna come lookin' for 'em.

I'll deal with him when he shows hisself." Smith's face hardened—"And he'll know he's been dealt with!" Smith said, as he rose to his feet.

Hattie fisted her left hand on her hip and shook the ladle she held in her right hand at her husband. "You'll do no such a thing. You gave up your fist-fightin' and wild ways and you not goin' back to 'em now! If there's any dealin' to be done with Deke Dunford, I'll do it myself."

Smith threw up both hands in mock surrender and backed up a step or two. "Honey, he don't know it yet, but somehow I think ol' Deke's met his match."

They smiled, then became somber as they realized the real issue was whether or not Mamie would survive.

Muhlenberg County, Kentucky
1932